A COURSE BOOK IN BRITISH SOCIAL AND ECONOMIC HISTORY FROM 1760

A COURSE BOOK IN BRITISH SOCIAL AND ECONOMIC HISTORY FROM 1760

P. F. SPEED

WHEATON
A Division of Pergamon Press

A. Wheaton & Co. Ltd
A Division of Pergamon Press
Hennock Road, Exeter EX2 8RP

Pergamon Press Ltd
Headington Hill Hall, Oxford OX3 0BW

Pergamon Press Inc.
Maxwell House, Fairview Park, Elmsford, New York 10523

Pergamon of Canada Ltd
Suite 104, 150 Consumers Road, Willowdale, Ontario M2J 1P9

Pergamon Press (Australia) Pty Ltd
Potts Point, N.S.W. 2011

Pergamon Press GmbH
Hammerweg 6, D-6242 Kronberg, Federal Republic of Germany

First Edition 1977
Reprinted 1978, 1979, 1981

ACKNOWLEDGEMENTS

The author and publishers are grateful to the following organisations who kindly provided photographs for use in this book:
Esso Petroleum Co. Ltd, Guildhall Art Gallery, International Computers Ltd, I.C.I. Ltd, The Mansell Collection, The Science Museum, Radio Times Hulton Picture Library.

Printed in Great Britain by A. Wheaton & Co. Ltd, Exeter

ISBN 0 08 020995 5

NOTES FOR THE TEACHER

This book provides a course leading to 'O' Level and C.S.E. The text gives the student the basic information; the documents encourage him to use his intelligence and imagination; the suggestions for further work show how he might broaden and deepen his studies. The twenty questions on each chapter need more explanation. They can be used in either, or both, of the following ways:

1 As preparation. The student answers the questions as he reads the chapter, so that they help his understanding and highlight any problems. Clearly, such work must be followed by explanation and discussion in class.

2 As catechisms, one of the oldest and best of teaching techniques. When a student can answer a set of questions from memory, he has gone most of the way towards learning the topic. He has, of course, not mastered it fully, until he can recall the essential information without any help.

A good knowledge of the facts is vital, if a student is to do well in his examinations, and, indeed, if he is to achieve the more liberal aims of the study of history.

P. F. Speed

TABLE OF CONTENTS

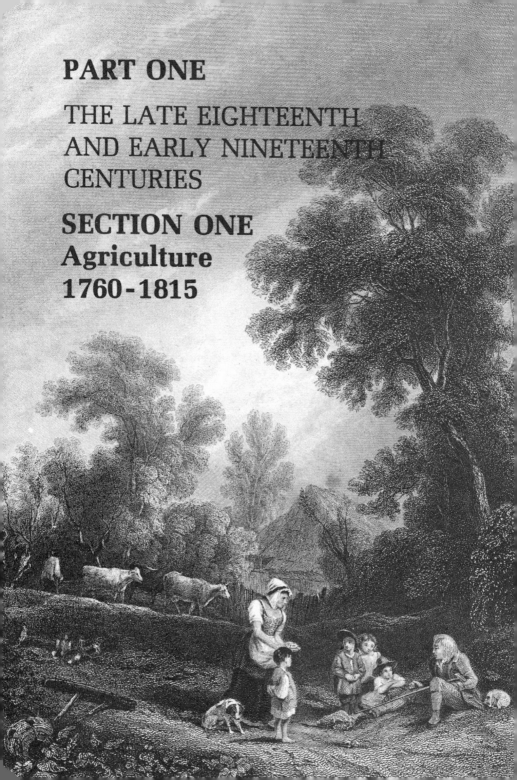

PART ONE

THE LATE EIGHTEENTH AND EARLY NINETEENTH CENTURIES

SECTION ONE
Agriculture 1760-1815

CHAPTER 1

The Village Before Enclosure

Long before the Norman Conquest the Saxons developed a system of farming that remained in general use until the eighteenth century, and survived in a few villages until the twentieth. There were changes, of course, but in all these centuries the fundamental idea remained the same. This was that the village was one large farm, with everyone working together in much the same way. In Saxon times particularly, there were wars and disorder, together with the constant danger of famine if the crops should fail. People were more worried about survival than they were about freedom, and no individual would want to strike out on his own.

The typical village, like most farms, divided its land into three. There was arable for crops, meadow for hay and pasture for grazing animals.

Arable Land—The Open Fields. Usually there were three huge fields surrounding the village. One of these grew barley, which they were able to sow in the autumn, because it was hardy enough to stand the winter: the second grew wheat, which was sown in the spring; the third field lay fallow. The idea of the fallow was to give the land a rest and allow it to recover its fertility. So that each field could do this in turn, they followed a three course rotation:

	Year One	Year Two	Year Three
Field One	Barley	Wheat	Fallow
Field Two	Fallow	Barley	Wheat
Field Three	Wheat	Fallow	Barley

Each field was about a mile across and was divided into acre strips about 220 yards by 22, or a furlong by a chain. On an average a family would own 30 of these strips, scattered all over the field. The boundary between one man's strip and another's was shown by a line left by the plough with a short stake at either end. There were no enclosures, that is fences, walls or hedges, which is why the fields were called "open fields".

All these arrangements had come about in logical and sensible ways though, unfortunately, there is not the space here to describe them, and we can only look at the disadvantages. They were many, but two were especially important.

In the first place the use of fallow meant that one third of the arable land was idle. Secondly, everyone had to farm in the same way. No-one could try a four course rotation, because the village had three fields: no-one could grow different crops because they would be planting and harvesting at different times from their neighbours.

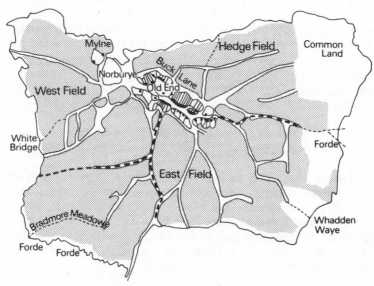

Plan of an open field village

Meadow Land. The meadow was kept for hay. Like the open fields it was divided into strips and each family owned a few scattered ones. No-one could change the use of his strips. Wheat might become highly profitable, but a farmer could not plough up his share of the meadow and increase his crop. Again we see the disadvantage of having land unenclosed.

2

The Common Land. This was an area of uncultivated land that lay between one village and the next. Farm animals would have destroyed many seedling trees, so there was a good deal of rough grass; otherwise it was in its natural state.

The common was important for the poorer villager, especially. Its main use was for grazing his animals. He and his family ate bread most of the time, but any extras like milk and meat came from the common. He would find wood and turf there for his fire, and timber and stone or clay if he wanted to mend his cottage. Obviously there was no attempt to divide the common. If it was a large one it was "unstinted", which meant that the villagers could graze all the beasts they wanted on it: if it was smaller, then it was "stinted" and each man was told how many beasts he could keep.

Usually, much of a common would be waste land, being marshy, or growing plants that were virtually useless, like bracken, gorse or brambles. It would have supported far more animals if it had been cleared, ploughed and sown with good grass. Moreover, no-one would think of keeping expensive pedigree stock on it. Cattle could be lost or injured, while the indiscriminate mixture of beasts meant they easily caught diseases from each other. It also meant that there could be little control over breeding.

We can see then, that the unenclosed village was meant for people who chose to live and work as a community. However, it was a frustrating place for anyone who wanted to forge ahead, and make himself money with new farming methods.

People in Agriculture. From the Middle Ages until well into the nineteenth century the people who mattered most were the aristocrats. Each one owned land scattered all over the country. The richest of them in about the year 1800 was the Duke of Devonshire with an income of £50 000 a year. At the bottom end of the scale came the Earl of Clarendon, with barely £3000 a year, and he only counted as an aristocrat because he had an ancient and honourable title.

Below the aristocrats came the gentry, or squires. A squire would own land in a few villages only. To belong to this class in about 1800, a man needed an income of £1000 a year at least and, very important, he must not work. He had to let his land and live on the rent.

Between them, the aristocracy and gentry owned most of the land in England, but there was a third group of landowners, the yeomen. Unlike the gentry they did not let their land to others, but worked it themselves with their families and some labourers. A rich yeoman might make himself £1000 a year, but many were quite poor. Most of their class vanished in the early eighteenth century.

Next came a most important group, the richer farmers, who were better off than many of the yeomen. They had less status, though, because they 3 did not own the land they worked, but rented it. It was their money that kept the gentry and aristocracy in style. Their farms were large enough to give them good incomes and they often held long leases. Usually they had good relations with their landlords and even when their leases expired they could count on having them renewed.

Below them came the smaller farmers. They worked their farms with the help of their families and could only afford to employ labourers, if at all, during harvest time. However, they made enough from their land to live on, and at least did not have to work for anyone else.

Next there were the cottagers. Each rented his house with its garden, together with some strips on the open fields. He would also have some beasts on the common. The cottager's wife would usually spin thread or work at whatever local industry was traditional, for instance, button making in Dorset. However, all this would not give a cottager enough to live on and he would have to work part of his time for one of the farmers.

There were a few villagers who owned nothing, and had to be full time labourers, but it was the tradition that they lived in the farm house. Farmer and labourer slept under the same roof and ate at the same table.

Out on the common there might well be a few squatters. These people had no rights and were only there on sufferance. The men would work as labourers, full time, while the wives and children looked after their few beasts.

Between the very rich and the very poor then, there was an enormous difference, but the important thing was that there was no clear division between one class and another. A big farmer would be more prosperous than many yeomen; there was little to choose between a small farmer and a cottager; if one met a poor cottager and a labourer in the fields they could well be doing the same work. All this gave rural society a unity and a stability which lasted until the agricultural revolution shattered it.

One way of sowing wheat was to scatter it broadcast on the surface of the ground and then cover it—or most of it—by harrowing. The other way was to dibble the wheat, as shown here.

Questions
1. What implements does a dibbler use?
2. Is the man working backwards or forwards? Why?
3. What will be the next operation? Which way will that person work?
4. What advantages does dibbling have over broadcast sowing?
5. What disadvantage does it have?

COTTAGERS

The cottagers have little parcels of land in the field, with a right of common for a cow and three or four sheep, by the help of which, and with the profits of a little trade or their daily labour, they make a comfortable living. Their land gives them wheat and barley for bread, and, in many places, beans to feed a hog for meat; with the straw they thatch their cottage, and winter their cow, which gives a breakfast and supper of milk, nine or ten months in the year. They have likewise a right to cut turf, roots and furze which is a great advantage to those who have not money to purchase other fuel.

(Addington—*Reasons For and Against Enclosing.*)

Questions

1. What two kinds of land do cottagers use?
2. What do they have from each kind of land?
3. What other work do they do? Why?

SQUATTERS

Jacob Johnson has about three roods of land, and no cow, only a pig. Edward Smith has two cows and a heifer. William Farr has a pig and very fine potatoes. Dolly has two cows and a heifer, and about two acres of land. They said the common was a very good one for feeding cows. Dolly has had 4lb of butter per week from one little Welsh cow that had the common only. They buy hay in winter, or hop bines, and straw, managing in this respect as well as they can.

(Arthur Young—*Annals of Agriculture*)

Questions

1. How do the squatters use the common?
2. These people have "encroached". What does that mean?
3. What problem do they have in winter?
4. How do they try and solve it?

COMMON LAND

On the moors, cottagers within a moderate distance from the common generally turn out a cow or two, perhaps a few geese, and I believe the latter are the only profitable stock. Not one in ten rent land to grow winter food. In summer the moor commons are frequently flooded; the cattle must be removed and temporary pasture rented at a considerable cost.

Owners of large estates, by turning out large numbers of cattle by day, and taking them home to feed by night have had the only benefit which an over-fed common could give.

The cattle of the cottager must unavoidably suffer. He must help them to recover by hiring better pasture, or leave them on the common in a stunted or starved condition. From this it is not easy to see how the cottager can have any benefit from keeping animals on the common, and when the cost of winter food is added, the question is decided, and it is clear he must make a loss.

(Sir John Sinclair—*General Report on Enclosures.*)

Questions

1. What use do the cottagers make of the common?
2. What problem do they have in winter?
3. How could they solve it? How many do?
4. What problem may they have in summer, from the weather?
5. What is the only way they can solve it?
6. Who are the only people to do well out of the common?
7. Why do they succeed?
8. What is the likely condition of the cottager's cattle?
9. According to Sinclair what makes it certain the cottagers lose by keeping cattle on the common?
10. On what points would Young and Addington disagree with Sinclair? Where would Young and Sinclair agree?·

Questions—Chapter One

1. What crop rotation was used on the open fields?
2. How big was each field? How was it divided?
3. Give two disadvantages of open field cultivation.

5

4. What disadvantage was there with the meadow?

5. Say where the common was and describe it.

6. What was its main use?

7. Why else was it important for the villagers?

8. Why was a common rarely good farm land?

9. Why was it unwise to keep pedigree stock there?

10. Who found unenclosed villages frustrating?

11. Name two aristocrats and give their incomes.

12. Give the minimum income for a squire.

13. What other qualification did he need?

14. How was a yeoman different from a squire?

15. How was a farmer different from a yeoman?

16. What labour force did a small farmer have?

17. What did a cottager own? How did he make a living?

18. What did a labourer own?

19. Where did he live?

20. What good feature did the class system have?

Further Work

1. Find other plans of open field villages.

2. Find and draw pictures of eighteenth century houses that belonged to: aristocrats, gentry, yeomen or rich farmers, poor villagers.

3. Look through art books to find pictures of eighteenth century aristocrats, gentry and ordinary country people.

4. Imagine you are a poor villager who has been told he may lose his common rights. Explain why you are worried.

5. Imagine you are a progressive farmer in an open field village. Explain why you are frustrated.

CHAPTER 2

Improvements in Farming

Between 1750 and 1800 the population of Great Britain increased. It was probably about seven million in 1750 and the first census in 1801 gave a count of nearly eleven million. To feed these extra people our farms had to produce more. Both arable farming and stock breeding improved, while land that had once been waste was brought into cultivation.

Arable Farming. Arable farming means ploughing the fields to grow crops. An important development here was the introduction of turnips as a field crop. They had come to this country from Holland in the sixteenth century, and had been grown in gardens, but it was not until the late seventeenth century that people began to realise how valuable they could be as feed for livestock. A man who did much of the pioneer work here was Viscount Townshend (1674-1738). He was so enthusiastic for the new crop, that they called him "Turnip" Townshend.

Another thing that was discovered was the value of growing grasses on arable land in rotation with other crops. On many soils it was an advantage to include a good deal of clover, as this is a leguminous plant. Such plants take nitrogen from the air. They store much of it in their roots and when they are ploughed in, it becomes available for the next crop.

The use of these new crops, turnips and grasses, was to have important results.

In the first place there was far more winter feed for the livestock. They no longer had to be slaughtered in the autumn, so that there was fresh meat and more milk all the year round. This was bound to mean a healthier population.

Secondly, Norfolk farmers began to use the new crops along with the old to make what became known as the "Norfolk Four Course Rotation". "Turnip" Townshend did not invent it, as is sometimes said, but he did do a   7 great deal towards making it well known. The sequence of crops was wheat, turnips, barley and grasses. The turnips and grasses kept the two straw crops from following each other and giving the soil a change was found to be as good as giving it a rest. Now all the arable land was sown every year instead of one third of it lying fallow.

Farm machinery began to improve, and one of the pioneers here was a Berkshire farmer called Jethro Tull. He had a theory that it was possible to keep land fertile by hoeing it regularly, so that there would be no need to spread manure. Tull disliked manure as it always contains the seeds of weeds. Tull was wrong. Regular hoeing does help keep land fertile, mainly by killing the weeds that would otherwise rob it, but it is essential to feed the land as well. However, Tull's work was not wasted, because to prove his theory he developed two useful machines. They were the horse hoe and the drill. He invented the horse hoe to save all the labour of hoeing by hand. However it was impossible to use it unless the seed was planted in straight rows which it never could be if it was sown broadcast, that is, scattered over the field by hand. Tull's answer was to make a drill which not only produced straight rows, but had the added advantage of putting the seed in the ground at just the right depth, and just the right distance apart. The result was a considerable saving. Sowing by drill took only one eighth of the seed used when sowing by hand, broadcast.

Partly because of his wrong idea about manure Tull's system spread slowly. When he died in 1741 few people had taken any notice of him. However, by the beginning of the nineteenth century all progressive farmers were drilling their wheat. The drill was improved too. Tull's had sown only three furrows at a time, but later machines like the Suffolk drill would sow fifteen.

Towards the end of the eighteenth century the threshing machine was invented. The old way was to thresh with the flail, a long job that kept the labourers busy through the winter. However, the new machines were powered by horse or water and they did the job much quicker, so that the farmer could save on his wages bill. The labourers, though, lost their winter job and what they thought of threshing machines is easily imagined.

Other, more traditional, pieces of equipment were improved. The plough was especially important. Formerly it had been made almost entirely of wood and turned the soil laboriously so that it needed four oxen to pull it. By the early nineteenth century there were ploughs like the Rotherham plough made entirely of iron. They were more efficient and much lighter, so that on ordinary soils, two horses could pull them quite easily.

Stock Breeding. We have already seen how the new crops of turnips and grasses meant there was much more food for the livestock, but this in itself 8 would not have improved their quality very much. It was important to develop new breeds, and here important work was done by a Leicestershire farmer, Robert Bakewell.

The usual method had been cross breeding. This was mating animals of different breeds and hoping their offspring would combine the qualities of both parents. Bakewell tried the other way which is in-breeding which meant that he mated "brothers" and "sisters" and "cousins". With sheep he had remarkable success and within a short time had produced an entirely new breed of Leicestershires. They had small bones, fattened quickly and made good mutton. They also had long fleece and produced large amounts of wool.

He tried the same method with the traditional English cattle, the longhorns, and he did improve them so that they had less bone and more meat, but on the whole they did not do well. However, a Durham farmer called Charles Colling used Bakewell's methods on shorthorns and was as successful with these as Bakewell had been with sheep. Eventually the new breeds of shorthorns ousted the longhorns, which are no longer common in this country, save in a few areas.

Other men took up the work and many breeds of animals were improved such as Jersey cattle, Southdown sheep, horses and even hunting dogs. Pigs had been quite small and active, and capable of a remarkably good turn of speed. However, their quality when they were bacon or pork was not good. With the new breeding methods they became much more like the ponderous animals we know today. They were especially important in the dairying counties where there was plenty of skimmed milk. This was milk from which the cream had been removed to make butter. Mixed with grain it made excellent pig food.

Improved Durham Shorthorns

9

The Cultivation of New Lands. A lot of the increased food production came not so much from improved methods as from bringing new land under the plough.

In the eighteenth century much of the Fenland was reclaimed. Dutch engineers like Cornelius Vermuyden had begun this work in the seventeenth century and they had concentrated on the inland areas. The eighteenth century engineers worked on the regions nearer the sea. They dug drainage ditches, straightened rivers and put in pumping stations. In the two centuries, a quarter of a million hectares were drained.

A good deal of marginal land was also reclaimed. This is land which is not barren like the tops of the Welsh mountains, nor fertile lowland as in a river valley. It comes in value between the two. Typical areas are the hills of the South-West of England, like the Mendips or much of Dartmoor. Such land came under the plough during the Napoleonic Wars when wheat prices soared so that it was possible to grow it almost anywhere and make a profit. Cultivation was pushed into quite unsuitable areas and wheat was grown in soggy clay lowlands and on semi-barren hilltops. However, what the landowners coveted most were the common lands surrounding their villages. Soon they had possession of nearly all of them and used them for cultivation. In so doing, they added greatly to the value of the farm land of this country, but they also destroyed the independence of their poorer neighbours. The enclosure movement that brought this about was the key to all the other changes.

BARRETT, EXALL AND ANDREWES'
PATENT TWO HORSE THRASHING MACHINE WITH PATENT GEAR WORK,
AS IN OPERATION.

Questions
1. What is meant by thrashing grain?
2. How is this machine powered?
3. What is missing from the right of the picture?
4. What other way was there of driving such machines?
5. What method was used before machines?
6. Why was the old method done by men?
7. What work is there on the machine for the women and the boy?
8. Why did labourers prefer the old method?
9. Why did farmers prefer machines?
10. What happened to many threshing machines in 1830? (page 108).

BROADCAST SOWING

Thursley, Surrey. They have sown their fields broad cast; they have no means of destroying the weeds by the horse-hoe; they have no intervals to bury them in, and they hoe, or scratch as Mr Tull calls it; and then comes St. Swithin and sets the weeds and the hoed-up turnips again. Then there is another hoeing or scratching; and then comes St. Swithin again; so that there is hoe, hoe, muddle, muddle and such a fretting and stewing; when, if that beautiful field had been sowed upon ridges at four feet apart, not a weed would have been seen in the field, the turnip plants would have been three times the size that they are now, the expense would not have been a fourth part of that which has already taken place, and all the muddling and poking about of weeds, and all the fretting and stewing would have been spared; and as for the amount of the crop, it would have been double.
(William Cobbett—*Rural Rides.*)

Questions
1. *How was this field sown?*
2. *What machine cannot now be used? Why not?*
3. *How are the people trying to destroy the weeds?*
4. *What problems does the rain cause?*
5. *How, says Cobbett, should turnips be sown?*
6. *Give five advantages he claims for his method.*

DRILLING BARLEY

They have a whimsical term about Holkham to denote a good crop; they call it "hat barley;" if a man throws his hat into the crop, it rests on the surface if good, but falls to the ground if bad. "All, Sir, is hat barley since the drill came."
(Arthur Young—*Agriculture of Norfolk.* 1813.)

Questions
1. *How do they test the quality of a crop?*
2. *Why have crops much improved in this part of Norfolk?*

CULTIVATION OF TURNIPS

Before the introduction of turnips, it was not possible to cultivate light soils successfully, or to devise suitable rotations for them. It was also difficult to support livestock through the winter and spring; and, as for feeding and preparing sheep and cattle for market during these inclement seasons, it was hardly thought of, and still more rarely attempted, unless there was plenty of hay, which only happened in a few instances. The benefits from turnip husbandry are therefore great.
(Robert Brown—*Treatise on Rural Affairs.* 1811.)

Questions
1. *On what soils are turnips grown?*
2. *What problems had there been with such soils?*
3. *What does a farmer do with his turnips?*
4. *When does he find them especially valuable?*
5. *What had been (a) difficult (b) nearly impossible, before turnips were cultivated?*
6. *How had the diet of humans been improved?*

CULTIVATION OF GRASSES

Artificial grasses include red and white clover, trefoil, cow-grass, and rye grass. Various mixtures of these grasses are sown with the Lent crops in most parts of the county; indeed it is very seldom that any of them are sown unmixed. The grass is usually mown for hay, but upon some farms it is fed, when it is hurdled off, the sheep having a fresh patch each day.
(Stevenson—*Agriculture of Dorset.* 1812.)

Questions
1. *What grasses are mentioned here?*
2. *How are they sown? When?*
3. *What is usually done with the grass?*
4. *What is meant by saying the grass is fed?*
5. *How would feeding the grass help the soil?*
6. *What rotation included turnips and grasses?*

Questions—Chapter Two
1. Say how the population of Great Britain grew.
2. Who helped make turnips popular?
3. How does clover improve the soil?
4. How did turnips and grasses help livestock?
5. What was the Norfolk Four Course Rotation?
6. How did Jethro Tull try to keep soil fertile?
7. Why did he invent the seed drill?
8. What advantages did it have?
9. How was it improved?
10. What new machine did labourers dislike?
11. How was the plough improved? Name a new kind.
12. What were Bakewell's ideas on breeding?
13. What sheep did he improve?
14. Who copied his methods? With what animals?
15. Name five other animals improved by breeding.
16. What marshland was reclaimed? By what means?

17. What is marginal land? Name typical areas.
18. When was marginal land cultivated? Why?
19. What land did landowners covet most?
20. Who suffered when they took it?

Further Work
1. From a geography book, find out what crop rotations are used in East Anglia today.
2. From a gardening book, find out the advantages of hoeing.
3. Find and copy pictures of farm machinery in use before 1830. Look out for pieces of old farm equipment in museums etc.
4. Read about Thomas Coke, Earl of Leicester.
5. Imagine it is the year 1800 and you have just rented a large Norfolk farm. Describe how you will run it.
6. A farmer and one of his labourers argue about thrashing machines. Write what they say.

CHAPTER 3

The Enclosure Movement

Enclosing a Village. We saw in the last chapter that promising new farming techniques were developed in the eighteenth century. Progressive farmers were anxious to use them, and landowners encouraged them, because prosperous tenants could pay higher rents. But we know, too, that it was next to impossible to employ the new methods in an unenclosed village. The only way to set individuals free to farm as they pleased was by enclosure. In the first place the common would be cleared of everything growing on it, and ploughed. Secondly, all the land in the village would be divided into compact farms, each fenced off from its neighbours, and made up of fields of a sensible size.

Though the landowner and the richer farmers might be keen, the humbler folk in the village were usually hostile. In the first place they were frightened of change, and just did not like new ideas. Secondly they had no wish to lose their common which meant so much to them. Many of them had good legal rights and if they could not be persuaded, then they would have to be compelled. The best way to do this was to ask Parliament to pass an Enclosure Act for the village.

The first step would be for the landowner to organise a petition and send it to Parliament. The House of Commons would ask a few M.P.s to form a committee to look at the scheme and report back. If the committee's report was favourable, which it usually was, Parliament would pass an Act ordering the village to be enclosed. It would appoint a commission of responsible local people to see that it was done fairly. The commission would listen to people who felt they had a good claim to a share of the land, and then give each one as much as seemed his legal right. Most of it would go to the squire or aristocrat who was lord of the manor and he would then divide it into compact farms.

All this was expensive. When Earl Fitzwilliam enclosed 1250 hectares (3000 acres) of his land in Northamptonshire he had to pay the following: 13

Parliamentary and legal expenses	£8000
Fences and hedges	£12000
New farm buildings and roads	£4000
Total	£24000

This was £8 an acre. However, it was all worth while since the rent for the 3000 acres went up £2800 a year. This was at a time when a farm labourer earned only 40p or 50p a week.

Enclosures brought important developments. The landscape became quite different, farming often became more efficient, and village society changed.

The New Landscape. Before enclosure a man going from one village to another would first of all leave behind all the houses grouped together round the church and village green. Next he would walk as much as two kilometres between the huge open fields, and finally he would come to untamed common land.

After enclosure there would still be plenty of houses in the village, but there would be isolated farms as well. Farms were compact blocks and some of them were a distance from the village. On these the landowner would build houses and barns, and make roads leading to them.

The huge open fields would have been divided into smaller ones surrounded by their hedges, and, as like as not, all growing different things. The common would have vanished, that, too, having been divided into fields, some arable, some meadow, and some pasture as their owners required. In fact, the countryside would look very much as we know it today.

Efficient Farming. A tenant of one of the enclosed farms was free to take advantage of the new farming techniques. He could have any crop rotation he wanted and some farmers went as far as twelve courses. If he wanted to use machinery his fields were big enough to make it worth while. If he bought expensive pedigree animals, then he could take good care of them. There was no waste land for fallow or common.

Enclosure did not always bring efficiency, though. As we saw in the last chapter the high price of wheat during the Napoleonic Wars encouraged farmers to grow it on land that was quite unsuitable. This was to cause problems later on.

14

Village Society. When a village was enclosed, it was likely to make important differences to the people living in it.

In the first place the squire was almost certain to gain, as he could let the new enclosed farms at higher rents. He had to invest a lot of money it is true, but as the figures for the Fitzwilliam estates show he could expect to have it all back in less than ten years.

A yeoman might find himself with a problem. He could not easily pay the heavy bill for enclosure, and he could see the advantages of the big new farms. His answer might well be to sell his land, and use the capital to set up as a tenant farmer. He would lose some status, but he would almost certainly add to his income. Some yeomen, like the Peel family, gave up farming altogether and set up in industry. Enclosures hastened the decline of the yeoman class.

The important farmers leased the enclosed farms. They took advantage of the new farming methods and, even more, the big increase in prices during the Napoleonic Wars. Many of them became rich and began to copy the gentry, buying carpets, pianos and other fancy furniture for their houses.

The Gentry

Smaller farmers were not always lucky. Sometimes the landowner would create a number of little farms for fear that he would not find enough wealthy tenants, but if he did not do that, the small man often had to give up. To meet all the expenses for taking on a large farm he would need to find four times its annual rent. There was machinery to buy, and livestock and seed corn. Also he would have to pay his labourers from his capital until he brought in his first harvest. If there was no small holding for him, he would have to become a labourer.

Cottagers suffered, too. The enclosure award might give a man a small share of land, but along with it he would get his bill for the enclosure expenses. The only way to meet it was to sell the land. As like as not he would soon have squandered the profits and become a labourer.

Following the enclosure of the commons, the squatters had nowhere to live. They would have to sell their livestock and become labourers, owning nothing.

As for the labourers themselves, it was quite likely that they would now have to leave the farm-house since the farmer and his wife would have made it too fine a place for people like them.

Rural society was now made up of three distinct groups. In the first place there were the landowners—the aristocrats and the squires—who were richer than they had ever been. Next there were the farmers, the tenants of the landowners. They had profitable, enclosed farms and made themselves prosperous. Thirdly there were the labourers, renting their cottages and gardens, but nothing more. There were far more of them than there had ever been, and they were unhappy with their lot. This was to have unfortunate results in the early nineteenth century.

16 *The Labourers*

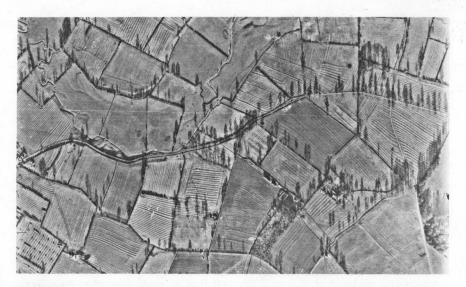

Questions

1. Locate the strips that once made up the open fields.
2. Count how many there are in one of the new fields.
3. Why do you suppose there are no strips showing beside the stream at the top left of the picture? What land was it probably?
4. How many isolated farms can you see?
5. Why were they built?
6. Locate the one or two clumps of trees. This is hunting country, so what use would they be?

THE POOR AND ENCLOSURES

Go to an alehouse kitchen of an old enclosed country, and there you will see the origin of poverty and poor rates. For whom are they to be sober? For whom are they to save? (Such are their questions.) "For the parish? If I am diligent shall I have leave to build a cottage? If I am sober shall I have land for a cow? If I am frugal shall I have half an acre for potatoes? You offer no motives; you have nothing but a parish officer and a workhouse! Bring me another pot!" The more the poor are encouraged to own property the less burthensome will they be found. He who cannot possess an acre may be the owner of a cow, and a man will love his country the better, even for a pig.
Effect of enclosures on the poor in several villages: *Eaton*. Injured. Their cows much fewer. *Alconbury*. Highly injurious to them. Many kept cows that have not since. They could not enclose and sold. *Abington*. Suffered greatly. All lands thrown to one person, and their cows vanished. *Heacham*. Much comfort from little properties of two to ten acres. They keep cows and grow corn.
(Arthur Young—*Annals of Agriculture*. 1801.)

Questions

1. According to Young, what are the things that poor people want to own?
2. In an enclosed village, what do the poor do with their money? Why?
3. How, according to Young, does owning property change a poor man's attitude?
4. How have the poor suffered as a result of enclosures at Eaton, Alconbury and Abington?
5. In what way was the enclosure of Heacham different from the other three villages?
6. What, in fact, is Young saying should be done for the poor whenever a village is enclosed?

FARMERS AND ENCLOSURES

As a general question, there can be no doubt of the superior profit to the farmer by cultivating enclosures, rather than open fields. In one case he is in chains; he can make no variations according to soil, or prices, or times. Whatever may be the advantage of varying the crops, he cannot change them—a mere horse in a team, he must jog on with the rest.

There is, however, one class of farmers which have undoubtedly suffered by enclosures; these are the little farmers. That it is a great hardship suddenly to turn many of these poor men out of their farms and reduce them to be day labourers, would be idle to deny; but it is doing no more than the rise of the price of labour, tithe, rates and taxes would be bound to do, though more gradually, without any enclosures. These little arable occupiers must give way to the progressive improvement of the kingdom.

(Sir John Sinclair—*General Report on Enclosures*.)

3. *Why was an Enclosure Act often necessary?*
4. *How did a landowner obtain an Act?*
5. *Who made up an enclosure commission?*
6. *What was its work?*
7. *What expenses had to be met?*
8. *How did enclosures change the landscape?*
9. *Why were isolated farms built?*
10. *What three new techniques were used on enclosed farms?*
11. *When and why was poor land used for wheat?*
12. *How did the landowners gain by enclosures?*
13. *What two things might a yeoman do?*
14. *Why were wealthy farmers able to make money?*
15. *How did they spend it?*
16. *Why did small farmers not rent enclosed farms?*
17. *How did enclosures affect cottagers?*
18. *How did squatters suffer?*
19. *What happened to labourers?*
20. *Name the three social groups found after enclosure.*

Questions

1. *What does Sinclair mean when he says "cultivating enclosures" brings a farmer "superior profits"?*
2. *For what reasons might a farmer want to vary his crops?*
3. *Under what conditions is the farmer "in chains"? What other expression does Sinclair use to describe his lack of freedom?*
4. *Who has suffered as a result of enclosures? What has happened to them?*
5. *According to Sinclair, what would have happened to them had there been no enclosures?*
6. *What does Sinclair say to justify their misfortune?*

Questions—Chapter Three

1. *What two groups of people wanted enclosures?*
2. *Who was against enclosures? Give two reasons.*

Further Work

1. *Look for "Parliamentary enclosures." Some of the signs are:*
   (a) Good sized fields, roughly square.
   (b) Hedges of nearly all the same species of shrub, usually blackthorn.
   (c) Wide verges to the lanes, sometimes. Ancient enclosures are usually small, close to the village, and irregular. Their hedges contain many species of bush, showing they are old.
2. *Find out if there was an Enclosure Act for your town or village.*
3. *Your village has been enclosed. Say how it has changed and what has happened to the people.*
4. *You are a wealthy farmer who has just taken over an enclosed farm. Why are you pleased?*
5. *A small farmer and a cottager meet in a pub and grumble about enclosures. Write what they say.*

SECTION TWO
Transport 1760-1830

CHAPTER 4

Road Transport

Seventeenth and Early Eighteenth Centuries. Generally roads were in a bad state. They had no proper surfaces and there were dangerous potholes. In summer they might be firm enough to take traffic, but in winter many of them were impassable.

One reason for this was that few people knew anything about the way to build roads; there had been no scientific road building in this country since Roman times and indeed where the old Roman roads had not been robbed of their stone they were still the best available. Another reason was that the parishes were responsible for the care of the roads. An Act of Parliament of 1563 had said that each villager was to give six days unpaid labour on the roads every year. This was known as "statute labour". Unpaid labour is not likely to be efficient and, anyway, the villagers saw no point in building good highways for the benefit of long-distance travellers. For themselves, they only needed the roads to go to and from their fields.

When they had to travel the poor went on foot while the rich went on horseback. Goods travelled on pack-horse trains. There were stage coaches for passengers, and stage wagons for goods, but they ran with difficulty and only in summer. With the growth of trade and industry in the eighteenth century, it was obvious that something would have to be done about the roads.

The Turnpike Trusts. As the parishes were unable and unwilling to make good roads, some other organisation had to be found. The turnpike trust was the answer.

A group of men, usually neighbouring landowners, would form a trust. They would obtain from Parliament a turnpike act which would give them authority to take over a stretch of road, usually about sixteen to twenty kilometres long. Between them they would find the capital to put the road in good order and then they would put gates across it. These gates had

The yard of a coaching house—1820

spikes, or pikes, stuck in the top to discourage men on horseback from jumping them. It was the pikes which gave the name "turnpike". Opening the gate was "turning the pike". The gate keeper would collect toll and some of the money was used to maintain the road, while the rest went to the members of the Trust as their profit.

The roads were improved in bits and pieces since, as we have seen, each trust only managed about sixteen kilometres or so. However, by 1830, 35000 kilometres had been "turnpiked" and there was a good network of main roads, especially those radiating from London. Minor roads were still as bad as they ever had been.

The Road Engineers. It was not enough to have the roads in the care of reasonably well-organised trusts. The science of road building had to be developed. There were a number of famous road engineers.

One of the first of these was John Metcalf (1717-1810), who did excellent work although he was blind. He believed in solid foundations and showed the importance of good drainage and easy gradients. Primitive trackways for horse and foot traffic run straight, but for horse drawn vehicles it is better to make detours, or to wind up the face of a hill if it is not possible to 21 avoid it. Metcalf did most of his work in the north, building for example, the Huddersfield to Manchester road. He was an important pioneer but, by the standards of the men who followed, he was not responsible for great distances.

Perhaps the greatest of the road engineers was Thomas Telford (1757-1834). By the early nineteenth century civil engineering had become an important profession, and this was recognised by the formation of the Institute of Civil Engineers. The Institute, in its turn, recognised the importance of Telford by making him their first President. He built canals, docks, harbours and bridges, but he was most famous for his roads. These included the Glasgow to Carlisle and, more important, the London to Holyhead. Telford saw that his roads were well drained and laid foundations of heavy stones with fine sand filling the gaps between them. The surface was of gravel. Roads like these proved very durable, but they were expensive and not all turnpike trusts were able to afford them.

The engineer who discovered how to make sound roads at a more reasonable cost was John Macadam (1756-1836). He believed that if the soil below the road was dry, there would be no need for foundations. He concentrated on good drainage, and on making his road surfaces waterproof. A typical Macadam road consisted of a twenty centimetre layer of stones, about seven centimetres across, and a five centimetre layer of stones, two and a half centimetres in size. The stones were angular and as the traffic went over them, they ground against each other. This made a fine powder that filled the spaces, and soon the whole became compact and water-tight. The theory was good and generally Macadam's roads lasted well, but they were not as durable as Telford's. However they were so much cheaper that most turnpike trusts preferred them.

Macadam worked first of all in Cornwall. Later he moved to the Bristol area, and finally to London. He built no great highway like the London to Holyhead, but he did improve hundreds of kilometres of existing roads.

The Results of the Turnpikes. Good roads made it possible to have good coaching services. Coaches themselves were improved; they were sprung and made lighter and more comfortable. Coaching inns were built alongside the turnpike roads. They gave accommodation and meals for people who were waiting and they acted as depots for goods and mail. However, they were most important for providing changes of horses. Everyone connected with coaching took a pride in being efficient. The companies saw that their vehicles were comfortable, and ran to a strict time-table. Ostlers at the inns would have the fresh horses ready waiting when a coach arrived, and could change them in two minutes. Coach drivers were veritable kings of the road, and their work became a fine art.

There was an important development in 1784 when John Palmer introduced a Mail Coach service. This replaced the post "boys" who had carried the mail on ponies, and had been thoroughly unreliable—often drunk and sometimes in league with highwaymen. To look at, mail coaches were much the same as ordinary coaches, but were lighter and faster.

All these changes cut travelling times considerably. Coaches could keep an average speed of sixteen or twenty kilometres an hour, which was five times as fast as before. The London to Edinburgh journey of 750 kilometres had been a ten day marathon. By 1830 it took two days.

There was now reliable transport for people and mail, which was invaluable for commerce and industry. Goods of many kinds travelled more freely as well, but for really bulky commodities water transport was the only way for the time being. The new roads were a good deal kinder to horses. Formerly a coach horse was unlikely to live more than two years. On the turnpike roads he would last for five years.

The Decline of the Roads. 1830 saw the beginning of the railway age with the opening of the Liverpool to Manchester line. At first it was thought that, in the main, railways would carry heavy goods, but they soon found their passenger traffic was highly profitable. The Liverpool to Manchester line, for example, was built to compete with the Bridgewater Canal, and so indeed it did. At the same time, though, it put the turnpike road between the two towns out of business. This was repeated all over the country, and by the middle years of the nineteenth century most of the turnpike trusts had vanished. Long distance transport by road was unimportant until the coming of the internal combustion engine.

The Royal Mail coming down hill—
1837

Questions
1. Who started the mail coach service and when? What did it replace?
2. How was a Mail Coach different from an ordinary coach?
3. Can you guess the use of the object hanging from a chain below the coach? What should the coachman have done with it?

BILLERICAY TO TILBURY IN 1769

Of all the cursed roads that ever disgraced this kingdom, none ever equalled this one. It is for 12 miles so narrow that a mouse cannot pass by any carriage; I saw a fellow creep under his wagon to help me lift my chaise over a hedge. The ruts are an incredible depth. Trees overgrow the road, so that it is impervious to the sun, and add to that the eternally meeting with chalk wagons, often stuck so fast that 30 horses may be tacked to each to draw them out. After this description can you believe that a Turnpike was opposed by the bruins of this country, numbers of farmers who are all perfectly well contented with their roads?

(Arthur Young—Tour Through the Southern Counties.)

Questions
1. Name the four faults Young finds with this road.
2. Why did the man have to crawl under his wagon?
3. What happens to chalk wagons?
4. Who opposes a turnpike? Can you suggest why?

COACHING ON MACADAM ROADS

The coach goes faster and faster and the old man becomes alarmed. He looks out of the window, but does he see death and destruction? No: he finds the coachman firm at his post, taking a pinch of snuff, his horses going at the rate of a mile in three minutes. "Bless me," exclaims the old man, "who has made all this improvement in your roads?" "A man called Macadam," was the reply, "but coachmen call him the Colossus of Roads. Great things have been done in cutting through hills and altering the course of roads, and it is no uncommon thing to see horses trotting merrily down hill where they were formerly seen walking up."

(Nimrod—The Road. 1822.)

Questions
1. How fast does the coach go? Is it safe?
2. Why did Macadam change the course of roads?
3. Explain the joke about the Colossus of Roads.

COACH RACING

At the top of Sheet Hill I overhauled my rival, and we went down broadside to broadside. At the bottom we met a postchaise, whose driver, staring with astonishment, pulled into the bank. A turnpike being just ahead I pulled in, or I do not know what might have been the result, but knowing my rival must be nearly beat, I went to pass him on the opposite hill. My leaders were again at his forewheel, when his passenger put his head out, and in a most angry tone said, "If I had a pistol I would shoot you!" "Put your b—— old head in, do!" said his coachman, and pulled his horses right across my leaders' heads, driving them up a bank. I was only able to reach his hind boot when he pulled up at Petersfield, and thus was ended our eight mile course in a few seconds over 20 minutes. Although my horses were none the worse, three of my rival's four never left the stable again.

(Cross—Autobiography of a Stage Coachman. 1861.)

Questions
1. What three accidents nearly happened?
2. How many miles an hour did the coaches go?
3. Why did the writer lose the race?
4. What happened to the horses?

COACHING ACCIDENT

On Friday, as the mail coach was passing over a bridge, a wheel hit the wall and the coach overset. Three of the outside passengers were thrown over the bridge, and a fourth hung by his hands on the top of the wall until rescued by the guard. One had a leg fractured and a rib broken, and another had several wounds and contusions. The coachman was seriously injured, and the guard slightly.

(West Briton Newspaper, Truro, August 14 1812.)

Questions
1. How was the coach overturned?
2. Where did the passengers fall?
3. What injuries were there?

24 Roads.

Questions—Chapter Four

1. Who had built the only good roads in Britain?
2. What was "statute labour"?
3. Give two reasons why it was inefficient.
4. How did people and goods normally travel?
5. What wheeled traffic was there? When did it run?
6. Why did better roads become essential?
7. What work did a Turnpike Trust do?
8. How many roads were "turnpiked" by 1830?
9. Give Metcalf's views on road building.
10. Name Telford's most famous road.
11. How did he build roads? (Four points).
12. Why did Macadam build without foundations?
13. How were his roads made? What did the traffic do to them?
14. Name three places where Macadam worked.
15. How were coaches improved?
16. What services did coaching inns give?
17. Who introduced a Mail Coach Service? Why?
18. How were travelling times improved?
19. What traffic profited most from the roads?
20. When and why did turnpike roads begin to decline?

Further Work

1. Look for traces of old pack-horse routes, especially pack-horse and clapper bridges.
2. Find and sketch pictures of coaches.
3. Look out for coaching inns and toll houses.
4. Read about coach travel in Dickens's novels:

Pickwick Papers, chapters 5, 9, 10, 28, 35.

David Copperfield, chapters 5, 19, 55.

The Uncommercial Traveller, chapters 12, 24.

Nicholas Nickleby, chapter 5.

5. It is 1820 and you have returned to England after many years abroad. Describe the differences you find in coaching—vehicles, horses, roads, riding in a coach.

CHAPTER 5

Inland Waterways

Navigable Rivers. Before the coming of the railways the only way to move bulky goods easily was by water. In the early part of the eighteenth century this meant using the rivers. There were five important river systems, between them serving much of the country:

1 Thames
2 Severn
3 Mersey and Dee
4 Humber, with its Yorkshire tributaries and the Trent.
5 The rivers that flow into the Wash.

Rivers have certain natural disadvantages. In their lower reaches they have large bends called meanders, they have sand bars and they vary a lot in their depth. Banks are often soft, so that towing by horse is out of the question. Sometimes they flood, sometimes they nearly dry up. Near their mouths the tide creates difficulties.

Some disadvantages were man-made There were mill weirs and low bridges. A town might block a river deliberately to stop trade going further upstream to a rival port. Nottingham played this trick on Burton-on-Trent.

However, rivers have two limitations far more important than any of these. In the first place they never flow from sea to sea so each one is bound to be a dead end. Moreover, there are many parts of the country that have no navigable rivers, and not only the mountainous areas. Birmingham, one of the most important cities in the country, has no river.

A good deal was done to improve the rivers by dredging them, building towpaths, and making cuts to avoid meanders, but the only real answer was to have canals.

Canals. The first canal of importance was the Bridgewater canal, opened in 1761. The Duke of Bridgewater owned mines at Worsley, eleven kilometres from Manchester, and he had two problems. One was that his mines contained too much water and the other was the high cost of taking the coal to Manchester by pack-horse train. He had the imaginative idea of building a canal which would both drain the mines and float the coal to Manchester. The Duke was helped by his agent, John Gilbert and they both had advice from a man famous in canal history, James Brindley.

The main obstacle to the canal was the River Irwell, but Brindley overcame this by building the Barton Aqueduct which, though a modest little structure by later standards, was considered a marvel in its day. It was 12 metres high. (An aqueduct is a series of bridges that carries water—unlike a viaduct which carries a road or railway.)

The canal proved its worth as soon as it opened, because the price of coal in Manchester was cut by one half.

Later it was extended along the south bank of the Mersey as far as Runcorn so barges could go to Liverpool.

Another important early canal was the Grand Trunk, opened in 1777. One man who was keen to have it built was Josiah Wedgwood, the manufacturer of the famous pottery that still bears his name. Wedgwood's factory was in North Staffordshire. He needed to bring china clay from Cornwall, which could come by sea as far as the Mersey, but was difficult to transport after that. He also used flintstone which came from Hull, but could only travel part of the way up the River Trent. Finally, he had to have transport for his finished goods, and barges would be ideal for carrying delicate pottery. The answer was to link the Trent and Mersey by Canal.

The engineer was James Brindley, who died in 1772, five years before the canal was finished. It was a much bigger task than the short Worsley to Manchester canal as it was over 160 kilometres long, and had 76 locks, five aqueducts and five tunnels. One of these, the Harecastle tunnel, ran for nearly three kilometres. When it was finished, the canal was of great help to the North Staffordshire potteries.

Following the success of these and other early canals, a good many more were built, especially during the "canal mania" of the years 1789-1793. People seemed to think that any canal would make money, and there were costly failures. In the main, though, most of them proved useful and profitable.

From a map it is easy to see the geographical importance of the canals. There were no longer five isolated river systems, but all were interconnected. At the same time most of the important towns and industrial regions were linked—London, Birmingham, the Black Country, Lancashire and the West Riding of Yorkshire. The Midlands were particularly well served. From being comparatively isolated, Birmingham was now the centre of almost the entire canal network.

Locks on the Regent's Canal

Barton Bridge, Lancs. —1761

The Benefits of the Canal System. For the first time it was possible to carry bulky goods, cheaply and easily, to many parts of the country not served by rivers. Industry flourished as a result—wool, cotton, pottery, iron and, above all, coal. Canals helped the growth of the towns, too. The new industrial cities could not have been built from local materials; there had to be large supplies of Welsh slate, Scandinavian timber, with bricks, stone, sand and lime from over a wide area. Canals were useful for agriculture as well, and would carry lime, marl, manure and grain. However, it was found that they would not pay if they were built to serve rural areas alone. The Southampton to Salisbury Canal was one of the failures of the canal mania.

Building the canals gave civil engineers valuable experience. They had to organise large gangs of land navigators, or "navvies" and they had to learn the techniques of shifting masses of spoil and of building aqueducts and tunnels. When the time came to build railways they already had the labour force, and most of the skills they needed.

Weaknesses of the Canal System. Not all canals were well made. Through trying to cut costs engineers failed to make them water tight, and they did not always build enough reservoirs. Some canals went dry if there was a drought.

Although they served far more of the country than the rivers, canals could not go into the mountainous areas. In many parts this hardly mattered but it did mean that the important industrial region of the north-east remained cut off from the rest of Britain, except for sea transport.

Canals were not built to one master plan. The network grew up piecemeal and each company chose its own gauge. This mattered most at locks or where, for ease of unloading, factories were built right to the canal edge. To widen them all to the size of the largest would have been too expensive, so where canals met, goods had to be off-loaded.

Barges were slow. The best they could do was about 5 km.p.h., and there would be delays at locks. For many cargoes this did not matter too much, but it did mean that canals were not popular with passengers. Some companies, like Pickfords, used "fly boats", which changed their horses frequently, but they could never match the stage coaches which, on the new turnpike roads, kept up an average speed four or five times faster than that of a barge. Canals failed to attract the passenger traffic from which the railways were later to make so much money.

However, these weaknesses only became important with the coming of the railways and until then canals were invaluable. They began to decline after 1840 as the railway network spread, but they proved much tougher rivals than the coaching companies. Many a railway found that the only way to kill a rival canal was to buy it, and then let it fall into disrepair. 29

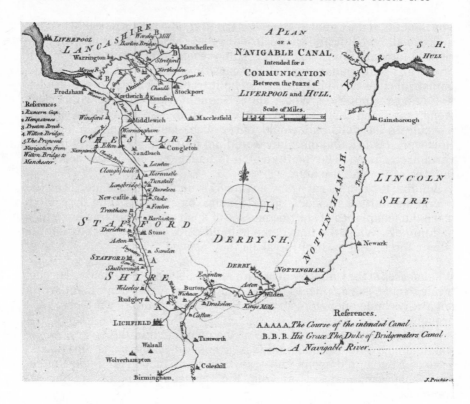

Questions

1. For which canal is this a plan?
2. Who was particularly interested in having this canal built?
3. Who engineered it?
4. When was it opened?
5. What two rivers does it link?
6. Why does it follow river valleys most of the way?
7. What happens near Harecastle? What had to be built here?
8. At what points were aqueducts needed?
9. What is made at Tunstall, Burslem and Stoke?
10. What materials did the canal take to these towns?
11. Trace the course of the Bridgewater Canal: a. in its original stretch b. the extension to Runcorn.
12. Find this area on a map of England so that you are sure where it is.

THE BRIDGEWATER CANAL

The primary object of the "Father of British Inland Navigation," as the Duke of Bridgewater has been justly styled, was to open his valuable mines at Worsley, and to supply the town of Manchester with coal at a much cheaper rate. Under an Act of 1760 the whole of the canal from Worsley to Manchester, together with the extensive underground works at his coal mines in Worsley, were executed. The aqueduct over the Irwell was opened in 1761, and shortly afterwards the line of canal to Manchester. The underground canals and tunnels at Worsley are said to be 18 miles in length. In 1762 this spirited and patriotic nobleman obtained from parliament the powers to enable him to extend his navigation, so as to open a better navigable communication with Liverpool.

All of these canals were executed in five years, under the direction of Mr. Brindley, at a cost of £220 000 to his noble patron, but as it all came from his private purse, the public have no means of knowing the exact amount, nor have they a much better idea of the annual income, though it was estimated at £130 000.

Although built at the Duke's private expense, the canals are of much greater importance to Manchester in reducing the price of minerals which before were nearly double their present cost.
(Priestley—*Rivers, Canals and Railways.*)

Questions
1. What is the Duke of Bridgewater called? Why?
2. Why did he want to build his canal?
3. Who gave him authority?
4. What was built in the mines themselves?
5. What extension was built?
6. How long did the work take?
7. Who supervised the work? Who else might Priestley have mentioned?
8. What were the estimated cost and income?
9. How was Manchester affected?
10. Why did this project encourage others?

CANALS AND RAILWAYS
We left Manchester and embarked upon the canal in a stage boat, bound for Chester. This was a new mode of travelling, and a delightful one it provided. Two horses, harnessed one before the other, tow it along at the rate of a league an hour; the very pace which it is pleasant to keep up with when walking on the bank. England is now intersected with canals. This is the district in which they were first

tried by the Duke of Bridgewater, whose fortune has been amply increased by the success of his experiment. His engineer Brindley was a man of real genius for this particular employment, who thought of nothing but locks and levels, perforating hills, and floating barges upon aqueduct bridges over unmanageable streams. When he had a plan to form he usually went to bed, and lay there working it out in his head till the design was completed. It is recorded of him, that being asked for what he supposed rivers were created, he answered, after a pause, to feed navigable canals.

Excellent as these canals are, railroads are found to accomplish the same purpose at less expense. It has been recommended that they should be universally introduced, and a hope held out that at some future time this will be done, and all carriages drawn along by the action of steam engines erected at proper distances.
(Southey—*Espriella's Letters from England.* 1807.)

Questions
1. What journey does the writer make?
2. How fast does he go? Does he enjoy the trip?
3. Why did travel by barge not become popular?
4. Why is the Manchester district important in the history of canals?
5. What problems has a canal engineer to overcome? How did Brindley overcome his?
6. What importance did he give to canals?
7. How accurately does Southey foresee the future of railways?

Questions—Chapter Five
1. Name five important river systems.
2. What disadvantages did they have, natural and man-made, and what geographical limitations?
3. How were rivers improved?
4. Why was the Bridgewater canal built?
5. Name three people involved in the work.
6. What was the main obstacle? How was it overcome?

7. What places did the canal link? (Two stages).

8. How did the canal prove its worth?

9. What canal opened in 1777? Who wanted it? Why?

10. How long was the canal? How many locks, tunnels and aqueducts did it have?

11. What was the "canal mania"? When was it?

12. Which area was well served by canals?

13. What was the most usual cargo? Name others.

14. Where did canals fail? Name one that did.

15. What experience did civil engineers gain?

16. In what ways were canals sometimes badly made?

17. What areas did not have canals?

18. Why would it have been useful to widen some canals? Why was it not done?

19. What traffic did canals fail to attract? Why?

20. When did canals begin to decline? Why?

Further Work

1. On a map of England, draw the main rivers. Put in the Trent-Mersey Canal. Link it to the Severn at Stourport and the Thames at Oxford. This was the start of the network; add any others you find.

2. Read about Telford's work as a canal builder.

3. Read about the labourers who built the canals. What were they called?

4. Find pictures of canals, the buildings that went with them, and canal boats.

5. What ways were there of changing levels?

6. You are a Midlands manufacturer of the 18th century. Explain why you are helping to pay for a canal to serve your town.

CHAPTER 6

Railways

Wagon-Ways. Modern railways developed from the wagon-ways of the sixteenth, seventeenth and eighteenth centuries.

At least as early as 1600 it had been found that it was much easier to move a loaded cart along rails, than along a road. The surface was smoother and consequently there was less friction.

Wagon-ways were particularly common on the Northumberland and Durham coal field. As the seams near the rivers were worked out, the mines moved inland and there was a problem of transport. The answer was to build a network of wagon-ways, some of the lines being twelve to sixteen kilometres long. Many other uses were found for wagon-ways, but the linking of mine and river was the most common.

The first rails were made of wood, which wore out quickly, so when iron became more plentiful they laid plates to protect it. Later on, rails were made entirely of cast iron. The first were produced at Coalbrookdale in 1767 and they were common by the 1790's. For extra strength they made them "fish-bellied". The invention of the steam locomotive meant rails had to take much heavier loads, and both wood and cast iron were likely to break. Thanks to the discoveries of Henry Cort there was now plenty of wrought iron which was generally used after 1810. Rails still kept the fish-bellied shape.

The usual way to move wagons was by horse, but there were other methods. Running down a slope they used gravity. The loaded wagons on their way down pulled up the empties, going the other way. At an incline that was too steep for a horse there would be a winch, powered in the late eighteenth century by a stationary steam engine.

The wagon-ways were privately owned and the general public could no more use them than we can use mineral lines that serve mines and quarries today. However, in 1801 the Surrey Iron Railway opened, so 33 named because its track was of iron. It ran from the Thames at Wandsworth to Croydon, a distance of about twelve kilometres. It was managed by a public company and was for public use. Anyone could run a wagon along the railway, on payment of a toll, just as he would on a turnpike road. People began to think about the possibilities of a network of public railways, but before the development of the steam locomotive, the advantage seemed to lie with canals.

Something must be said about the Stockton to Darlington line, though since it connected coal mines to the River Tees, it was safely in the tradition of the old wagon-ways. It was engineered by George Stephenson, and opened in 1825. It was 40 kilometres long and at various stages relied on horses, stationary engines and gravity. To cover part of the distance was a locomotive, the *Locomotion*. The line was different from many wagon-ways in that the owners allowed outsiders to run their wagons along it, on payment of a toll. As with the Surrey Iron Railway, this was treating the railway as if it were a road. Unfortunately vehicles cannot pass or avoid each other on a railway, so allowing the public on it was bound to lead to confusion.

Stockton to Darlington is important in railway history for a curious reason. Stephenson fixed the gauge of 4' 8½" inches by taking the average of the wagon-ways in the area. It became the standard gauge for the north-east, then for the rest of Great Britain and is now used on half the railways of the world.

The Steam Locomotive. One of the first men to make a moving steam engine was a Frenchman called Cugnot. He intended it to draw artillery. In England the early experiments were the work of Murdock and Trevithick who, like Cugnot, meant their machines to run on roads. Then, in 1804, Richard Trevithick made a locomotive that ran on rails for a Welsh iron works. Later, in 1808 he made his *Catch-me-who-can*. It was simply a locomotive running round on a circular track for the amusement of the London crowds, but it was a most important development in that it showed the possibility of running steam locomotives on rails.

A problem that taxed the early inventors was the problem of "slip" between wheels and rails, so in 1812 Blenkinsop made his *Salamanca*. It had a large cog wheel, engaging pinions on the rail. He used it at the Middleton colliery in Yorkshire, from where he built a line eight kilometres into Leeds. The *Salamanca* pulled 20 wagons at a time, doing, it was claimed, the work of 50 horses.

In 1813, however, Hedley made his *Puffing Billy*, which hauled eight wagons at 8 km.p.h. along a smooth track, thus showing there was no need of the rack and pinion, as long as gradients were gentle.

We now come to the work of George Stephenson. In 1814 he made the
34 *Blucher*, which had two pistons and so gave a smoother action than the

single piston and flywheel. In 1825 he made his *Locomotion* for the Stockton to Darlington line and this engine could run at about 12 km.p.h.

Finally, there was his most famous locomotive of all, the *Rocket*. The promoters of the Liverpool to Manchester railway, wondering whether to use locomotives or stationary engines, offered a prize of £500 for the best locomotive. The trials were held at Rainhill and the *Rocket* beat its four competitors, running at an average speed of 22 km.p.h. and going as fast as 50 km.p.h. There was nothing new about the engine, but Stephenson did make good use of three ideas that he and others had already developed.

In the first place he used a tubular boiler, which gave a large heating surface making it possible to raise steam quickly. Secondly he directed his steam exhaust up the chimney, which created a strong draught for the fire. These two things together gave such a good head of steam that the pistons could be connected directly to the driving wheels. There was no longer any need for "grasshopper" motion and the complicated system of levers and cogs that the earlier locomotives had needed.

Stephenson's Rocket

The Liverpool to Manchester Line 1830. This was the most important of the early railways. It was built because the promoters thought it could compete with the extension of the Bridgewater canal which joined the two towns. They commissioned George Stephenson as engineer and work began in 1826. The line ran for 48 kilometres and in making it Stephenson had to bore the Edgehill tunnel almost 2 kilometres long, dig a deep cutting, construct a bridge over a canal and cross a notorious marsh called Chat Moss. In doing all this he showed it was possible to build a railway over many different obstacles.

The track was made of the strong, durable wrought iron rails that had already been developed and we have seen how Stephenson produced the first really efficient steam locomotive.

The organisation of the line was important, too. It was a public line in the sense that anyone could use it, unlike the traditional wagon ways. However, the company decided they would not have private vehicles causing confusion. They owned all the rolling stock, so keeping control over the traffic. Another important idea was to carry passengers. It was only an afterthought, but they soon found that the fares made up a great deal of their income.

The Liverpool to Manchester line had the three essentials for success—strong track, well-built locomotives, and efficient organisation. Its opening marks the beginning of the railway age.

Questions

1. When was this engine built? For what railway? (Look at the letters on the wall.)

2. Locate the tops of the two cylinders, standing vertically above the top of the boiler. Trace the drive to the wheels, noting the levers at the top which gave the "grasshopper" motion.

3. What was the reason for having a tall chimney?
4. Where did the driver and fireman stand? What protection had they from the weather?
5. What shape are the rails? From what material would they be made?
6. What does the brake on the wagon tell you?
7. What would the wagon have carried?
8. In what ways was the Rocket an improvement on the Locomotion?

TRANSPORT BETWEEN LIVERPOOL AND MANCHESTER

In 1760 the number of vessels which docked at Liverpool was 2560. In 1824 it was 10 000. In 1784 an American vessel arrived having for part of her cargo eight bags of cotton. In 1824 there were imported to Liverpool 409 670 bags. In 1760 the population of Liverpool was 26 000 and in 1824 125 000. The same stupendous increase was found in the trade and population of Manchester. In 1760 the population was 22 000. In 1824 it was 150 000. The first steam engine was used in Manchester in 1790. In 1824, 200 steam engines were at work. In 1824 there were 30 000 power looms, while ten years previous there was none. The canals which carry the merchandise between the two towns are the Mersey and Irwell and the Bridgewater Canal. The barges have to navigate the River Mersey from Liverpool to Runcorn, a distance of about 20 miles, and thence by separate routes to Manchester, the whole distance being about 50 miles.
(Booth—*Liverpool and Manchester Railway* 1831.)

RAILWAY COMPANY'S PETITION FOR AN ACT

The charge upon goods has been 15s a ton. It is not that the water companies have not been able to give more reasonable terms, but strong in their monopoly they have not thought proper to do so.
It is Competition that is Wanted
But it is not just because of high canal charges that a Railway is desirable. The Canals are inadequate to the regular and punctual conveyance of goods at all periods and seasons.

Questions
1. Draw diagrams to show the growth of:
a. Trade in Liverpool. b. Industry in Manchester. c. Population in both towns.
2. What industry has caused this growth?
3. Why is good transport needed between the towns?
4. How have the canals taken advantage?
5. How and why are they unreliable?

BUILDING THE LIVERPOOL-MANCHESTER RAILWAY

Chat Moss. Chat Moss is a huge bog, in some places 35 feet deep, and so fluid that an iron rod would sink through. The Railway floats on the surface, its compactness and buoyancy in the most fluid places being assisted by hurdles of brushwood and heather, laid under the wooden sleepers.
The Edgehill Tunnel. In some places the substance excavated was a soft blue shale, with a lot of water; in other places a wet sand presented itself and sometimes the miners refused to work. Nor is this surprising for they were boring their way in the dark, with the water streaming round them, and uncertain whether the props and stays would bear the pressure till the arch-work was completed. Other portions were through fine sandstone, clean, dry and substantial, needing no props or arches. The Tunnel was built in eight separate lengths, connecting with the surface by upright shafts. The accuracy with which these lengths were joined is most creditable to the engineer.
The Sankey Viaduct. Two hundred piles, 30 feet in length, were driven hard into the foundations of each of the ten piers. The heavy ram, hoisted up with snail's pace, and then falling down like a thunderbolt on the head of the devoted timber, driving it perhaps a single half inch into the stratum below well illustrates the old adage "slow but sure." The viaduct is nine arches, each of 50 feet span and 70 feet above the Sankey Canal.
(Booth—*Liverpool and Manchester Railway.* 1831.)

Questions

1. How does the railway cross Chat Moss?
2. Name three rocks the tunnel passes through.
3. On what plan was the tunnel made?
4. What was "most creditable to the engineer"?
5. How many piles were driven for the viaduct?
6. What does the viaduct cross? Why is it famous? (use a reference book.)

14. What did "Puffing Billy" prove?
15. When and where was the "Rocket" proved?
16. Give three reasons for its success.
17. Why was the Liverpool to Manchester line built?
18. Give four engineering works found on it.
19. What rails were used?
20. How was this railway organised?

Questions—Chapter Six

1. Where were wagon-ways common? Why?
2. What were the first rails make from?
3. What iron was first used? What replaced it?
4. What shape were iron rails?
5. Give three ways of hauling wagons.
6. Where did the Surrey Iron Railway run?
7. How was it different from other wagon-ways?
8. Why was the Stockton to Darlington line built? When? Who was its engineer?
9. Name a locomotive that ran on it.
10. Why was there sometimes confusion on this line?
11. What was important about its gauge?
12. Who built "Catch-me-who-can"?
13. How did Blenkinsop overcome slip?

Further Work

1. Find pictures of the early wagon-ways and the vehicles that ran on them.
2. What are the differences between cast and wrought iron. Why is wrought iron better for rails? (Chapter Eight).
3. Find out more about railway lines and sleepers.
4. What other countries have the same railway gauge as Britain? Which have a different gauge?
5. Read more about early locomotives and their makers.
6. It is 1820 and you are a Manchester cotton manufacturer. Say why you would like a railway to Liverpool, but also why you think the idea is almost impossible.
7. You have just seen the opening of the Liverpool to Manchester Railway. Say what future you think railways have.

SECTION THREE
Industry 1760-1815

CHAPTER 7

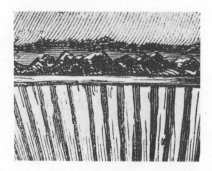

Coal Mining

At the beginning of the eighteenth century Great Britain produced, perhaps, 2½ million tonnes of coal each year; by the end of the century it was 10 million tonnes. The increase was due to greater demand, improved mining techniques and better transport.

Demand. Coal is burnt in private homes, and in industry. In the eighteenth century most people lived in the countryside and no villager would be willing to pay for coal when he could go to the common and have wood, furze or peat for nothing. Only a few industries burnt coal. It was used for brick making, sugar refining, soap boiling and glass. However, there were plenty of other industries that needed heat, but were unable to use it. Brewers for example, found that if they dried hops with it, the beer tasted of sulphur. Even more important, it was not a lot of use to the iron industry. Some kinds would heat iron in the forge without ruining it, but all attempts to smelt with it were failures. Generally speaking, the ordinary householder burnt wood, and in industry they burnt charcoal. However, as time went on, more and more coal was needed.

In the first place, the forests dwindled away. The agricultural revolution hastened their going, for the enclosure movement meant that the commons were cleared of their timber and cultivated.

At the same time, the population grew, and the towns along with it. London had been a great consumer of coal for some time. It was the first city to grow to any size and, being a port, it was easy to supply it from the Northumberland and Durham coalfield. This trade in "sea coal" had flourished since the Middle Ages. Now other towns began to spread, and their inhabitants found that coal was the only practical fuel for cooking and heating.

In industry there was a most important development when the Darby family of Coalbrookdale discovered how to use coke to smelt iron. By 1790, 97% of the iron produced in Britain was smelted in coke furnaces. The coal industry had found an important customer.

Something must be said about the steam engine. Obviously the fact that there was plenty of coal at hand encouraged Newcomen, Watt and others to develop the new form of power. However, before 1800 steam engines were few, and it was not until well into the nineteenth century that they were burning coal in quantity.

Improved Techniques. The industry met the increased demand for coal partly by employing more labour, but also by using new techniques.

Probably the most important development was the use of Newcomen engines for pumping. The early miners preferred open cast workings, but they also dug shallow bell-pits to seams just below the surface. If they had to go far into the ground they made pits that could be drained by adits. Eventually, though, all the easily mined coal was won and they had to sink deep shafts that would not drain naturally. Immediately they had the problem of water. They had pumps of a kind, such as buckets attached to an endless chain, but they could only raise water a short distance. The atmospheric engine of Thomas Newcomen was the answer. It was simple to the point of being crude, and its fuel consumption was alarming. None the less, it was effective, as was shown by one that was installed at Barnsley. It raised three and a half million litres of water every day and made it possible to mine four million tonnes of coal.

In addition to water, miners had to contend with gas. There was "choke damp", or carbon dioxide, which would suffocate them, and "fire damp", or methane, which would explode. One way of dealing with it was by "wafting" which meant waving a stout piece of cloth at the entrance to the mine. Another way was to send in a man covered with a wet sack and holding a long taper ahead of him. He exploded the pockets of gas that collected under the roof. It was a great improvement when, in the larger mines, some owners used two shafts. One of these, the "upcast" shaft, had a fire at the bottom which drew air down the downcast shaft and through the workings. Even with this improvement gas remained a serious problem and many seams were unworkable because of it.

Underground, carrying the coal from the face to the bottom of the shaft was the work of women and children. They had tubs, or sometimes wicker baskets, which they pushed and pulled on sledges. Towards the end of the eighteenth century some pits had iron rails and the tubs were mounted on wheels. Pit ponies were used increasingly in the larger mines.

There were several ways of bringing the coal up the shaft. Sometimes there was a windlass turned by hand, but the most advanced method they had was the horse capstan. Whichever was used, the coal, and indeed 41

Children hauled coal tubs through narrow underground passages

miners, came up the shaft swinging dangerously on the end of a hemp rope. There were mines where girl bearers carried the coal up ladders, or a kind of spiral staircase.

At the coal face itself there was no change. Men still hewed it from the rock with hand tools. Indeed it is obvious from what has been said that almost all the work in bringing the coal to the surface was done by hand.

Transport. We have seen how the demand for coal increased and how output increased in order to meet it. There was, however, the problem of carrying the coal from the mines to the customers. Before the building of the railways the only way to do this at all cheaply was by water. It was because it was so well served by river and sea transport that the Northumberland and Durham coalfield was the first to produce coal in quantity. Elsewhere the industry could not expand. Transport by packhorse made coal too expensive.

The first development came in the north-east where the mine owners found they were losing their natural advantages because the seams near the rivers were being worked out. As the mines moved back from the water, they built wagon-ways. Horse-drawn wagons were good enough to link mines with rivers, but for long distances something more was needed. The answer was to build canals. In 1761 the Duke of Bridgewater opened his famous canal from his mines at Worsley to Manchester, and halved the price of coal in that town. Other canals followed and although they carried a great variety of goods, they took far more coal than anything else. Wherever the coal went, industry followed.

Results. The coal industry allowed people to live in large cities and continue to cook and heat their homes quite easily. Coal created the modern iron industry, and it encouraged the use of steam power. Because of these three things, coal made the industrial revolution possible.

Questions on Picture
1. What is the man doing? How is he dressed?
2. What is causing the light ahead of him?
3. What improvements were made in some mines to make such work unnecessary?

EXPLOSIONS
Explosions from fire damp are well known wherever mines have been worked into a competent cavity. One which happened near Newcastle was very remarkable; 70 men were blown out of the pit and a large piece of timber about ten yards long and ten inches thick was blown a considerable distance and stuck into the side of a hill. (Sharp—*Treatise on Coal Mines.* 1769.)

Questions on Extract
1. What causes explosions? In what kind of mine?
2. How does the writer show the power of the explosions?

TRANSPORT UNDERGROUND—USE OF CHILDREN
The hurriers who haul the coal buckle round their naked persons a broad leather strap, to which is attached in front a ring and about 4 feet of chain ending in a hook. As soon as they enter the main gates, they detach their harness from the corve, change their position by getting behind it, and become 'thrusters''. The vehicle is

43

then placed upon the rail, a candle is stuck fast by a piece of wet clay, and away they run, pushing their load with their heads and hands. The command they hold over it at every curve and angle, considering the pace, the unevenness of the floors and rails, and the mud, water and stones, is truly astonishing. I know few gates that will allow the use of horses; hence has arisen the substitution of children. In some I have had to creep upon my hands and knees, the height barely twenty inches, and then have gone still lower upon my breast, and crawled like a turtle. In others I have been able to accomplish my journey stooping. They are sometimes of great length. In the Booth Town Pit I walked, crept and rode 1800 yards to one of the nearest faces; the most distant was 200 yards further; the floor of the gate was every here and there three and four inches deep in water and muddy throughout. The roofs and walls are sometimes even, at other rough, rocky and loose, requiring proppings to prevent their falling; despite, however, the utmost precautions, large masses occasionally fall.
(*Royal Commission on Mines.*)

Questions
1. What does the child use to pull his corve?
2. Why do you suppose he is called a "hurrier"?
3. What is a "main gate"? What has been put there to make hauling the coal easier?
4. Why are horses not much used?
5. Describe a gate: size, length, floor, roof.
6. What is the most likely accident. What others do you suppose are possible?

WINDING GEAR
Gins are turned by horses. Those of the very worst kind, broken-winded, spavined and blind, are made to perform the work. Gins are not too dangerous as the strength of the horse is seldom enough either to draw the corve over the pulley or to break the rope. The motion in coming up or down the shaft is, of course, regulated by the animal or the attention of the child that

drives it; it is sometimes quick, at others slow and jerking. Sometimes a swinging motion is given to the corve; the chances then are that you get a blow from the other ascending or descending corve, or strike the sides of the shaft with the danger of being thrown out.
The turn-wheel is more dangerous, as you are, at all times dependent upon the man or woman who works it. It is nothing more than a common well-winch, with a fly-wheel. In getting off the corve you are at the mercy of the winder. As soon as you arrive at the top, the handle is made fast by a bolt drawn from the upright post; the winder then grasps your hand and brings you by main force to land. The unfortunate case of David Pellett who was drawn over the roller by his own uncle and grandfather, just when their attention was drawn to a passing funeral, is a painful illustration of their unsafety.
(*Royal Commission on Mines.*)

Questions
1. Find a picture of a horse gin.
2. Who controls a gin?
3. Describe the horses that work gins.
4. What accidents are unlikely with one? What can go wrong?
5. Describe a turn-wheel. Give two ways in which it is particularly dangerous.

Questions—Chapter Seven
1. How much did coal production increase in the eighteenth century?
2. Give three reasons for this increase.
3. Explain the low demand for coal in the early eighteenth century. (Domestic and industrial.)
4. What was happening to the forests?
5. Describe London's coal trade.
6. Why did domestic demand increase?
7. What new form of power needed coal?
8. What industry began to use coal? Why?
9. Why did drainage of mines become a problem?
10. How was it solved?
11. What two gases gave problems?
12. How was mine ventilation improved?
13. What was the old way of carrying coal underground?

14. How was it improved?
15. Give three ways of bringing coal up the shaft.
16. How did miners hew coal?
17. Where was most coal produced? Why?
18. What form of transport developed in the north-east?
19. What was built elsewhere?
20. How did coal make the industrial revolution possible?

Further Work
1. Find pictures of child miners. Read more about their work, and work done by women.

2. How did Newcomen's engine work? (Chapter 9).
3. Read about the use of coal to make iron. (Chapter 8).
4. Read more about the transport of coal. (Chapters 5 and 6).
5. You are an 18th century mine owner and you want to increase the size and depth of your mine. What are your problems and how will you overcome them?
6. Imagine you are a child miner. Describe the mine, your work and the dangers you face.

CHAPTER 8

The Iron Industry

The Early Eighteenth Century. First of all we must look, briefly, at the way iron was made. For fuel they used charcoal from oak trees. They mixed it with the iron ore and some limestone and put it in a blast furnace to smelt it. The furnace had this name because they blasted air into the bottom of it in order to make the fire hot. When it was tapped, the iron ran out into hollows made in a bed of sand. After the ingots had set, and had been turned over, they looked like a litter of piglets lying side by side. For this reason the iron that came straight from the blast furnace was known as pig iron. It was so hard that the only way to shape it was to melt it and cast it and in this form it was known as cast iron.

Pig iron contains a good deal of carbon which it absorbs from the fuel in the blast furnace. Carbon makes iron hard, but too much of it also makes it brittle. Though suitable for such things as the cylinder of a steam engine cast iron would not for example be any use for the moving parts of a machine. Here wrought iron was used and this was made by removing much of the carbon. They did this by heating the iron and then beating it under heavy trip hammers, a process which took a good deal of time. Wrought iron, though softer than cast iron, is easy to work, and is not brittle. In the eighteenth century it took the place of steel for almost everything but the cutting edges of tools.

The iron industry was found in places where there was ore, and plenty of oak trees to make charcoal. Two typical areas were the Weald of Kent and Sussex and the Forest of Dean in Gloucestershire. The manufacturers needed water power to drive the blast furnace bellows and the trip hammers, so the works were fairly well scattered along the banks of fast flowing streams. Because of this most iron firms were family affairs, each owning little more than a small blast furnace and a forge with its trip hammer.

In the first half of the eighteenth century the British iron industry had problems. It suffered from poor transport and foreign competition. Swedish and Russian iron was better than our own. However, the main problem was fuel. Only oak charcoal would burn with enough heat to smelt iron and it took six large trees to make one tonne of iron. Not surprisingly the forests were vanishing and it was clear that unless someone found another fuel, the industry would decline.

Technical Changes. In the first place the fuel problem was solved by the Darby family. There were three Abraham Darbys, father, son and grandson. Their works at Coalbrookdale in Shropshire is one of the most famous.

It is obvious that coal will burn with enough heat for smelting, but it contains so many impurities that it will ruin the iron. The answer which the Darbys found was to turn it into coke, which is nearly pure carbon. To change to the new fuel, though, was by no means quick and easy. It was important to find the right type of coal for coking and the right type of ore to go with it. Abraham Darby the first began the work soon after 1700, but he left it to his son to finish. It was not until the 1750's that smelting with coke became at all usual, and indeed many iron works went on burning charcoal until the end of the century. The Darbys' discovery did mean, however, that there was no immediate danger of running out of fuel.

The need now was to speed up the manufacture of wrought iron. In the early 1780's important discoveries were made by Henry Cort at his iron works at Fareham in Hampshire. First of all Cort used a puddling furnace, which was a form of reverberatory furnace. The idea is to

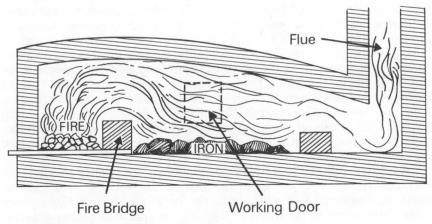

Fire Bridge   Working Door

Section through a reverberatory furnace

47

keep the fire away from the molten iron, otherwise carbon will be added to it not taken away. The furnace has a low wall across it with the fire on one side and the iron on the other. The heat from the fire is reflected down on to the iron from the roof of the furnace—it "reverberates"—like noise in an empty room. When it was molten the iron on the surface rapidly lost its carbon since it combined with the oxygen in the air and went away as carbon dioxide. By stirring, or puddling, all the iron in the furnace would lose as much carbon as was wanted. A workman did this through a hole in the front of the furnace.

The iron that came from the puddling furnace was still far from good, but Cort found he could bring it up to standard by passing it between heavy rollers.

Cort was in business in a small way, but in 1787 his discovery was taken up by Richard Crawshay and used in his works at Cyfarthfa in South Wales. Soon Crawshay had shown quite clearly the value of Cort's discoveries, and had made himself a fortune. By the early nineteenth century Great Britain could produce wrought iron more cheaply than Sweden or Russia.

There were other changes that helped the industry. One of these was the invention of the steam engine which could be used to work the bellows to blast furnaces and drive the rolling mills. Another was the building of canals, since water transport was the only way to move the raw materials and finished goods in bulk.

Results of the Technical Changes. In the first place, the iron industry itself was transformed. It moved from the oak forests to its new source of fuel, the coal fields. Important works grew up in South Wales, the West Midlands, South Yorkshire and on Clydeside. The industry became larger, and employed far more people. Large firms appeared under the control of wealthy ironmasters. There were the Darbys in Shropshire, the Guests and the Crawshays in South Wales, Roebuck in Falkirk and the most colourful personality of them all, John Wilkinson. He was so enthusiastic that they called him "iron mad". He even had an iron coffin made, though he had outgrown it before he died. In 1787 he proved it was possible to have an iron ship, by making one and floating it on the Severn. Also he greatly improved the technique of boring castings. His works at Bersham supplied James Watt with accurately bored cylinders, before which all Watt's attempts to build a full sized engine were failures.

The growth of the industry was important for transport. In 1787 Abraham Darby built the first iron bridge. He wanted it to link his works at Coalbrookdale with those on the other side of the Severn. Later there were structures like Telford's suspension bridge over the Menai Straits. Iron was even more important for railways; without it they would never have been built. Again the Darby family were the pioneers, as the third Abraham cast the first iron rails in 1767.

Iron was important for other industries. The production of cannon and other weapons increased, especially during the Seven Years War (1756-1763) and the Napoleonic Wars. There could have been no steam engine without it, and no machinery for textiles or anything else. A new departure was the use of iron in building. The textile manufacturers were anxious to have fire-proof mills and were pleased to have an ample supply of iron that could be used instead of timber.

In the early years of the eighteenth century iron was the hand-maid of wood. The industry did little more than supply the odds and ends of iron needed on the farms or on the ships. By the end of the century it was making possible a revolution in transport and in industry.

Questions
1. Who invented puddling? What is its purpose?
2. What use are the openings in front of the furnaces?
3. What is the use of the long iron bar, with the handle, lying on top of the furnace?
4. The workman is taking an iron bloom out of the furnace. Where will it be taken next?
5. What fuel does the furnace burn? Why does it not contaminate the iron?

COALBROOKDALE IRON WORKS
It was my husband's father, Abraham Darby that attempted to mould and cast Iron pots etc. in sand instead of Loam (as they were wont to do, which made it a tedious and expensive process) in which he succeeded. About the year 1709 he came into Shropshire to Coalbrookdale. He here cast Iron Goods in sand out of the Blast Furnace that blow'd with wood charcoal; for it was not yet thought of to blow with Pit Coal. Some time after he thought that it might be practable to smelt the Iron from the ore in the blast Furnace with Pit Coal. Upon this he first try'd with raw coal as it came out of the Mines, but it did not answer. He was not discouraged, had the coal coak'd into Cynder as is done for drying Malt, and then succeeded to his satisfaction. These were beneficial discoveries. My Husband Abraham Darby was but six years old when his Father died, but he inherited his genius and made many improvements. One of Consequence to the prosperity of these Works was as they were very short of water that in the Summer or dry Seasons they were obliged to blow very slow, and generally blow out   49

the furnaces once a year, which was attended with great loss. But my Husband proposed to Erecting a Fire Engine to draw up the Water from the lower Works and convey it back into the upper pools, that by continual rotation of the Water the furnaces might be plentifully supplied. But all this time the making of Barr Iron at forges from Pit Coal pigs was not thought of. My husband conceived the happy thought that it might be possible to make bar from pit coal pigs. Upon this he Sent some of our pigs to be tryed at the Forges, and a good account being given of them, he erected a blast furnace for Pig Iron for Forges. Had not these dicoveries been made the Iron trade of our produce would have dwindled away, for woods for charcoal became very Scarce and landed Gentlemen rose the price of cord wood exceeding high—indeed it would not have been to be got. But from Pit Coal being introduced in its stead the demand for wood charcoal is much lessn'd, and in a few years I apprehend will set the use of that article aside.

Many other improvements he was the author of. One of Service to these Works here they used to carry all their mine and coal upon horses' backs but he got roads made and laid with Sleepers and rails as they have them in the North of England. And one wagon will bring as much as twenty horses used to bring on horses' backs. Of late years the laying of rails of cast Iron was substituted for wood, which altho' expensive, answers well for Ware and Duration. We have in the different Works near twenty miles of this road which cost upwards of Eight hundred pounds a mile. That of Iron Wheels and axle trees for these wagons was I believe my Husband's Invention.

(Letter of wife of Abraham Darby II, Abiah Darby.)

Questions

1. When did Abraham Darby I go to Coalbrookdale?
2. What did he manufacture?
3. How did he improve the casting process?
4. What happened when he first tried smelting with coal?
5. How did he succeed?
6. Why did the works need water power?
7. What happened when there was no rain?
8. How was the problem solved?
9. Where was wrought iron made? (Bar iron).
10. What iron had always been used to make it?
11. What did Abraham Darby try?
12. Why was the discovery of the use of coal important?
13. Where did the idea of railways come from?
14. How did they improve efficiency?
15. What were they first made from?
16. What did Abraham Darby use instead?
17. How much was invested in railways?
18. How were wagons improved?
19. List the improvements of the first two Darbys.
20. Why was Abraham Darby III famous?

Questions—Chapter Eight

1. What fuel was first used in blast furnaces?
2. What is iron straight from the furnace called?
3. What does it contain? What does this make it?
4. How was wrought iron made? What are its qualities?
5. Give two important iron producing areas of the early 18th century. Why was iron made there?
6. Why were most iron firms small?
7. Why was there a fuel problem?
8. Who solved the fuel problem? How?
9. Who speeded up the making of wrought iron?
10. What furnace did he use? How did it work?
11. What happened to the iron when it left the furnace?
12. Who first used the new process on a big scale?
13. Name two ways the steam engine helped.

14. What form of transport was especially useful?
15. Name four areas where the iron industry became important.
16. Which iron master was called "iron mad"?
17. How did he help Boulton and Watt?
18. Who built the first iron bridge? Where?
19. How else did iron help transport?
20. Name four ways iron helped other industries.

Further Work

1. Look for 18th century iron goods in museums.

2. Find out about the art of charcoal burning.
3. Find and copy a diagram of the inside of a blast furnace.
4. Draw a map to show (a) where the iron industry was in the early 18th century (b) where it was in 1800.
5. Find pictures of iron bridges built about 1800.
6. What is the difference between steel and cast iron and wrought iron? Why was steel little used in the 18th century? (Chapter 23).
7. You are a worker at Coalbrookdale in 1800. Say why your firm has been important in the history of the iron industry and the history of transport.

CHAPTER 9

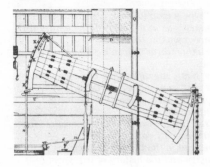

The
Steam Engine

It had been known for a long time that there was power in steam, but no-one managed to use it in an engine until just before the beginning of the eighteenth century.

Savery's Engine 1698. This was a pump rather than an engine, and apart from its valves it had no moving parts. The inventor meant it to drain mines, but it had so many drawbacks that it was not much used. It was only 0.05% efficient, so it burnt a lot of fuel. It had little power and could not be used for mines of any great depth. The boiler had no safety valve and was likely to explode.

Newcomen's Engine 1708. This engine worked by atmospheric pressure. It had a cylinder and a piston. The cylinder filled with steam which was condensed with a spray of cold water, so creating a partial vacuum. Atmospheric pressure then drove the piston down.

This engine could work the bellows to a blast furnace, but it was used mainly for pumping, sometimes in Cornish tin mines, though mainly in coal mines. It could drive an effective pump and make new supplies of coal available from the deeper seams.

Newcomen engines were simple and there was little to go wrong. Even if one did, the local blacksmith could usually do the repair. They remained in use until the 1830's.

One weakness was that they burnt a lot of fuel, so they were not much used away from coalfields. Also, since they could not give rotary motion, they could not drive machinery directly. The best they could do 52 was to pump water into the reservoir of a water wheel.

Watt's Engine 1769. James Watt was instrument maker to Glasgow University. He was given a model of a Newcomen engine to repair and decided to improve it. He saw it used a lot of fuel because the steam was condensed by cooling the cylinder, which, as a result, had to be reheated at every stroke of the engine. To overcome this, Watt built a separate condenser, connected to the cylinder by a tube. The cylinder could now remain hot all the time as the steam was condensed elsewhere.

Watt went into partnership with Matthew Boulton who owned the Soho Works at Birmingham, Boulton providing the capital to develop the engine. The engine itself was not a success until John Wilkinson supplied a cylinder bored accurately at his Bersham works.

Watt now had an efficient pumping engine, but he wanted to develop it so that it would drive machinery. The up and down pumping motion had to be converted to rotary motion. The obvious way was with a crank, but the crank had already been patented by Pickard. On the suggestion of his assistant, William Murdock, Watt used the "sun and planet" device until Pickard's patent expired.

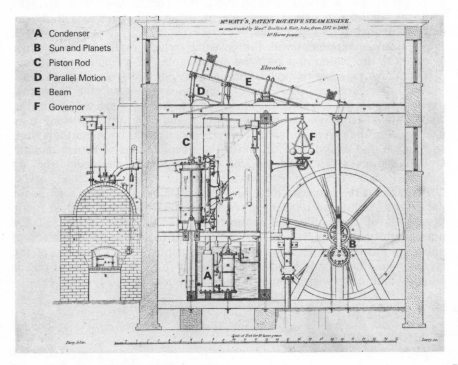

A   Condenser
B   Sun and Planets
C   Piston Rod
D   Parallel Motion
E   Beam
F   Governor

James Watt's rotative steam engine

Important changes were made to the piston. In the earlier engines only the down stroke was a working stroke, which was all that was needed for pumping. For rotary motion, though, it was better to have the engine working on the up stroke as well. To achieve this Watt did three things. In the first place he closed in the cylinder head, and made the upper half of the cylinder steam-tight. Secondly he admitted steam at each side of the piston alternately. Thirdly, the steam was under slight pressure and it was this, not the force of the atmosphere, which drove the piston. The condenser was still essential because it meant that the steam was pushing against a partial vacuum, instead of the full weight of the atmosphere.

There was now a problem where the piston rod met the beam. Formerly there had been a chain, which was quite good enough for a downward pull, but, obviously it could not take an upward thrust. There could not be a direct connection because the end of the beam moved through the arc of a circle and the piston rod would be swung out of the upright position. This could not be, as the cylinder head was closed in. To solve his problem Watt invented parallel motion. This was a system of levers which allowed the piston rod to move in a straight line and, at the same time, push and pull the end of a beam that was moving through part of a circle.

The final development was the governor which regulated the supply of steam to the piston and kept the engine going at a regular speed.

It was now possible to have a steady rotary action from steam power.

The early Boulton and Watt engines were used for pumping, particularly in the Cornish tin mines, which were a long way from the coal fields. Coal owners, on the other hand, had all the fuel they needed, and they went on using Newcomen engines, because they were so reliable and easy to repair. With the development of rotary motion, steam engines were used in iron works, textile factories and on wagon-ways for drawing trucks with cables.

Throughout the eighteenth century, however, steam power was never important. As late as 1800 there were only 1200 engines, against many thousands of windmills and water mills. By the second half of the nineteenth century, however, steam was the most important source of power in most major industries and in transport. The inventors of the steam engine had made it possible to unlock the vast reserves of power which would otherwise have lain idle in the coal fields.

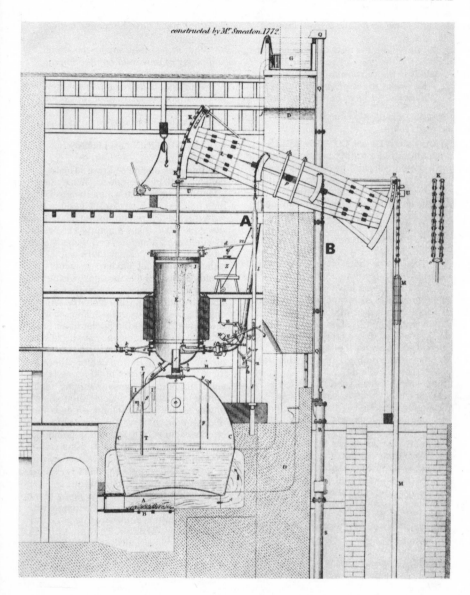

constructed by Mr Smeaton. 1772.

Questions

1. This is an atmospheric engine. Who built it? When? Who built the first of this kind?

2. Locate: pump rod (on far right); beam; chain linking beam to piston; piston; cylinder; "haystack" boiler; steam inlet to cylinder; outlet for water from cylinder.

3. Why are the ends of the beam curved?

4. Why is water being sprayed into the cylinder?
5. What will be the next thing to happen?
6. What is the work of rods A and B?
7. What is the purpose of this engine?
8. Why would it not drive machinery?
9. Why would it have burnt a lot of fuel?

5. What might have happened without steam power?
6. What is meant by saying the steam engine is "of universal application and unlimited extent"?
7. What limit is there on its use? How was this to affect the location of the cotton industry?
8. How many processes go on in a mill?

STEAM POWER IN COTTON MILLS

Seven hundred and fifty people are enough for a cotton mill, and by the assistance of the steam-engine, they will spin as much thread as 200 000 could do without machinery. The invention of the steam engine has changed industry as the invention of gunpowder changed warfare. (Farey—Treatise on the Steam Engine.)

Amazing as was the progress which had taken place in the cotton industry prior to 1790, it would soon have found a check upon its further extension if a power more efficient than water had not been discovered. Happily, a power was discovered, of almost universal application and unlimited extent, adapted to every locality where fuel was cheap. This power was the steam engine.
It is by iron fingers, teeth and wheels, moving with exhaustless energy and devouring speed, that the cotton is opened, cleaned, spread, carded, drawn, roved, spun, wound, warped, dressed and woven. All the machines move at once and all derive their motion from the mighty engine, which firmly seated in the lower part of the building and constantly fed with water and fuel, toils through the day with the strength of perhaps a hundred horses.
(Baines—History of the Cotton Manufacture.)

Questions

1. How many people may work in a cotton mill?
2. How many would be needed to do the same work without machinery?
3. What does Farey compare with the steam engine?
4. What power had the cotton industry used before 1790? Why was it unreliable?

STEAM POWER IN COLLIERIES

(Tyneside.)
The pumping engine at Friar's Goose colliery is 180 horse-power. The cylinder is 6 feet in diameter, in which the stroke is nine feet. At each stroke 195 gallons of water are delivered on the surface, and as there are six strokes a minute 1170 gallons are delivered a minute, or 1 444 800 a day. At South Hetton colliery there is a pumping engine of 300 horse-power. Winding engines are used for raising the coals and for lowering the men and boys. They are quite separate from the pumping engines which have quite enough work of their own to do. At the Eppleton pit they raise 50 score of tubs per day, or 333 tons, the winding engine being of 100 horse-power. At South Hetton Colliery there are three winding engines of 90 horse-power each, adjoining the great pumping engine before named. The concentration of steam power at this establishment exceeds that of any other colliery. The power of 570 horses is constantly exerted in pumping out the water and drawing up the coal. I found that the engineers were very proud of their engines and kept them very much cleaner than they cared to keep themselves. They are always going about them, pouring oil here, and wiping with tow or hemp there, loosing this part and screwing up the other. They always called the engine "She" and seem to have great affection for "Her".
(Leifchild—Our Coal Fields and Our Coal Pits.)

Questions

1. What is the size of the Friar's Goose cylinder?
2. What is the "stroke" of an engine?

3. How much water does this engine pump in a day?
4. How much might the one at South Hetton pump?
5. What are winding engines for?
6. How powerful are they in comparison?
7. How do the engineers show pride in their engines?
8. How did the use of steam engines make mining more efficient?

Questions—Chapter Nine
1. What was the purpose of Savery's engine?
2. Name three drawbacks it had.
3. What force drove Newcomen's engine?
4. How was steam used in it?
5. Where was the engine most used?
6. What happened if one went wrong?
7. Why did it burn a lot of fuel?
8. How did Watt show fuel could be saved?
9. How did (a) Boulton (b) Wilkinson help Watt?
10. What did Watt use instead of the crank? Why?
11. Name three changes made to the piston.
12. What connected beam and piston in an atmospheric engine?
13. What device did Watt invent to join the piston rod and the beam? Why was it needed?

14. What device kept the engine speed steady?
15. What action did all Watt's improvements make possible in a steam engine?
16. Who went on using Newcomen's engines? Why?
17. Where were many Boulton and Watt pumping engines used? Why?
18. Name two of the first industries to use the rotary engine.
19. What were the main sources of power in 1800?
20. When did the steam engine become really important?

Further Work
1. Read more about James Watt and Matthew Boulton.
2. Find out about water and wind power. What disadvantages did both have?
3. What work did John Smeaton do in improving water wheels and steam engines?
4. Read about the Cornish mining industry.
5. How was the steam engine improved after Watt? Look especially at the work of Murdock.
6. It is 1800 and you are a retired engineer. Say how the steam engine has developed in your lifetime and how you see its future.

CHAPTER 10

The Cotton Industry

A small cotton industry was established in this country in the late sixteenth century, but for a long time after that most of our cottons were imported from India. By the eighteenth century they were becoming very popular and the demand for them grew. English manufacturers saw there was a lot of money to be made and they were determined to compete both with their Indian rivals, and with the well-established woollen industry in this country. They were successful in both because they took advantage of a good many important inventions and because they developed the factory system.

Inventions. The first of these was John Kay's flying shuttle, patented in 1733. It was a simple enough attachment to the hand loom, but it made it possible for a weaver to work twice as quickly as before. The weavers were afraid it would cost them their jobs and they were so hostile to Kay that he fled abroad. However, they soon found the value of his flying shuttle and made themselves a good deal richer by using it.

The weavers did run into a problem, though, in that they were now working so quickly that they often ran out of yarn. The spinners could not keep up with them as they were still using the old fashioned wheel that produced only one thread at a time. It was necessary to invent something better.

In 1765 James Hargreaves patented his spinning jenny. Cotton thread has to be stretched as it is spun, which the spinners had done by holding it in their fingers and pulling. For the spinners' fingers Hargreaves substituted a moving clasp that would hold several threads at once. His first jenny spun six threads at a time and later models as many as eighty. Jenny thread was reasonably fine, but was soft and
58 weak. It was quite suitable for weft which goes the width of the cloth,

but was not strong enough for warp which runs the whole length.

The next machine was the water frame patented by Richard Arkwright in 1769. How far it was Arkwright's original invention is open to doubt and we do know that the most important idea in it had been developed some years before by Lewis Paul. This was to draw out the thread by rollers. Water frame thread was stronger than jenny thread so it was ideal for warp.

A most important thing about the water frame was that, as its name suggests, it needed water to drive it. Arkwright first tried a horse gin, but he preferred the smooth, steady power that only a water wheel could give. As we shall see, this was to have important results on the organisation of the industry.

In 1779 Samuel Crompton patented his mule, so called because it was a cross between the jenny and the water frame. It used both moving clasp and rollers with the result that its thread was fine and strong. For the first time manufacturers in this country were able to produce muslin which is the most delicate of the cotton fabrics.

There was now so much thread being made that it was difficult to find enough weavers. To solve this problem a clergyman, Edmund Cartwright, invented a power driven loom in 1785.

Unfortunately it had to be stopped so frequently that it was no quicker than a handloom. However, early in the nineteenth century other inventors, notably William Radcliffe, perfected Cartwright's work.

There were other inventions, as for example scutching machines that opened the bales and cleaned the raw cotton, and carding and roving machines that prepared it for spinning. Finishing was also speeded up. In 1784 Thomas Bell invented roller printing so that cloth was no longer printed laboriously by hand. In 1785 James Watt introduced bleaching with chlorine to this country and a process that had taken weeks could be done in a few hours.

The Organisation of the Industry—The Factory System. In the early eighteenth century, the equipment for making cotton cloth was simple enough and small enough to be used in the home. The industry was organised on the domestic system. This did not mean, however, that the workers were entirely their own masters. They stood somewhere between independent craftsmen who provide everything for themselves, and employees, such as the factory hands that are common today, who have only their labour to give. There might have been a time when the textile workers had bought their own materials and equipment and sold their finished goods, as well as finding working space in their own homes. However, by the eighteenth century, wealthy capitalists had a good deal of control. These were merchants who bought the raw cotton 59 and had it delivered to the spinners. Their agents then collected the thread and delivered it to the weavers. They took the woven cloth and usually did the bleaching and printing in their own works. Finally they sold it from their warehouses.

Domestic spinning

60 *Factory spinning*

The spinners and weavers had nothing to do with buying the raw material, or with the organisation of the trade, but they did provide their own equipment and place of work. Above all they still had a good deal of independence, and could work just as and when they liked. Spinners were usually the wives and daughters of farm labourers who had to look after their homes and help outside at busy times like haymaking. Most weavers had a small amount of land, and owned a cow or a pig.

The new inventions brought changes, since complicated machines needing water power could not be used in the home. In 1771 Richard Arkwright and his partner Jedediah Strutt set up the first cotton mill, where they spun thread with water frames. This was at Cromford on the River Derwent. Other such mills followed and domestic spinning ended. Power looms came later, in the early nineteenth century.

It was at this time that the more progressive manufacturers began to build huge mills, iron framed so that they were strong and fireproof, and with steam engines to power the machines. One floor would be for preparation, with others for spinning, weaving and finishing. The factory was planned so that every piece of equipment was in full use all the time. These were completely integrated works, taking in raw cotton, and sending out finished cloth.

The workers had to keep pace with the machines. The days were gone when the craftsman, in the independence of his own home, could finish work when he felt like it, to milk his cow or have a drink with his friends.

The Importance of the Cotton Industry. The cotton industry brought prosperity. It gave employment to thousands of people, and the skilled men in the factories were among the most highly paid workers in the country. It stimulated other industries—coal, iron, engineering, building and chemicals all grew along with cotton. Since we were the only country mass producing cotton goods, they had a ready sale all over the world and our export trade greatly increased. In those days British manufacturers put Germans out of business!

The large supply of cheap clothing was important for the working classes. We have seen how the population grew and it was most important there should be plenty of sensible clothing, easy to wash and at prices ordinary people could afford. The cotton industry met this need.

Unfortunately, there were social problems as well. The industrial towns grew, and we still do not know how to keep up standards of civilisation in these places. A new type of employer and worker appeared—the employer owning everything, and the worker providing nothing but his labour. The two came into conflict, and still do. There were the death agonies of the old craft industries, the handloom weavers suffering particularly, because they either would not or could not take factory work. For a time there was the mass employment of children, who were exploited by parents and factory owners alike.

It was no accident that the period after the Napoleonic Wars, when the cotton industry was reaching its peak, was also a period of great unrest.

Questions

1. Who invented the power loom? When?
2. Name one of the men who improved it in the early nineteenth century.
3. What are nearly all the workers in the picture? Why would an employer prefer this kind of labour?
4. How many workers are there to each loom, roughly?
5. What do the man and woman at the front of the picture seem to be discussing?
6. What do you imagine was the man's work in the factory?
7. How are the looms driven? What is dangerous about such an arrangement?
8. What, probably, provided the power for the factory?

CROMPTON'S MULE

Samuel Crompton's father held a small farm, and, according to the custom of those days, spent part of his time in spinning and weaving. Samuel learned to spin on a jenny, but being dissatisfied with the yarn, he made his own spinning machine. What annoyed him most was that he was not allowed to use his little invention by himself in his garret. He became an object of the curiosity of the people for miles around, many of whom climbed up at the windows to see him at work. He resolved to be rid of the mystery by showing his machine to a number of gentlemen who chose to pay a guinea a-piece. In this way he collected £50 and

was able to make a better and larger machine. In 1812 he estimated the number of mule spindles at work as between four and five million, and in 1829 about seven. He asked Parliament for some reward for the national advantage derived from his invention, and was given £5000. This sum was given to his sons to carry on a bleaching concern, but they mismanaged the business and went bankrupt, reducing their father to poverty.
(Ure—*Cotton Manufacture of Great Britain.* 1836.)

Questions
1. How did Crompton's father make a living?
2. Why did Crompton make his mule?
3. Why do you suppose people were so interested?
4. Why did he give away his secret?
5. Who gave him £5000? Why? What happened to it?

Hours Needed to Spin 100lb. of Cotton
Indian hand spinners (18th century) 50 000
Crompton's mule, worked by hand,
  1780   2000
Power assisted mule, 1795   300
Roberts's automatic mule, 1825   135
Most efficient modern machinery,
  1972   40

Questions
1. How much has spinning been speeded up?
2. How was the mule made more efficient?

A COTTON MILL OF THE 1830's
The building consists of a main body, and two lateral wings, the former being 300 feet long and 50 feet wide, the latter projecting 50 feet in front of the body. The moving power consists of two 80 horse engines, which are mounted on the ground floor. The boilers for supplying steam to the engines and the warming pipes are in an exterior building. As the looms require the utmost stability they are on the ground floor to the number of one thousand. The throstle frames occupy the first and second storeys and the mules the fourth and fifth. The third storey is the preparation gallery, between the throstles and mules. From here the rovings are carried downstairs to be spun into warp on the throstles, and upstairs to be spun into weft on the mules.
(Baines—*History of the Cotton Manufacture.*)

Questions
1. What is the size of this building?
2. How is it powered and heated?
3. Where are the boilers? Why?
4. Where are the looms? Why?
5. Why is preparation done on the third floor?
6. What are warp and weft?
7. The throstle is an improved version of an earlier machine that spun warp. What was that machine?
8. Draw a diagram showing the use of each floor.

COTTON EXPORTS IN THE 1830's
The fabrics of cotton exported in one year would form a girdle passing eleven times round the equator. This manufacture furnishes nearly one half of British exports, and it supplies almost every nation of the world with some portion of its clothing.
(Baines—*History of the Cotton Manufacture.*)

Questions
1. How much cloth is exported? Where does it go?
2. Why are these exports important for Britain?

Questions—Chapter Ten
1. When did the British cotton industry start? What two competitors did it have?
2. Give two reasons for its success.
3. Who invented the flying shuttle?
4. What problem did it create for spinners?
5. Who invented the spinning jenny? How many threads would it spin?
6. How did Arkwright's machine draw out the thread? How was it powered?
7. Who invented the mule? Why was it so named? What quality thread did it produce?

8. Who invented the first power loom?
What was wrong with it? When was it
improved?

9. Name two machines invented to
prepare cotton for spinning and two ways
finishing was improved.

10. Where was cloth made under the
domestic system?

11. Who controlled the industry? How did
they organise it, through their agents?

12. Which processes went on in their own
works?

13. How did domestic workers use their
independence?

14. Who built the first cotton mill?
Where?

15. Describe later cotton mills.

16. How did the new mills affect the
workers?

17. Name five industries stimulated by
cotton.

18. How did cotton affect exports?

19. How did the cotton industry help
ordinary people?

20. Name four social problems the cotton
industry created.

Further Work

1. Find out more about Richard
Arkwright.

2. Why was Watt's engine important for
the cotton industry? (Chapter 9).

3. Read more about child workers
(Chapter 31) and domestic workers
(Chapter 15).

4. Why is the cotton industry less
important today? (Chapters 25 and 40).

5. You are an elderly cotton worker in
1830. What changes have you seen in the
industry?

SECTION FOUR
Social Changes 1760-1815

CHAPTER 11

Population

In 1695 Gregory King estimated that there were 5.5 million people in England and Wales. He worked this out carefully from figures for taxation and most people agree that he was not far wrong. The first census was held in 1801 and this gave a count of just over nine millions. We can see that the population increased, we know that it grew considerably, but after that, everything is uncertain. We do not understand why the population grew, nor can we discover what connection there was with the important economic changes which were taking place. We can only speculate.

The Increase in Population—Birth Rate. A population is likely to grow if children are born in increasing numbers. This can be for a variety of reasons. The age structure of the population is important. In a country in which most of the women are over fifty, the birth rate will be low. On the other hand, if most of the women are under fifty, it might well be high. The age at which women marry makes a difference, for the younger they are, the more children they are likely to have. Fertility is important. Women might be able, on an average, to have children every three years: on the other hand it might be possible every fifteen months, or even every year. We must expect a high birth rate then, if a large proportion of women are of child bearing age, if they marry young, and if they are fertile. Were any of these things true of the eighteenth century?

There are a great many general statistics, but none of them are reliable, and we have to depend on a few detailed studies, one made on the peerage, and others on the parish registers of a few villages. From these it would seem that women did become more fertile and that among 66 the common people the average age of marriage did fall. However, we cannot be sure that these changes were general, and it is only a possibility that the increase in population was due to an increase in the birth rate.

The Increase in Population—Death Rate. There seems to be good reason for believing that the death rate fell, particularly in the second half of the eighteenth century. Records of insurance companies and studies of individual families seem to show that people were living longer. Why this should be is not easy to understand.

Some years ago it was thought that there was a high death rate at the beginning of the eighteenth century, largely because of spirit drinking. Hogarth's cartoon *Gin Lane* was taken as evidence of this. Then Parliament put a high tax on spirits and people cut down their drinking. On top of that, it was said, there were important developments in medical science and doctors became much more skilled. In the first place, though, we have no way of knowing how widespread gin drinking was and, more important, it is highly unlikely that eighteenth century medicine was good enough to explain the very considerable increase in population. There are other suggestions.

In the Middle Ages, and indeed until the seventeenth century, it would seem that the two greatest killers were the bubonic plague, or

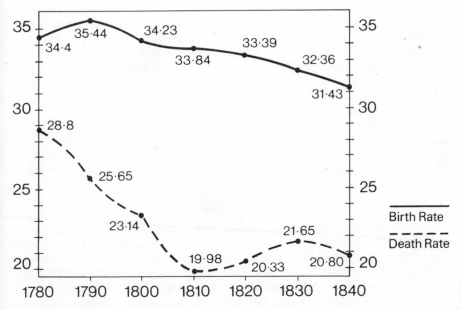

Birth and death rate per thousand—1780 to 1840

Black Death, and famine. The plague last visited this country in 1666. Furthermore, though individuals died of hunger in the eighteenth century, there was no general famine.

It has been suggested, too, that towns may have been healthier because they had better water supplies and because of the work of improvement commissions. Inoculation may have cut down smallpox. Mothers may have known more about the care of infants.

We can be sure about the plague and famine, but not about any of the other ideas.

Population and the Economy. We know that farming, industry and trade all grew in the eighteenth century. We know, too, that the population increased. Was there any connection? Did the growth of the economy encourage the growth of the population, or was it the other way round? Can it have been that the two things grew together, each helping the other? We could begin to answer these questions if we knew when it was that the population began to increase, and the economy to expand. As it is, we know neither, and we are driven back to guesswork.

Surely, though, there must have been some link between population and farming. Without the extra food there could not have been the extra people. Moreover, the growing demand for food certainly encouraged the agricultural revolution, though this does not mean that it caused it.

Much the same can be said of industry. More people meant a growing need for basic goods like coal and cotton and, as we have seen, these industries expanded in order to meet the demand. Again, though, this does not mean that industry could not have developed without the population increase; in fact, having a large population can slow technical changes. An employer is unlikely to buy expensive machinery when he can find plenty of cheap labour. Here is one reason why coal was hewn by hand until well into the twentieth century.

Could it have been that the growth of industry encouraged population? It is possible that people were more willing to have large families if they thought their own jobs were safe, and that their children, when they grew up, could find employment. There is no clear proof, however, that this is what happened.

Conclusions. To sum up, we can say with certainty that the population increased considerably in the eighteenth century. We think it possible that this was due to a higher birth rate, but more probably it was due to a falling death rate. It is clear that there must have been some link between population growth and economic growth, but as soon as we try to find out what the link was we meet an "egg and chicken" argument
68 which no-one has yet settled.

For I have heard a voice as of a woman in travail, and the anguish as of her that bringeth forth her first child. *Jeremiah 4 v.31.*

Questions
1. What kind of hospital is this?
2. Who manages it?
3. What does the figure on the left suggest the rich should do?
4. What is the purpose of the Bible quotation?
5. Describe the hospital building.

VANISHING DISEASES
Some of the most fatal of illnesses are now extinct, or rarely seen. At the head of these is the Plague, which last visited England in 1665. Within the century preceding this, four dreadful outbreaks occurred in London, in 1593, 1603, 1625 and 1636, and besides these epidemics there were few years at that period in which some deaths from plague are not enumerated. Two other diseases, now almost unknown, are the Rickets and the Scurvy.
(Thomas Bateman—*Diseases of London.* 1819.)

Questions
1. When did the Plague last appear?
2. How frequent had epidemics been?
3. What is an endemic disease? Was the plague one?
4. Find out the cause of rickets and scurvy and suggest reasons for their decline.

69

Population of England and Wales in Thousands

	Rickman 1801	McCulloch 1839	Griffith 1926
1700	5475	5135	5835
1710	5240	5066	6013
1720	5565	5345	6048
1730	5796	5688	6008
1740	6064	5830	6013
1750	6467	6140	6253
1760	6736	6480	6665
1770	7428	7228	7124
1780	7953	7815	7581
1790	8675	8541	8216
1801	9168	9187 (1800)	9168

Questions
1. Draw a graph for each of these tables.
2. Why are the tables different?
3. In what ways are they roughly similar?
4. Why do Rickman and Griffith agree on the 1801 figure?

A COUNTRY DOCTOR

We have a quack of the highest and most extended reputation in Dr. Tubbs, inventor and compounder of medicines, bleeder, shaver and physicker of man and beast. His skill he inherited from his aunt, the wise woman of the village who bequeathed to her favourite nephew her blessing, Culpepper's Herbal, a famous salve for cuts and chilblains and a still. This legacy decided his fate. A man who possessed a herbal, could read it without much spelling, who had a still and could use it, had already the great requisites for his calling. He was also blest with an endowment which is equally essential to the success of quackery, namely a prodigious stock of impudence. Patients come to him from near and far; he is the celebrated person of the place.

The only patient I ever won from the worthy empiric was his own wife, who had languished under his prescriptions for three mortal years, and at last stole down in the dusk of evening to hold a private consultation with me. I offered her a ticket to the Basingstoke dispensary, an excellent charity, which has rescued many a victim from the clutches of our herbalist. But she said her husband would never forgive such an affront to his skill. My next suggestion was to "throw physic to the dogs." She did so, and by the end of the week she was another woman. I never saw such a cure. By just throwing away her husband's decoctions, she is become as strong and as hearty as I am.
(Mary Russel Mitford—*Our Village.*)

Questions
1. What is a "quack"?
2. What are Dr. Tubbs's occupations?
3. How did he qualify as a doctor?
4. What is a Herbal?
5. How can we tell Tubbs is uneducated?
6. How did Miss Mitford cure his wife?
7. What was a dispensary? How was it financed?
8. How can you tell Miss Mitford has some prejudice against Tubbs?

Questions—Chapter Eleven
1. What was the estimated population of England and Wales in 1695?
2. Who made this estimate?
3. When was the first census?
4. What did it give as the population?
5. What three things must be true of the women of a country, if there is to be an increase in population?
6. What evidence have we that birth rate increased?
7. What seems to show that people were living longer?
8. Give two theories for the fall in the death rate that no longer seem correct.
9. What were the two great killer diseases until the seventeenth century?
10. What happened about them?
11. What might have happened to the towns?
12. What might have happened with smallpox?
13. How did farming help population?
14. How did population help farming?
15. How did population help industry?
16. How can a large population slow progress in an industry?
17. Name an industry where this happened.
18. How might industry have helped population?
19. Which is the more likely reason for the

increase in population—higher birth rate,
or lower death rate?

20. What can be said about population
growth and economic growth?

Further Work

1. Read about outbreaks of the Plague.
2. Find a picture of Hogarth's Gin Lane.
3. Find out who introduced inoculation to this country. How is it different from vaccination?

4. What changes in farming produced more and better food? (Look back to Chapter Two).

5. What growing industries might have been helped by growing population? (Chapters 7-10).

CHAPTER 12

The
Old Poor Law

By the Old Poor Law we mean the system of giving help to those who were in need, as it was until reformed by an Act of Parliament in 1834. It began in the reign of Elizabeth I and lasted, with some changes, for over two hundred years.

The Elizabethan Poor Law 1601. The first really important Poor Law Act was passed in 1601, towards the end of the reign of Elizabeth I. It said that each parish had to take care of its own poor. To do this they would need money, so they had to raise a special rate, called the poor rate. People who fell on hard times and came to the parish for help were known as paupers. They were divided into two groups, the "impotent" and the "able-bodied". The impotent paupers were the elderly, the orphans and the sick. They were supposed to have food, clothing and shelter. The able-bodied were those who were physically fit and capable of earning their own living. They were to be provided with work.

Each year the ratepayers of the parish, meeting in the vestry of the church, elected one or more overseers of the poor. The overseers decided in the first place how much money they were going to need for the year. They then worked out how much each of the ratepayers should contribute and collected the money from them. Every week they met the paupers, listened to their requests for help, and then paid them what they thought fit.

In general this meant that no poor person need ever die of hunger or neglect, but the system was far from perfect.

In the first place, parishes varied in size and in wealth. In a large parish, with plenty of rich ratepayers, a pauper might expect reasonable treatment. However, in the eighteenth century, two thirds of the parishes in the country had 200 families or less, nearly all of them poor, and grudging every penny in poor rates. Going "on the parish" meant living off neighbours who could ill afford to keep you, and it was made to seem a disgrace.

Overseers were not efficient. The job was unpaid, and they had to do it on top of their work. They were likely to make themselves unpopular because the ratepayers would be sure they were giving too much, and the paupers would be sure they were getting too little. They found it difficult to make the able-bodied do any work. In some parishes one might find small groups half-heartedly mending the roads, but most overseers found it easier—and indeed cheaper—to pay them a small sum of money and be rid of them.

The Act of Settlement 1662. Settlement was an important part of the old poor law. Paupers had been moving from parish to parish looking for more generous treatment, but after the Act of 1662 they could only have relief where they belonged, or, in legal terms, where they had a settlement. The usual way to gain a settlement in a parish was to be born there, but one could also earn it by working there for more than one year. A woman would have a change of settlement if she married a man from another place.

Workhouses. John Cary of Bristol started the first workhouse in 1695 and they became fairly common in the eighteenth century. The idea was to make the poor work for their living, but in most places it was a forlorn hope. The paupers spoilt the materials given them and once

The Workhouse

again it was found cheaper and easier to feed them and leave it at that. Workhouses became places of refuge for the impotent poor, while the able-bodied drew "out-door" relief. This meant they took their money from the overseers and lived at home.

One difficulty was that only a rich parish could afford to build a workhouse. Accordingly, in 1782, an M.P. called Gilbert persuaded Parliament to pass an Act to solve this problem. Gilbert's Act allowed any group of neighbouring parishes to pool their resources and build one workhouse between them. There was no compulsion and parishes only co-operated if they wanted.

The Speenhamland System. Probably this was the most criticised feature of the old poor law. It began in 1795. There was war with France, prices were rising rapidly and the poor were finding it hard to live. A group of Berkshire magistrates met at the village of Speen to see what could be done to help in their area. Magistrates had the right to fix minimum wages, and they were going to decide what they should be. However they came up with quite a different idea. They decided that wages could stay as they were, but that if a poor family did not have enough to live on, then they could come to the parish for an allowance. The poor ate bread and little else, so the allowance was tied to the price of bread. When the gallon loaf cost 5p they felt that a man should have 15p a week for himself, and 7½p each for his wife and children. A couple with three children would be entitled to 45p a week. If their wages were only 35p then the parish would pay 10p. If the price of bread rose or fell, then the allowance would move with it, and however poor the wages, no family need starve.

Soon other areas were copying Berkshire and the system became quite common in the South of England, the Midlands and East Anglia. It was hardly used at all in the north.

In 1775 the poor rates for the whole country were £1½ millions. In 1818 they were £8m. Much of this rise was inevitable as there was a lot of distress brought by high prices during the war, but people finding themselves paying more and more in rates looked round for something to blame. Their favourite target was the Speenhamland system. It was said that it kept wages low. If a man complained to his employer that he was not earning enough then he would be told to go and get the extra from the parish. The system was said to be unfair to poorer ratepayers. A man who did not employ labour had to pay his rates and these went, in effect, to subsidise the wages bills of his richer neighbours. The poor were demoralised. It had always been thought a disgrace to go "on the parish", but in some villages nearly all the labourers had to, for at least part of each year. However, the biggest complaint of all was that it
74 encouraged malingering. Whatever a man earned, the parish would

make up his wages, enough for him to buy his bread. There was little point in working hard; in fact some saw no point in working at all.

None the less the Speenhamland system lasted for fifty years, and proved very difficult to destroy. There seem to be two reasons for this. In the first place the wealthy employers in a village, that is the richer farmers, did well out of it. They could pay their men starvation wages knowing the parish would make them up. They could buy threshing machines and put their men out of work for the winter. The parish would keep them alive and the Act of Settlement would keep them in the village, so that they would still be there when they were wanted again in the spring. The second reason was that many people were afraid of the labourers. The enclosure movement, the use of threshing machines and the high price of bread all caused discontent that led to rick burning and even a small rebellion in 1830 known as the Swing riots. It was felt that if the employers would not pay the labourers to keep them quiet, then the parish must.

This picture is from the lid of a tobacco box.

Questions

1. Who are the people standing on the left of the picture?
2. Why have they come to this room?
3. Who are the men sitting at the table?
4. How did they obtain their office?
5. How long are they likely to keep it?
6. What questions are they asking, probably?

7. What should they do about the two men on the left?
8. What are they more likely to do?
9. Why is there mention of a church? (Top right of picture).

ALLOWANCES IN SUSSEX 1825

They give a single man sevenpence a day, enough to buy two pounds and a quarter of bread for six days in the week, and as he does not work on Sunday, there is no allowance. The poor creature has seven pence a day to find food, clothes, washing and lodging! We hear of the efforts of Mrs. Fry and others to improve the situation of felons in the gaols, but never do they give one single pious sigh for those sufferers, who are driven to become felons or waste away by hunger.

(Cobbett—Rural Rides.)

Questions

1. What is the allowance? What bread will it buy?
2. How much does that amount of bread cost today?
3. What must this money buy?

75

4. *What happens about Sunday?*
5. *What does Cobbett think of Mrs. Fry?*
6. *Why are labourers "doomed to become felons"?*

POOR RATES

The farmer will say, "If you compel me to pay £100 a year to unemployed labourers, I must reduce my wages and that will ease me in one way while you burthen me in another." There is a parish in Suffolk where the rates are 25s an acre; now the farmer who is doing justice to his land cannot possibly pay this enormous rate and pay his own labourers too, and he must say to his men, "Instead of 10s I can only give you 5s a week, and you must go to the parish and have the rest made up."

Questions
1. *Why are the poor rates so high?*
2. *What are they in the parish mentioned here?*
3. *Why does the farmer lower wages?*
4. *How do the labourers find the extra money?*
5. *What is the name of this system?*

LABOURERS AND POOR RELIEF

A great change has taken place in the spirit of the lower classes of people. Many would struggle on with large families never applying for relief, but that spirit is dead. The motives to industry and frugality are cut up by the roots when the poor man knows that if he do not feed himself, the parish must do it for him. He has not the most distant hope of being independent, however hard-working he may be. To acquire enough land to build a cottage is a hopeless aim in ninety-nine parishes out of a hundred.
(*Arthur Young—Annals of Agriculture.* 1801.)

Questions
1. *How did the poor once think of parish relief?*
2. *What is meant by "industry and frugality"?*
3. *What happens if a poor man does not work?*

4. *What might encourage him to work?*

WORKHOUSE INMATES

We usually find 60 or 80 children, 20 or 30 able-bodied paupers, and an equal number of aged and impotent paupers, the proper objects of relief. The mothers of bastard children and prostitutes live among the children who also have the examples of the poacher, the vagrant and the decayed beggar. There is often a solitary blind person, one or two idiots, and not infrequently are heard the ravings of some neglected lunatic. In such receptacles the sick poor are often immured.
(*Poor Law Commissioners' Report.* 1834.)

Questions
1. *List all the different people in the workhouse.*
2. *Who are "the proper objects of relief"?*
3. *How many people might there be all together?*
4. *Which is the largest group?*
5. *What is the writer afraid will happen to them?*

Questions—Chapter Twelve
1. *Who was made responsible for the care of the poor by the Elizabethan Poor Law of 1601?*
2. *How was money found to help the poor?*
3. *Name two classes of pauper and what was done for each.*
4. *Who were the officers elected to care for the poor?*
5. *Describe their work.*
6. *Why were paupers treated differently in different places?*
7. *In what ways were the parish officers inefficient?*
8. *What did the Act of Settlement prevent?*
9. *What was a "settlement"? Name the ways of acquiring one.*
10. *Who started the first workhouse? Where?*
11. *What was the original idea for a workhouse?*
12. *What, in fact, did workhouses become?*
13. *What was "outdoor relief"? Who drew it?"*

14. What did Gilbert's Act allow?
15. When did the Speenhamland System begin? In which county?
16. Describe how it worked.
17. Into which parts of England did it spread?
18. What happened to the poor rates between 1775 and 1818?
19. What were the four main criticisms of the Speenhamland System?
20. Give two reasons why it survived.

Further Work
1. Find out about the Roundsman System, used by some parishes instead of Speenhamland.

2. How did changes in agriculture make the problem of poverty worse?
3. You have been elected a poor law overseer. Say what your work and problems will be.
4. You are a farmer. Write a letter to a newspaper complaining about your poor rates.
5. You are a labourer on poor relief. Say how you are treated, and what you think of the system.

CHAPTER 13

Police
and Prisons

PART 1 *Police*

Parochial Police. Ever since the Middle Ages it had been the duty of each parish to keep its own inhabitants in order so that there were as many police forces as there were parishes, and few of them were efficient.

The men in charge were the magistrates, or Justices of the Peace, and it was their duty to appoint the constables and see that they did their work. They also questioned criminals as senior police officers do today. In the eighteenth century anyone who was arrested would go to the justice's house and be questioned, probably by the same man who would try him when he appeared in court. Magistrates were unpaid, and some were "trading justices" which meant they took bribes.

Constables, too, were unpaid. They were ordinary citizens who had to take the job for one year, each in turn. It was highly inconvenient as they still had to earn their living.

In the larger towns there were usually watchmen. They served under the constables and did most of the routine patrolling. They had wages, and if good men were employed the watch was efficient, as indeed it was in the City of London. However, in most places, including outer London, wages were so poor that no-one who was any use would want to join the watch. Old men were given the job to stop them going "on the parish".

London Police. London was the only really big town in eighteenth century England, so keeping order here was a special problem. We have seen that in the City they solved it by having well-paid, efficient watchmen, but the City is only a small part of London. Something had to be done about the remainder.

Two magistrates who realised this were Henry Fielding and his blind half-brother, John. In 1753 Henry gathered together some of the men who had been constables and had done their work conscientiously. He suggested they should become a force of detectives. He had some public money with which he could pay them small salaries, and they were able to make quite a lot more from rewards, and from working as private detectives. They called these men the Bow Street Runners, after the street in which the Fieldings had their office.

Henry Fielding soon died, but John went on with the work and in 1763 he organised the Bow Street Horse and Foot Patrols. They wore uniform and did the same work as policemen on the beat. The foot patrol covered an area of between eight and ten kilometres from Charing Cross, while the horse patrol went twenty-five kilometres.

All this was a success, so in 1792 Parliament passed the Middlesex Justices Act which set up seven police offices modelled on Bow Street. In each one there were three salaried magistrates and six police officers who were detectives, like the Bow Street Runners. In 1800 Parliament created yet another police office, which was responsible for the shipping on the Thames.

Alternatives to the Police. As the police were, with a few exceptions, quite inefficient, there were attempts to find alternatives. One way was to make the penalties for crime so savage that people would be frightened into good behaviour. Parliament made one crime after another punishable by death until, in theory, a man could be hung for any of 200 offences, some of them quite trivial. This did not stop crime, mainly because the average criminal does not worry too much about punishment. He does worry about being caught, but with practically no police this was most unlikely. Moreover only a tiny proportion of criminals who were arrested were ever hung. Courts were unwilling to condemn people to death for petty offences, and even when the sentence was hanging, it was usually changed to transportation.

Another alternative to having a good police force was to encourage ordinary people to help, by offering rewards. For the conviction of a criminal you could expect anything from £5 to £40, depending on how important he was. However, it was not enough to give information. You might have to arrest the criminal yourself, and you would certainly have to bring the prosecution, taking on all the work in court that today is done by the police. All in all, if you caught a criminal it was usually cheaper, in the long run, to let him escape. It was almost certainly safer.

PART 2 *Prisons*

Prison Conditions. In the eighteenth century they punished their criminals with the pillory, by whipping, by transporting them overseas, or by hanging them. Only rarely did they give prison sentences, and if a criminal *was* in gaol, he was likely to be either awaiting trial, or the punishment the court had given him. Indeed the majority of people in prison were not criminals at all, but debtors.

Most prisons belonged to the towns in which they were situated, although a few were private property. The local magistrates were supposed to inspect them from time to time, but rarely did. They were left almost entirely to their gaolers. A gaoler had no salary, so he made what he could out of his prisoners. He would charge fees for such things as admission, discharge, putting on irons and removing them. He would sell drink, and indeed anything else the prisoners could afford. A large prison would have a "master's side" where those who could pay lived in comfort and a "common side" where the poor lived in absolute misery.

Some prisons were specially built, like Newgate in London, but in a small town the prison might be in a gatehouse, a ruined castle or even a disused stable. These places were damp, without sanitation or proper water supplies and bare of furniture. They were also insecure and the gaolers made up for this by loading the criminals with irons. Disease was common, typhus, or gaol fever, being especially dangerous.

80 *Inside Newgate*

Prison Reformers. Two people took the lead in trying to reform prisons. They were John Howard and Elizabeth Fry.

John Howard became Sheriff of Bedfordshire in 1773. This led him to visit Bedford gaol and he was so horrified at what he found that he determined to inspect other prisons to see if they were all as bad. He found that they were.

Howard worked on his own, and his method was to collect and publish facts so that people were made aware of what was wrong. He wrote a book called the "State of the Prisons" and he also gave evidence to the House of Commons. Practically nothing effective was done in Howard's life time, but his work was important because it showed the need for reform.

Elizabeth Fry was a Quaker who started her work for prisons as a result of a visit to Newgate in 1813. Her methods were different from Howard's in that she did more than collect information. She went among the female prisoners at Newgate and tried to help them lead better lives. She encouraged them to draw up a code of behaviour that they all kept voluntarily; she brought in sewing materials and sold the clothes they made. She set up a prison school, with the prisoners who knew how to read teaching the others; above all she tried to teach religion because she thought that this was the only real answer to the problem of crime. To help, she gathered together a group of ladies, and she also toured the country organising Ladies' Prison Associations wherever she could.

Parliament passed a few Prisons Acts at this time, and these are described in chapter 29. However, nothing at all effective was done officially until 1835. Until then prison reform depended on the good will of private individuals and a handful of reforming magistrates.

Elizabeth Fry visiting Newgate prisoners

Questions
1. Why did John Howard visit prisons?
2. What prisoners are there here?
3. Describe the walls, floor, lighting and bedding.
4. Who is the man to whom Howard is speaking?
5. How did such men make their money?
6. Write the account you imagine Howard might have made of this visit.

A SOCIETY FOR THE PROSECUTION OF THIEVES AT TRURO

The Society offers rewards for the apprehension of such persons as shall be convicted as follows: burglary, highway robbery, stealing horses or cattle, stealing corn or lead, £5; stealing hogs or husbandry equipment or shop-lifting, £2; robbing orchards or gardens, or barking or cutting trees, £1: breaking hedges, stealing gates, garden vegetables or hay, or robbing fish ponds, 10s.

82 (*West Briton* Newspaper 16.7.1813.)

Questions
1. What is the object of this society?
2. What rewards are offered?
3. How do they compare with government rewards?
4. In the main, what property are they protecting?
5. Why were societies like this needed?
6. What dangers can you see in offering rewards?

INTERVIEW WITH A LONDON CONSTABLE

What parochial force have you?—Only watchmen. What is the regulation as to their age?—There is none. We have one man 70 years old and deaf. How often do they patrol?—Every half hour. Where do they pass the night between patrols?— Partly round the coffee stands, which is a great nuisance; they are there nearly all night talking with prostitutes and other bad characters. Is there any enquiry into the qualifications of a constable?—No. He must be a householder. I had been

scarcely two years a householder, when I was named by the vestry, by way of punishment as I supposed, for my influence against the vestry.
(*Committe on the Police of the Metropolis.* 1828.)

Questions
1. What does the word "parochial" mean?
2. Whom does the constable supervise?
3. What does he say about them?
4. What is the only qualification for a constable?
5. Who chooses the constables?
6. Why does this man think he was made one?

KING'S BENCH PRISON FOR DEBTORS, LONDON
It is like a town in miniature, only surrounded by 30 ft walls. Cookshops, circulating libraries, coffee houses, dealers and artisans of all kinds, dwellings of different degrees, even a market-place; nothing is wanting. When I went in a noisy game of ball was going on in the latter. A man who has money lives as well and as agreeably as possible within these walls— bating liberty, but he who has nothing fares ill enough; to him, however, every spot on the globe is a prison.
(Prince Puckler-Muskau—*A Regency Visitor.*)

COUNTY GAOL AT LAUNCESTON
The prison is a room 23½ ft by 7½ ft, with only one small window, 2 ft by 1½ ft, and three dungeons on the side opposite the window; these are about 6½ ft deep, one 9 ft long, one about 8, one not 5; this last for women. They were all very offensive. No chimney; no water; no sewers; damp earth floors; no infirmary. The court not secure, and the prisoners seldom permitted to go out to it. Indeed the whole place is out of repair, and yet the gaoler lives distant. I once found the prisoners chained two or three together. Their provision was put down to them through a hole in the floor of the room above, and those who served them often caught the fatal fever.
(Howard—*The State of the Prisons.*)

Questions
1. What is the King's Bench Prison compared with?
2. Who is imprisoned there?
3. Why is life pleasant for them?
4. What is meant by "bating liberty"?
5. Who does find life there unpleasant?
6. Draw a plan of Launceston Prison.
7. In what ways is the prison offensive?
8. Why are chains needed to stop escapes?
9. What was the "fatal fever"?
10. Account for the differences between these prisons.

Questions—Chapter Thirteen
1. What local government area was responsible for law and order?
2. What duties did magistrates have?
3. Why were constables unlikely to be efficient?
4. What work did watchmen do? Why were they often inefficient?
5. Who started the Bow Street Runners?
6. What were they? How did they make their money?
7. Name two Bow Street Patrols and their areas.
8. What were created in 1792 and 1800?
9. What was done to frighten criminals into good behaviour?
10. Give two reasons for its failure.
11. What had to be done to earn a government reward?
12. How were criminals punished?
13. What were most people in prison?
14. Who was responsible for prisons?
15. How did gaolers make their money?
16. What buildings might be used as prisons? Describe their condition.
17. What roused John Howard's interest in prisons?
18. What book did he write? How did he find his information?
19. Where did Elizabeth Fry do most of her work?
20. Describe what she did. What did she feel was the best answer to crime?

Further Work
1. Read about 18th century criminals, especially highwaymen.
2. Find out what you can about Jonathan Wild.

3. *Read about debtors' prisons in Dickens —Little Dorrit, chapters 6-8 and Pickwick Papers 40-42.*
4. *Read more about the lives and work of John Howard and Elizabeth Fry.*

5. *You are an 18th century criminal. Describe the police force in your town and say why you are not frightened of it.*
6. *You have visited an 18th century prison. Say what you saw, and what changes you think should be made.*

CHAPTER 14

Elementary Education

Elementary education was the kind given to the children of the poor. The idea behind it was to encourage them to grow up into honest, reliable workmen and servants who would be content with their humble place in life. Education was not meant to help them get on in the world; on the contrary, they were expected to be submissive, and obedient to their betters. This was to be achieved by teaching them religion which was the most important subject in the schools. Reading came next, because children had to study their Bibles and Prayer Books. To help them in their daily lives they had writing and arithmetic, but that was about all. It was thought dangerous to teach the poor too much as they might then have ideas above their station. Other things might be done, but they would not include more advanced education.

The Eighteenth Century. There were three types of school for the children of the poor—Charity Schools, Sunday Schools and Dame Schools.

In 1699 some important members of the Church of England started the Society for the Promotion of Christian Knowledge—the S.P.C.K. One of its aims was to encourage the founding of Charity Schools, and this happened in many towns. The clergy and their richer followers would raise money and build a school. People would then agree to pay annual subscriptions which would be used for running expenses. Each year the subscribers would elect a group of managers and it was their duty to see the school was conducted properly. They ordered its equipment— such as it was—they appointed the teachers, they paid their salaries, and they visited the school regularly to see they were doing their job.

Religion was, of course the main subject, with reading, but most Charity Schools tried to do more. They taught not only writing and arithmetic, but useful crafts like spinning for girls or gardening for boys. They gave their pupils free uniform and the school was often known by the colour of it—the Blue School, the Green School etc. When the children left, the managers saw they were apprenticed to good masters, by which they usually meant the ones who attended church regularly.

Charity schools did useful work, but there were too few of them. A country town might have only one, and that would be for about twenty pupils. It was hard to get into one of these schools. Conditions varied, but the sort of thing they required was that the parents should be members of the Church of England, sober and well behaved. They also had to be poor, thus really needing free education for their children. Even so, the child would have to wait for someone to leave the school, and then find a subscriber who was willing to nominate him.

Sunday Schools, on the other hand, did not select their pupils. They would teach any child that came along. The credit for starting them has gone to Robert Raikes who opened one in Gloucester in 1780. Certainly there were Sunday Schools before this, but Raikes did a lot to make them popular.

86 *A Charity School*

Sunday Schools concentrated on teaching religion and reading, partly because they were open on only one day a week and partly because many of the teachers could not write. They were unpaid and untrained people from all walks of life—some were well-educated gentle folk, some were tradesmen, and others, perhaps, were foremen from the local factory. These schools taught very little and children could attend them for years and hardly learn a thing. However, there is a lot of credit due to the people who gave up their Sundays to teach in them, because they were the first in this country to try and give an education to every child that wanted one, even though it was just part-time.

Here we must mention Dame Schools. Any child could attend these, if his parents could afford a small fee. The teacher wanted to make money, and the parents often wanted to be rid of their young children. There may have been some good Dame Schools, but most of them were just baby-minding establishments, overcrowded and insanitary into the bargain.

The Early Nineteenth Century—Monitorial Schools. In the market towns, and in the villages even more so, the poor were under the eye of the parson and the squire. They did not live together in large numbers, so they were fairly easy to control. However, the new industrial towns were different. There were no squires and few parsons, while police forces hardly existed. Moreover, the poor were massed in their thousands. They were often discontented, and there was a growing fear that there might be a revolution as there had been in France. It seemed more important than ever to bring the working classes under the influence of the Church. To do this they needed schools, but there were few teachers and little money.

Faced with this problem two men came forward independently, with the same answer, which was to use the monitorial system. They claimed that with their method one master could control a very large school, perhaps of several hundreds. He would select his brightest pupils and make them his monitors. He would teach them early in the morning and when the others arrived the monitors would pass on what they had learnt to groups of about eight or ten.

The schools would have their money from subscribers, as Charity Schools did, but children who could afford it also paid a small fee, though this might only be ½p a week.

One of the men who introduced the system was a Quaker called Joseph Lancaster. With the help of some wealthy supporters, including King George III, he opened a school in the Borough Road in London. In 1809 he founded the Royal Lancasterian Society to encourage the spread of his ideas. Unfortunately Lancaster was an impossible man who fell out with almost everyone. In 1814 his Society expelled him and 87 went on with the work without him. They now called themselves the British and Foreign Schools Society and their schools were known as British Schools for short. People who supported them were Nonconformists—Methodists, Baptists, Congregationalists and Quakers. The idea was that the children should learn non-denominational religion during the week, and the beliefs of their own particular church at Sunday School.

The other man who developed the monitorial system was a clergyman of the Church of England, Andrew Bell. Having a lot of time to spare from his duties as an Army Chaplain in India, he started a school in an orphanage in Madras. He had no adult teachers, so he used children. When he came back to England, he tried his ideas here, and in 1811 founded the National Society for Promoting the Education of the Poor in the Principles of the Established Church. This became known as the National Society, and its schools as National Schools. The religion they taught was that of the Church of England.

Because of the religious difference there was a good deal of rivalry, which in some ways was no bad thing. If in any town the Noncomformists raised money and built a British School, it was highly likely that the members of the Church of England would build a National School. The parent Societies gave their followers encouragement, advice and even small amounts of money. They also started Training Colleges for teachers. The British Society, for example, founded one in the Borough Road, where Lancaster had his first school.

It is doubtful whether children learnt much in monitorial schools, but none the less they were important. The people who started them were looking forward to the day when every child in the country should have full time education.

Questions for picture on page 89.

1. Where is this school?
2. When was it opened?
3. How many boys were to attend?
4. What system of teaching is used?
5. Explain the reference to Madras.
6. What Society might have had a hand in starting this school?
7. What religion would be taught here?
8. How is the room heated and ventilated?
9. Why would good ventilation be essential? (Look at the "central" heating.)
10. What furniture is there?
11. One of the adults is the teacher. Who might the other be? (Not a parent).
12. Locate the sand table on which the youngest children learn to write. Why should they use this method?

AN INTERNAL VIEW OF CLAPHAM SCHOOL.
Conducted on the System of the MADRAS SCHOOL Invented by Andrew Bell D.D. &c.
This School was erected in 1810 for the Education of 200 Boys.

POEM FOR SCHOOL CHILDREN
On those days spent in riot,
No bread you brought home;
Had you spent them in labour
You must have had some.
A dinner of herbs, says the wise man with
   quiet,
Is better than beef amid discord and riot.
So I'll work the whole day,
And on Sunday I'll seek
At the church how to bear
All the wants of the week.
The gentlefolk too will afford us supplies,
They'll subscribe and they'll give up
Their puddings and pies.
(Hannah More—*The Riot.*)

Questions
1. *What should a hungry man do rather
than riot?*
2. *How can he console himself?*
3. *What is the duty of the rich?*
4. *What does the writer want schools to
teach?*

A CHARITY SCHOOL
I leave my money for the clothing and
schooling of 25 boys of indigent parents of
the Church of England. Each boy to be
allowed annually a green cloth coat,
waistcoat and breeches, one shirt of
flaxen cloth, with stockings, cap etc., and
the residue yearly paid to teach the boys

89

reading, writing and arithmetic, and singing of psalms and toning the responses in divine service in the parish church. No boy to be admitted if the parents receive relief from the parish.
(Will of Gabriel Newton of Northampton.)

Questions
1. How many boys will attend this school?
2. What three conditions must the parents meet?
3. What clothing are they to have? How often?
4. What subjects will they study?
5. Which seems more important—the clothing or the education?

MONITORIAL SCHOOLS
A. The Boys' School in Borough Road was opened by Joseph Lancaster in 1801, and is actually extended to 700 boys who are instructed upon a Plan entirely new, by means of which one master alone can educate 1000 boys in Reading, Writing and Arithmetic as effectually and with as little Trouble as Twenty or Thirty have ever been taught by the usual modes. The school is arranged in classes; a monitor is appointed to each, who is responsible for the cleanliness, order and improvement of every boy in it.
(Lancaster—Improvements in Education.)

B. The poor teacher has the sole charge of 150 little dirty, ragged, ignorant urchins, assembled in the miserable building dignified by the name of a National School, and he is expected to convert them into clean, well-bred, intelligent children. He cannot educate them all himself, and therefore he is obliged to use the monitorial system; the result of which is, that while a portion of the children are vain, conceited and puffed up, a larger proportion are left in ignorance. I have known children who have been two years at a National School and left it unable to read.
(Walter Hook—Letter to Bishop of St. David's.)

Questions
1. Who started Borough Road School?
2. What claims does he make for it?
3. What does he give as the reason for success?
4. What is a National School?
5. How many children may attend?
6. What sort of children are they?
7. What is the teacher expected to do?
8. What system must he use?
9. What are the results, for the majority?
10. Who will be "vain, conceited and puffed-up"?
11. Is two years long enough to learn to read?
12. Which of these two writers do you think gives the more accurate idea of a monitorial school?

Questions—Chapter Fourteen
1. What was elementary education?
2. What were its aims? How were they to be achieved?
3. What subjects were taught?
4. What Society encouraged Charity Schools?
5. How was such a school financed and run?
6. Which subjects were taught?
7. Describe the uniforms.
8. What happened when a child left school?
9. How was it possible to go to a Charity School?
10. Who could go to a Sunday School?
11. Who helped make them popular?
12. What did they teach? Why did they have little success?
13. What was wrong with most Dame Schools?
14. Why, in the early 19th century, did it seem more important to give everyone an education?
15. What two things were lacking?
16. What was the monitorial system?
17. How were monitorial schools financed?
18. Name two men who developed the monitorial system. What religion were they?
19. What Societies did they found? What work did these Societies do?

20. Why were monitorial schools important?

Further Work

1. Find out if there was a Charity School in your area. If old people talk of a "Blue School" that was probably one.
2. How are modern Sunday Schools similar, and how are they different from those of the 18th century?

3. Find pictures of schools, children and teachers.
4. Read more about the lives of Bell and Lancaster. What happened to Lancaster after his Society expelled him? What happened to Bell?
5. You have visited a monitorial school. Write what you have seen.
6. You are a wealthy townsman in 1810. Explain why you are giving money to help pay for a school.

CHAPTER 15

Working Class Discontent 1790-1820— Causes

During the Napoleonic Wars and just after, there was a lot of unrest. It was because of problems brought by the industrial revolution, by the war, and by the attitude of the government.

Problems of the Industrial Revolution. In the first place there was the trade cycle. We have seen how industry grew, but it did not progress at a steady pace. Instead it went forward in six or seven year cycles, each one made up of a boom and a slump. A boom was a time of rapid growth, in which business was brisk and more and more people found jobs. During the slump which followed trade and industry declined, and as employers cut back their production, so they dismissed their workers. Unemployment brought hunger and discontent.

The reorganisation of industry caused difficulties. New machines brought hardship to people who made their livings by old-fashioned methods. In the eighteenth century spinning machines took work from the farm labourers' wives and in the early nineteenth century power looms began to threaten the livelihood of the handloom weavers. In the woollen finishing trades simple little pieces of equipment made skilled men redundant. One of these gadgets was the shearing frame which cropped the cloth so that it was an even thickness all over. Shearing by hand had been a highly skilled and well-paid occupation. In the stocking making counties of Leicestershire, Nottinghamshire and Derbyshire, the manufacturers brought in what was known as the "wide frame", which could be worked by unskilled people and wove cheap but poor quality stockings. Such cheap stockings ruined the market for the better ones and the skilled knitters could not find work.

92　　As important as the new machinery, was the change from the domestic system to the factory system. The old way was to have master craftsmen, each employing at most a journeyman or two, and a handful of apprentices. They worked in the masters' homes or in their workshops, and though there may have been harsh discipline and drudgery for the employees, the masters at least had a good deal of freedom. If an industry went over to the factory system the little workshops would not pay. What happened then, for example, to a master weaver? He would never submit to the discipline of a factory and in any case the owner would have no use for his skills. The only thing he could do was to go on working in the same old way, but for longer and longer hours, and less and less money.

Factory workers themselves were not always happy. There were some excellent mills, but there were others that were dirty, uncomfortable and dangerous. Moreover, a slump would bring unemployment, while during a boom the working day could be unbearably long. An employer who was anxious to make money might drive his workers for sixteen hours or even longer.

Problems caused by the War 1793-1815. War interrupts trade. Fortunately for us our navy controlled the seas and our merchants were able to find new markets when they needed them. It was at this time that we began to trade with South America. European countries welcomed our goods, too, and we even did business with France through the German port of Hamburg. However, the fact that Napoleon controlled almost the entire coastline of the continent meant that he could hurt us when it suited him. From 1806 to 1812 he tried, with his Continental System, to stop all British goods entering Europe. There was so much smuggling that he had little success, but he did manage to create difficulties for certain industries like pottery, which lost some of its best markets for a while.

More seriously, the war brought inflation. From time to time the British government made loans to its European allies so that they could keep their armies in the field against Napoleon. The loans usually went abroad in the form of goods, which created shortages in this country and, as a result, high prices.

Food became dear, too. For some reason there was a whole series of bad harvests that lasted until 1813 and the war made it difficult to make up supplies by importing from Europe. Grain was scarce and from being about £2.70 a quarter in the early 1790's rose to an average price of £4.70 in the years 1811-1814. In 1812 it reached a peak of £6.30. Bread, which was about the only thing the labourer ate, became exceedingly expensive. It is true that wages rose as well, but they limped far behind the prices of manufactured goods and food.

The end of the war should have made things easier, and it seemed for 93

Food Riots—1816

a time that it might. In 1813 there was a bumper harvest and wheat prices fell, alarmingly to the farmers, but to the glee of ordinary people. European ports were wide open to English goods, trade and industry boomed and there was full employment. However, they had opened their presents before Christmas, as it were, and when peace came in 1815 prosperity and plenty did not last long. Almost at once there was a slump made worse by an end to the fighting. There were no more government orders for ships, guns, munitions, uniforms and all the materials of war, while 300 000 demobilised soldiers and sailors were looking for jobs.

Attitude of the Government. The ruling classes had little sympathy for the workers. The people who ran the country were the landed gentry, whose main idea was to look after farming. They showed their attitude quite clearly after the war when wheat prices began to tumble. In 1815 Parliament passed a Corn Law which was meant to keep prices high by controlling imports. The gentry were quite prepared to make working class people go on paying dearly for their food, so as to safeguard their own fortunes.

Not only were they selfish, but they were frightened as well. The grey masses of discontented, unpoliced workers in the industrial towns seemed a new threat. On top of that, there was the French Revolution and with all the unrest in this country it seemed there might be a British

Revolution as well. Under these conditions both workers and government turned all too quickly to violence.

Questions

1. What does this factory make?
2. What impression is the artist trying to create of factory life?
3. Who, probably, is the man in the top hat? How is he dressed? What is he holding?
4. Who, probably, is the man in the cap? How is he made to seem?
5. How are the workers clothed? How well do they seem to eat?
6. What were some of the unpleasant features of factory life?
7. Find other pictures of factory interiors. Try and decide whether the artist here has exaggerated.

INTERVIEW WITH A HANDLOOM WEAVER

What are your wages?—Ten shillings a week, with deductions of 2/6 from it, leaving 7/6.

Is yours the worst paid branch of weaving in Manchester?—The best.

How long have you been a weaver?—Twenty-three years.

What did you get when you began?—I was but a boy then; I could earn 12/- per week.

What is the effect upon you of the fall in wages?—It deprives me of all the comforts of life entirely; I can get nothing but the coarsest of food, and less in quantity than I used to do.

What do you do for clothing?—As well as I can; sometimes I have some, and sometimes very little.

How do you pay the doctor, when you are ill?—I have to work myself well again.

What do you pay for your church-seat?—I am not prepared to go. I would if I had got decent clothing. When I was a young man I did get more wages; I had three suits of clothes, and a good watch in my pocket, and two or three good pairs of shoes, and one or two good hats.

What does your wife earn?—About 5/- a week.

Does she go to the cotton factory?—Yes.

Is it not painful to you to have to send her to a factory?—Yes, it causes great grief to me.

(Gaskell—*Artisans and Machinery.*)

Questions

1. What invention is the cause of this man's problem?
2. What can he earn a week? (One shilling = 5p.)
3. What did he earn as a boy?
4. What has he had to give up?
5. What does he mean by, "I have to work myself well again"?
6. Why does he not go to church?
7. How did he spend his money when his wages were better?
8. Why would he be particularly unhappy about his wife working in a cotton factory?

DURING A SLUMP AT COLNE

In all I visited 83 dwellings. They were without furniture, save old boxes for tables, and stools, or even large stones, for chairs; the beds were of straw and shavings, sometimes with torn pieces of carpet or packing canvas for a covering, and sometimes without any kind of covering whatever. The food was oatmeal and water for breakfast; flour and water, with a little skimmed milk, for dinner; oatmeal and water again for those who had three meals a day. I was informed in fifteen families that their children went without the "blue milk", or milk from which the cream had been taken, on alternate days. I saw children appeasing the cravings of the stomach by the refuse of decayed vegetables in the root-market. I saw a woman in the very last stage of extenuation suckling an infant which could scarcely draw a single drop of nutriment from her exhausted breast. I inquired the child's age—"Fifteen months". "Why was it not weaned?" Another mouth would have been added to the number of those for whom the supply of oatmeal was insufficient. I was told that there had been several instances of death by sheer starvation.

(Cooke-Taylor—*Tour in the Manufacturing Districts of Lancashire.*)

Questions

1. How many houses were visited?
2. What furniture did they have?
3. What food were they eating?
4. How many meals a day did they have?
5. What is "blue milk"?
6. What were some children driven to eat?
7. Why did the mother breast feed her child?
8. What had happened to some people?
9. What happens to the economy during a slump?
10. Why were these people so poor?
11. Where is Colne?
12. What indusry do you suppose had been hit?

Questions—Chapter Fifteen

1. Give three things that caused problems during and after the Napoleonic Wars.
2. Why did the slump cause hardship?
3. Who suffered because of (a) spinning machines (b) power looms?
4. What inventions caused trouble in (a) cloth finishing (b) stocking manufacture?
5. What was the old way of organising industry?
6. What did craftsmen have to do when faced with competition from factories?
7. Why were factory workers sometimes unhappy?
8. What does war do to trade?
9. What advantage did Britain have during the war with France?
10. Name a new area of trade for Britain.
11. What did Napoleon attempt with his Continental System? When?
12. Why did he have little success? What industry did suffer?
13. How did the war cause inflation?
14. Give two reasons why wheat was dear during the war.

15. Why was dear wheat especially unfortunate in those days?
16. What problems came with the end of the war?
17. Who controlled the government?
18. What was their main concern?
19. What did Parliament do to please them?
20. Give two reasons why the ruling classes were frightened.

Further Work

1. In what ways were Britain's problems of the early 19th century like those of today?
2. It is 1815. Some working men meet and talk about their problems and worries. They have had a hard time during the war and are disappointed now peace has come. Write what they say.
3. You are a member of the government in 1815. Say why you think the workers are discontented and why you are going to keep an eye on them.

CHAPTER 16

Working Class Discontent 1790-1820— Events

Having looked at the causes of discontent we must now see how the working classes reacted, and how the government tried to hold them in check.

Trade Clubs. A few workers had already organised themselves into trade clubs which were the forerunners of the modern trade unions. Clubs would help members who were sick or out of work and they also bargained with employers for higher wages. If they did not have their way, and if they had enough money, they might call a strike. However, they were not nearly as strong as modern trade unions.

In the first place each club was quite local, rarely covering more than one town. Its members usually met in a public house which is why so many of these have names like "The Carpenters' Arms".

Secondly, all the trade clubs put together would have accounted for only a fraction of the working people in the country. Their members were skilled craftsmen working in the towns. Farm labourers, domestic servants and unskilled town labourers had no trade clubs and they were the most numerous by far.

A third weakness was that trade clubs were illegal. Theoretically they were "conspiracies in restraint of trade". In fact, the authorities tolerated them, but if the men in a particular industry became too demanding, then the employers might prosecute. The only problem was that it was a complicated legal process involving a judge and jury. It took a lot of time and was likely to be expensive.

Petitions. Sometimes a group of working people would send a petition to Parliament. For example, in 1816 a group of disgruntled cotton workers decided to march to London to complain. Each man carried a blanket to sleep in, so their expedition was known as the March of the Blanketeers. They were dispersed by troops long before they reached London.

Most petitions failed like this one. As working men did not have the vote, Parliament was not sensitive to their opinions.

Political Activities. The working classes had no party of their own, but there was a small group of middle class politicians who had ideas that appealed to the ordinary man. They were the Radicals. Two of their leaders were William Cobbett and Henry Hunt. Cobbett was a journalist and he encouraged discontent with his newspaper the "Weekly Political Register". Hunt was good at raising violent passions with his speeches. They called him "Orator" Hunt.

During the early years of the French Revolution various Corresponding Societies were formed, which met to discuss politics and exchange letters with the Jacobin Clubs in Paris. They wanted to reform Parliament and give every man the vote. One of the most important was the London Corresponding Society whose secretary was a shoemaker called Thomas Hardy. Naturally enough the government thought societies like these were plotting revolution.

Violence. Groups of working people became violent from time to time, largely because they could not have their way by legal means. Sometimes they attacked employers and fellow workers who refused to strike. There were assaults, beatings, vitriol throwings and even murder. However, most industrial violence was not against people, but against mills and machinery. It culminated in an organised campaign of destruction by men called Luddites.

The Luddites took their name from their mythical leader, Ned Ludd, who was supposed to have his headquarters in Sherwood Forest. They were active in three parts of the country. In 1811 the Midland Luddites smashed wide frames for making stockings, throughout Nottinghamshire, Derbyshire and Leicestershire. In 1812 the Lancashire Luddites attacked mills using power looms and the Yorkshire Luddites mills using shearing frames. Finally they were put down by the army and sixteen were hanged while many more were transported.

There was political violence as well as industrial. In 1816 there were riots at the Spa Fields in London and in 1820 there was the Cato Street Conspiracy, which was a plot to murder the entire Cabinet. These things were the work of a few crazy fanatics but they made the working classes look more dangerous than they were.

Government Action. As we have seen the Government was hostile to the working classes and did its best to hold them down.

One way was by legislation. For example in 1799 and 1800 the Combination Acts made it illegal to form trade clubs in order to press for higher wages. This had always been so; the difference was that offenders could now be tried quickly and easily before magistrates. How far the Combination Acts were used is not clear, though it does seem that they were fairly well enforced in parts of the country where the workers were feared, like the northern industrial towns. Elsewhere the trade clubs went on much as before.

Then there were the Six Acts of 1819 which followed the Peterloo incident described below. They gave magistrates extra powers to search for weapons, and made it illegal to do arms drill. This sort of thing was reasonable enough, but they also made it difficult to organise effective public meetings and they put a tax on periodicals. The idea here was to make publications like Cobbett's "Political Register" too dear for ordinary people to buy.

As there was no proper police force the Government was glad to use the war as an excuse to form bodies of voluntary cavalry called the Yeomanry. They were made up of wealthy men, hostile to the workers and eager for a fight. Some of them had the chance in 1819 at what was known sarcastically as "Peterloo", after the battle of Waterloo. A crowd had assembled in St. Peter's Fields, Manchester to hear "Orator" Hunt. It was behaving perfectly, but the yeomanry charged it, killing eleven people and injuring many others. The whole affair was quite disgraceful, but the Government congratulated the magistrates who ordered the charge, and Parliament passed the Six Acts.

Again because there was no police force the Government used spies. In order to show results these men sometimes acted as "agents provocateurs", which means they encouraged people to conspire and then had them arrested. A spy called Oliver even stirred up a small rebellion in Derbyshire in 1817 as a result of which three men were hanged.

Things began to improve after the war ended in 1815 and the worst of the post-war problems were solved. It was recognised that the working classes had no intention of starting a revolution in the French style with aristocrats hanging from lamp-posts and the guillotine hard at work. The Government began to be more tolerant in the early 1820's when "New Tories" like Huskisson and Peel joined the Cabinet. In 1824, thanks largely to agitation by the Radical politician Francis Place, Parliament repealed the Combination Acts. It not only swept away the legislation of 1799 and 1800, but all the old laws that had gone before. It was now legal to form a trade club.

The ruling classes still kept a wary eye on the workers, but the worst of the repression was over.

The Peterloo Massacre

A MEETING OF THE TRADES' UNIONS.

Questions

1. Is the artist in favour of trade clubs, or against them? Give reasons for your answer.
2. How many different trades are shown here?
3. Which ones were, in fact, likely to have trade clubs? Why are the others included?
4. Would they have all met as one body?
5. What things is the speaker against? What fear is the artist playing on here?
6. What Acts were passed against Trade Clubs? When and why?

Luddites

In November 1811 frames were broken at Bulwell and all the furniture in a house destroyed. Someone shot one of the assailants and there was great excitement at his funeral; the riot act was read, the high sheriff, magistrates and military being present. The next day the enraged rioters broke a wagon load of frames near Arnold and 37 frames at Sutton. Here the yeomanry cavalry caught four. Stacks were burnt of members of that force. The daring of the Luddites was shown by one who entered a house in Nottingham one evening, went upstairs and smashed a frame in a minute or two; but that short time was enough to cause an alarm; constables were at the front of the house. The man threw himself on the roof, where he saw in the dim light that the earth had just been dug in a garden below, and leaped from the eaves of a three storey house, upon it. He ran through a kitchen where a family were at table and escaped. At one trial eight were found guilty and six were hanged while two were transported for life. The former showed great firmness, addressing the spectators, and all joined in singing a hymn. Fifteen thousand people saw the execution. After this scene Luddism seems to have become extinct. About 1000 stocking-frames and 80 lace machines were destroyed during this outburst of popular frenzy.

(Felkin—Hosiery and Lace Manufacture.)

Questions
1. In what county were these disturbances?
2. What things did the Luddites destroy?
3. Who tried to put them down?
4. How did the Luddites retaliate?
5. Give two examples of Luddite courage.
6. How much damage did they do?
7. What punishments were given?
8. What other counties had Luddites?

Questions
1. When and where was this incident?
2. Why had the crowd gathered?
3. Had they done anything to provoke a charge?
4. What people were killed?
5. What did the yeomanry do after the charge?
6. Who were the yeomanry?
7. Why were they keen to charge a crowd like this?
8. How did the government react?

PETERLOO

"Stand fast," I said, "they are riding upon us." The cavalry were in confusion; they could not, with all the weight of man and horse, penetrate that compact mass of human beings; and their sabres were plied to hew a way through naked held-up hands and defenceless heads; and then chopped limbs and wound-gaping skulls were seen; and cries and groans were mingled with the din of that horrid confusion. "For shame! For shame!" was shouted. Then "Break! Break! They are killing them in front and they cannot get away." For a moment the crowd held back as in a pause; then there was a rush, heavy and resistless as a headlong sea, and a sound like low thunder, with screams, prayers, and imprecations from the sabre-doomed crowd who could not escape. On the crowd breaking the yeomanry wheeled, and, dashing whenever there was an opening, they rode, pressing and wounding. Women, maids and tender youths were indiscriminately sabred or trampled. In ten minutes from the beginning of the havoc the field was an almost deserted space. The hustings remained, with a few broken flag staves and a torn banner or two; whilst over the whole field were strewed caps, bonnets, hats, shawls and shoes all trampled, torn and bloody. The yeomanry had dismounted—some were easing their horses' girths others adjusting their accoutrements, and some were wiping their sabres. Several mounds of human beings were where they had fallen, crushed down.
(Bamford—*The Life of a Radical*.)

Questions—Chapter Sixteen
1. What work did trade clubs do?
2. What area would one cover?
3. What men joined trade clubs?
4. What were they in the eyes of the law?
5. Why did employers rarely prosecute them?
6. Name a famous march to London, to present a petition.
7. Why did most petitions fail?
8. What political party appealed to working men?
9. Name two of its leaders.
10. What societies were formed during the French Revolution?
11. Why were working men sometimes violent?
12. What group attacked machinery?
13. Name three areas where they were active. What happened to them in the end?
14. Name a famous riot and a plot.
15. What Acts were passed to make it easy to prosecute Trade Clubs? How far were they used?
16. What were the Six Acts?
17. What happened at Peterloo and afterwards?
18. Describe the activities of government spies.
19. Why did the government change its policy?
20. What did Francis Place achieve?

Further Work
1. List any public houses in your area, named after trades.
2. Read more about William Cobbett and Henry Hunt.
3. Find out more about the Cato Street Conspiracy. How was it discovered?

103

4. Read Charlotte Bronte's novel Shirley chapters 2 and 19, for descriptions of Luddites.
5. Imagine you were living in Nottingham in 1811. Describe what was happening.
6. Imagine you were one of the yeomanry cavalry at Peterloo. Say what you did and why.

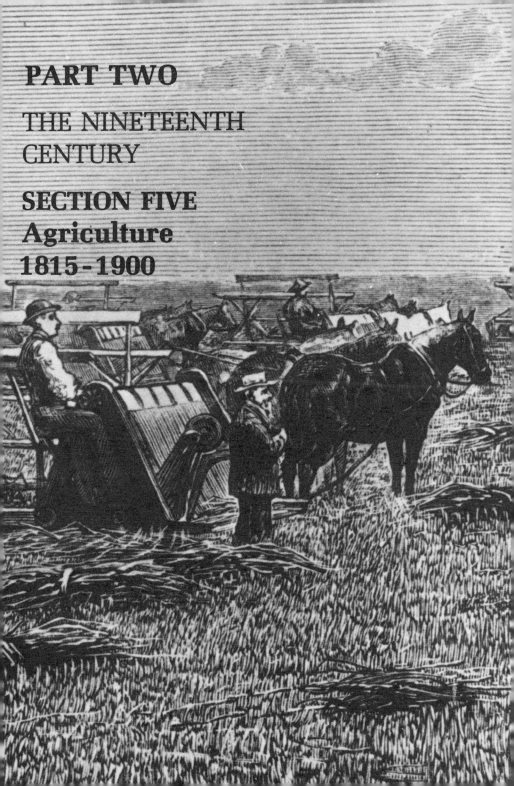

PART TWO

THE NINETEENTH CENTURY

SECTION FIVE
Agriculture
1815-1900

CHAPTER 17

Farming
1815-1850

During this period prices for almost everything went down, and farm produce was no exception. Food from animals became cheaper, but the most drastic fall was in wheat prices. To take two extreme examples, the average price for wheat during the years 1808-1813 was £5.15 a quarter, with a peak of £6.32 in 1812, while in the middle 1830's the average was £2.45, the lowest price being £1.97 in 1835. We must look at the reasons for this fall and show how it affected farming and the policy of the Government.

The Fall in Wheat Prices—Causes. It all began with a sharp drop in price just after 1813 which is easy enough to explain. The harvest of that year was a bumper one, so grain was plentiful and cheap. In fact the ending of the war saw a run of good harvests and cheap food. Also, after 1815, the Government was no longer in the market buying large amounts of grain for the army and navy. Both of these things, though, could only explain a fall in prices over a short period. There was a long-term reason as well.

Farming is not one industry as, say, coal mining or shipbuilding. We can think of it as being more like the textile industry which is made up of cotton, linen, wool and so forth. Sometimes these separate groups will compete with one another, and this was what was happening in farming.

We saw in Chapter Two how wheat growing had been attempted in unsuitable areas, like clay lands, and marginal lands. As long as prices were high, farmers cultivating such soils could make a profit, but in normal times they found themselves in competition with men in the more favoured wheat lands, for example, East Anglia. With good soil and the right climate, such men were increasing their production and forcing down prices. As prices fell, so they stepped up production even more. They were paid less money for every quarter of wheat, but they kept their incomes high by selling more of it. The farmers with the poor soils could not increase their output, so they saw their war-time prosperity wither away. What they did not see was the reason. The war had ended and British ports were open once again to foreign wheat. Farmers who were in difficulty looked to places like France, Poland and Russia as the cause of their troubles; they need have looked no further than East Anglia.

Results. As has already been suggested, one result of the fall in prices was greater efficiency, in areas where it was possible. Farmers already knew the way, because men like Coke of Norfolk had shown them in the early days of the agricultural revolution. More land was enclosed, there were experiments with new crop rotations, better breeds of cattle were reared, and there was mechanisation. Threshing machines became especially popular. Farmers who owned them did not have to employ men through the winter, threshing laboriously with the flail.

Greater efficiency was good for the country as a whole. Although the population grew as it has never done before or since, there was food for everyone, and at falling prices. For the people in farming, though, there were problems. Landlords, farmers and labourers were all affected.

As it was no longer so easy to make money from a farm, landlords had to show consideration for their tenants. Leases were more generous, with the landlords undertaking such things as the repairs of buildings and roads. Wealthier landowners kept up their incomes by investing capital in their farms. Obviously, the better the farm, the higher the rent it would attract. Life was not so easy for the smaller squires. They could not afford expensive improvements so they had to accept lower rents.

Some tenants found themselves in difficulties. During the war they had leased farms at high rents, thinking the good days would never end. Now they found they had peace-time prices for their wheat, but had to pay war-time rents for their farms. Some went bankrupt, while others just left their farms and ran away.

Labourers suffered, too. If a farmer loses his profits, he has to pay lower wages. As we have seen, farmers also economised by buying threshing machines, and giving their men the sack during the winter. They then had to seek help from the parish. The farm labourers showed their dislike of threshing machines and the poor law authorities very clearly in 1830.

That year a rebellion we know as the Swing riots broke out in the corn growing counties of the South of England, the Midlands and East Anglia. There was no organisation. It began in Kent and then spread 107 like a bush fire. As men in one village heard what their neighbours were doing, they followed suit. The rebels smashed threshing machines, attacked workhouses and drove unpopular overseers from their homes or ducked them in the village ponds. Few people were hurt, however, and no-one was killed. The government showed less restraint. It sent in troops, there were mass arrests and nine labourers were hung while 450 were transported.

Burning hayricks in Kent—1830

Government Action—The Corn Laws. Before the Reform Act of 1832 the landed interest controlled the House of Commons, and even afterwards it was very strong there. It dominated the House of Lords throughout. Not surprisingly the Government did what it could to protect farming and stop the price of wheat from falling. It seemed to them that the best way to do so was to control imports. In 1815 a Corn Law prohibited all imports of wheat if the price in Great Britain was below £4.00 a quarter. In 1828, Wellington's Government made the law less severe by introducing a sliding scale of tariffs. If wheat was cheap, imports were discouraged by a high tariff; if wheat was dear, the tariff was low.

The attempt to keep up the price of wheat pleased landlords and farmers, but no-one else. Working people in the towns hated the Corn Laws because they seemed to mean high prices for food. The most dangerous group, though, were the manufacturers who had enough intelligence and organisation to mount a proper campaign. It began in 1839 when a group of Manchester business men headed by Cobden and Bright formed the Anti-Corn Law League. Their main argument was that if Britain did not buy foreign corn, foreigners could not buy British goods. Their opponents said they wanted bread to be cheap so that they could pay their workers lower wages.

The argument over the Corn Laws brought to a head the conflict between the traditional rulers of the country, the landed gentry, and the newer class of wealthy manufacturers who were eager for power.

Events began to move in favour of the League when Peel became Prime Minister in 1841. He was a Tory and he had promised in his election speeches to keep the Corn Laws. Peel, however, was a cotton manufacturer and he also believed in Free Trade, which meant the abolition of all tariffs. At first he felt he could not fly in the face of his own party, but in 1845 there was a famine in Ireland when blight struck the potato crop. Cheap food was needed in abundance, and it seemed that the Corn Laws stood in the way. Peel asked for them to be repealed, and enough of the Tories reluctantly agreed, though they felt sure the ruin of British agriculture would follow.

In the event, all the strife over the Corn Laws turned out to be irrelevant. When they were in force, they did not stop prices falling; after they had gone, agriculture certainly did not decline. Indeed by the early 1850's it had entered what came to be known as its golden age.

Questions
1. What event is this cartoon celebrating?
2. What is the League that is mentioned? (See top of boot).
3. Who is the small figure at the top?
4. Why are the words "Free Trade" written on his shield?
5. Why is the dead giant shown as a nobleman?
6. Why is the word "Monopoly" written on his cudgel?

109

INTERVIEWS WITH LAND AGENTS 1833

Essex. In 1825 I valued a property which I then estimated at £22 000; in 1832 I was requested to revalue it, when I could only set it at about £12 000. The depreciation arose entirely from the tenacity of the soil and the expense of cultivating it was more than the value of the produce it would bear.

What land is it?—A strong, retentive clay.
Have you any farms of this strong land untenanted?—Yes, many.
How does land sell?—We cannot find purchasers.
Norfolk. What is the state of cultivation?—In as good a state as ever I knew it.
As well cultivated?—Yes, and as well stocked.
Is it yielding as much profit?—Farming is much less profitable than it was, but the land is in a progressive state of improvement.
Cambridgeshire. There is a great deal of fenland?—Yes, that land is better than it ever was and I never knew a greater spirit of improvement than there is now.
There has been an immense outlay in drainage?—Yes.
The great improvement has been at the expense of the landlords and not the tenants?—Certainly.
(*Royal Commission on Agriculture.* 1833.)

Questions
1. *How much had the Essex farm fallen in value?*
2. *What is the soil there? What do you imagine farmers had been growing on it?*
3. *What is happening in Essex when farms are offered to let or for sale?*
4. *What is the state of farming in Norfolk?*
5. *What is happening in the Fens?*
6. *Who has been meeting the expenses? Why?*
7. *Why has farming in these two counties remained profitable?*
8. *How will the progress in Norfolk and the Fens affect Essex?*

THE SWING RIOTS 1830

There were stilly gatherings of the misguided peasantry amongst the wild hills, in the gloom of evening, and open and noisy meetings of determined men at noontide in the streets and greens of our Berkshire villages, sallying forth to collect money or destroy machinery. There were daylight marches on the high road, regular and orderly as an army, and midnight visits to lonely houses, lawless and terrific as the descent of pirates. With the approach of night came the red glow of fires gleaming on the horizon, the tolling of bells, and the rumbling sound of the engines clattering along, and too often rendered useless by the cutting of the pipes after they had begun to play. The blow seemed to fall just where it might least have been looked for, on the charitable. One of the objects of attack was a widow of ninety, the best of the good, the kindest of the kind. The rioters made us fear, and such fear comes near to hate.

Then the time came when the fires were quenched, the riots were put down, the chief of the rioters was taken. The crowded gaols groaned with their overload of wretched prisoners; soldiers were posted at every avenue to guard against escape and every door was watched night and day by miserable women, the wives, mothers or daughters of the culprits, praying for admission to their unfortunate relatives. The danger was fairly over and pity had succeeded to fear.
(Mary Russel Mitford—*Our Village.*)

Questions
1. *When and where do the rioters meet?*
2. *What does the writer seem to suggest is odd?*
3. *What things do they do? How do they interfere with fire engines?*
4. *What kind of people do they often attack?*
5. *Why did "pity succeed to fear"?*
6. *Why were the farm labourers rioting?*
7. *What punishments did they receive?*

Questions—Chapter Seventeen
1. *Give two short-term reasons for the fall in wheat prices after 1813.*
2. *Why had wheat growing on unsuitable land been profitable during the war?*

3. How did farmers on good wheat soil cope with falling prices? Which part of England was this?

4. What did farmers on poor soils blame for falling prices?

5. How did farming become more efficient?

6. Why were landlords more generous to tenants?

7. How did they try to keep up their rents?

8. What problem did some farmers have with their leases?

9. Give two reasons why labourers were unhappy.

10. Describe the Swing Riots.

11. How were the rebels punished?

12. Why did the government protect the landed interest?

13. Describe the Corn Laws passed in 1815 and 1828.

14. Who formed the Anti-Corn Law League? Name two of its leaders.

15. Why did they want the Corn Laws repealed?

16. What two social groups were in conflict?

17. Which Tory Prime Minister wanted Free Trade?

18. Why did he not abolish the Corn Laws at once?

19. What event forced their repeal?

20. What happened to farming after repeal?

Further Work

1. Read more about Cobden and Bright and the Anti-Corn Law League.

2. Find out more about Sir Robert Peel. What happened to him after the repeal of the Corn Laws?

3. Read about the Irish Potato Famine.

4. You are a Norfolk farmer in 1840. Explain how you are coping with the fall in wheat prices, and how your landlord is helping you.

5. You are a labourer who has taken part in the Swing Riots. Explain why you rioted, say what you did and what happened afterwards.

CHAPTER 18

The Golden Age of British Farming 1850-1875

The third quarter of the nineteenth century was a prosperous time for British farmers. Profits were higher than they had been during the Napoleonic Wars and higher than they would ever be again in peace time until after World War II.

We have to look at the reasons for this prosperity, the people who took advantage of it and the techniques that they used.

Causes. In the first place there was little competition from abroad. The repeal of the Corn Laws had been expected to bring wheat prices to a ruinous level, but it did not do so because there were no foreign countries with large quantities of surplus grain. Even existing supplies might be interrupted. For example, the Crimean War of 1854-1856 stopped trade with Russia and gave wheat growers three very agreeable years. With livestock the situation was even better because practically no animals were imported and British farmers had the market to themselves.

On top of this, industry was prosperous. People in the towns had good wages, so they no longer needed to live almost entirely on bread. They could now afford foods that had once been luxuries, such as milk, butter, cheese and meat, and they also wanted better clothing which meant more wool and leather. The main reason for the prosperity in farming was this demand for animal products, coupled as it was with an almost complete absence of foreign competition.

However, industry did more than supply a market; it also provided goods and services. In the first place there was the manufacture of artificial fertilisers which were becoming widely used. Also there were ample supplies of cheap iron so that it was possible to manufacture all

sorts of farm machinery, including steam engines.

Most important of all was the railway. The "mania" of the 1840's gave the country a fairly complete network and it provided farmers with an excellent service. In the first place, fresh milk could now travel a fair distance. Formerly, city dwellers had had their milk from cows kept in stalls in the towns themselves, or from farms in the immediate neighbourhood. A dairy farmer further away could only use his milk for butter and cheese, feeding the skimmed milk and the whey to his pigs. With a railway it was quite possible to send milk, for example, from Wiltshire to London. Railways were also important for meat. Droves of cattle had once been a common sight, making their way along "green lanes" to the London markets. After a hundred kilometres or so of walking they had lost some of their weight and had to be grazed on the outskirts of the city until they had recovered it. With a railway, cattle could go from farm to market in a day.

Farmers and Landowners who Profited. The men who were best placed to profit from the golden age were those who were lucky enough to own land in the light-soil areas of East Anglia, the Cotswolds and the chalk downs of the South. The Norfolk four course rotation was well suited to such land, so farmers had their turnips and grass leys to feed cattle, as well as cereals. They found it easy enough to rear more cattle and sheep, but at the same time continue to produce wheat, which was still a valuable crop. It is true that wheat prices fell unpleasantly low from time to time, but this did not worry them unduly as they could feed the surplus to their animals.

Landlords in these areas were particularly willing to invest money in their land, because good farms meant high rents and there were now tenants who were willing to pay well. There was no more enclosing to be done, so the usual investment was in land drainage.

New Techniques. When it came to making improvements, the farming community found there were plenty of people willing to give advice. One of these was a journalist called James Caird, who had failed as a farmer. In 1848 he wrote a book called "High Farming, the Best Substitute for Protection". In it he explained how, by being more efficient, farmers need fear nothing from the repeal of the Corn Laws. There were also important-sounding organisations. The Royal Agricultural Society had been founded in 1838; the Board of Agriculture started an experimental station at Rothamsted in Hertfordshire in 1843, and in 1845 the Cirencester College of Agriculture opened. It is difficult to say how much direct influence all this had, but its very existence reflected the mood of the more progressive men—a willingness to meet a challenge or an opportunity with a spirit of enterprise. We can see that "high farming" aptly describes the golden age when we look at the 113 improvements that were being made.

Land drainage has already been mentioned. If soil is waterlogged it will grow the wrong herbage, it is difficult to plough and it wastes manure. Also the growing season is short, because wet land is cold. Foremost among the progressive farmers was a Scot, Smith of Deanston. By putting in drains and by deep ploughing he converted soggy wasteland into a productive farm. This was in the 1820's. Smith's drains were ditches, filled with stones and then covered over, and although they were efficient they were expensive. In 1843 John Reade produced a clay pipe drain, which was much easier to lay, and shortly afterwards a pipe making machine was patented.

A new departure was the use of artificial fertilisers, encouraged, partly, by a German chemist called Liebig. In 1840 he published a book called "Organic Chemistry in its application to Agriculture". At about this time the first cargoes of Peruvian guano began to arrive. Guano is the accumulated droppings of sea birds and bats, built up for centuries in Peruvian caves. Strictly speaking it is not an artificial fertiliser, but it is used in the same way. They also had bone manure, superphosphates, and sodium nitrate. Much of the nitrate was imported from Chile. Basic slag, an important source of phosphates, came after the discovery of the Gilchrist-Thomas process of steel making, but that was in 1878 when the golden age was over.

As most of the profits came from animals, it is not surprising that stock breeding was important. The older breeds developed by Bakewell and others survived, but there were new ones as well, for example improved Lincoln sheep and Aberdeen Angus beef cattle. There were huge work horses, too, like the Shire, Clydesdale and the Suffolk Punch.

The large mixed-farms were mechanised. By 1850 steam power was common in industry, and now it was applied to the farm. In the yards, engines drove all manner of equipment—threshing machines, chaff cutters, turnip slicers and water pumps. They were also used for ploughing. They could not pull a plough like a horse, but drew it across the field on the end of a cable. They could make several furrows at once and stir the soil more deeply than was possible with draught animals. The disadvantage of the method was that it was only economical on large, regular fields.

One particularly useful machine was the reaper. Patrick Bell had made an efficient one in the 1820's but it was too expensive to buy in those difficult times. In 1851 an American, McCormick, brought his reaper to the Great Exhibition and this revived interest in Bell's machine. In 1853, Crosskill improved the reaper by making it lay the wheat in sheaves, so that it was easier to collect and bind.

Such then was "high farming", but in the midst of all their prosperity, 114 the mixed farms had a fatal weakness. They still depended far too much

Steam-powered threshing

on wheat and the day was fast coming when anyone relying on that crop would face overwhelming competition.

Questions

1. What method of reaping did this replace? Why is it better?

2. Locate the cutters. They have "reciprocating" knives which means they work like many pairs of scissors side by side, or like a hedge trimmer. How did other, less successful, machines work?

3. What is the purpose of (a) the canvas sheet behind the cutters (b) the sails i.e. the propellor like object at the front?

115

4. Why do the horses walk behind the machine?
5. How does the machine lay the corn? What will happen to it next?
6. How did later reapers deal with the corn?
7. What work does a combine harvester do?
8. When did Bell invent his reaper?
9. Why did it not come into general use at that time?
10. What revived interest in it?

GUANO

Guano is the dung of sea birds brought to this country from the rocky shores of Peru where, under the influence of a placid clime and dry atmosphere, it has accumulated in vast beds. It has been analysed and found to contain phosphates, urates and other salts. It is, beyond question, the most valuable of all the animal manures which have been imported into this country. It is calculated to add in a material degree of the produce of the British Isles, and, from its portable nature, to afford increased facilities to cultivation in the remoter districts.
(Low—Elements of Practical Agriculture. 1847.)

Questions

1. What is guano? Where is it from?
2. What plant foods does it contain?
3. How will it "add in a material degree to the produce of the British Isles"?
4. How will it help remoter districts?
5. What other new fertilisers were there?

LAND DRAINAGE IN BERKSHIRE

Every acre of the farm was drained with pipes laid four feet deep, the drains being 15 feet apart in the stiffer lands and 30 feet in those which were drier. Following the drainers the whole farm was trenched by forks to a depth of 22 inches. The cost of both operations, drainage and trenching, was nearly £12 an acre; so that if a great improvement has been effected, it must not be overlooked that it has been done by a large outlay of capital.
(James Caird—English Agriculture in 1850-1851.)

Questions

1. How deep and how far apart are the drains?
2. Why was the soil trenched as well as drained?
3. What was the cost?
4. What misgiving does Caird seem to have?
5. What are the advantages of drainage?

A STEAM ENGINE ON A DORSET FARM

It thrashes and winnows the corn, cuts the straw into chaff, turns the stones for grinding the cattle food, and works a bone crusher in which also the hard American oilcake is broken down. Over the furnace is a drying loft, where corn is dried by the waste heat of the engine fire. The chaff is carried to the root house where turnips are sliced by machine and the roots and the chaff are then mixed together. This mixture is the winter food of the cattle and sheep, cake and corn being added as needed. A large steaming-chest is being erected in which the steam from the engine boiler will be employed in preparing all the food.
(Ibid.)

Questions

1. What work does the engine do?
2. What use is made of the surplus heat and steam?
3. What use are crushed bones?
4. Find out what oil cake is made from.
5. What is the winter feed for the cattle?
6. What crop rotation does this farm have?

RAILWAYS FROM NORFOLK TO LONDON

Formerly, when several days were occupied in driving to London, a sheep was found to have lost on the average 10lb. and a bullock 28lb. This was waste, entirely lost to everybody. On the quantity of stock sent out by Mr. Hudson this loss was, in value, £600 a year; nearly the whole amount now finds its way to the market, as the stock are put in the trucks in the morning, and reach London in the afternoon without fatigue.
(Ibid.)

Questions

1. How had animals once reached London?
2. How much weight did they lose?
3. How long does it take them by rail?
4. How much money does the railway save this farmer?

Questions—Chapter Eighteen

1. When was the Golden Age of British farming?
2. What happened after the repeal of the Corn Laws?
3. Why were people in towns able to buy better food?
4. What foods did they want?
5. What did industry produce for farmers?
6. How did railways help the supply of milk and meat?
7. What areas were the most prosperous?
8. What system of cropping was used there?
9. Which products were the most profitable?
10. How did landlords help?
11. Name a writer on farming and his book.
12. Name three organisations founded to encourage and help farming.
13. Who showed the value of land drainage?
14. What was his method? How was it improved?
15. Name a German chemist and his book.
16. Name four new fertilisers.
17. What new breeds of cattle were there?
18. How were steam engines used (a) in the yards (b) for ploughing.
19. Name two men who invented reapers.
20. How was the farmers' prosperity in danger?

Further Work

1. On an outline map of England, mark the light soil areas that did well during the Golden Age.
2. On your visits to the country look out for stacks of clay pipes used for drainage. What is "mole drainage"?
3. List the fertilisers mentioned in Chapter 18 and find out the particular value of each. A gardening book will help.
4. Find pictures of (a) the different breeds of livestock mentioned in Chapter 18 (b) farm machinery used in the middle of the 19th century.
5. Imagine you are a Norfolk farmer during the Golden Age. Explain how you run your farm and why you are prosperous.

CHAPTER 19

Farming
1875-1900

For many farmers these were years of depression. We have seen that the golden age came about because of the success of mixed farming. The larger profits were from stock, but the system also depended upon wheat. Sometimes there was a glut of grain, but they could cope by feeding the surplus to cattle. However, consistently low prices for year after year would mean ruin. This was just what did happen in the last quarter of the nineteenth century. In the best year of the golden age, 1854, wheat sold for £6.70 a quarter; in 1894, the worst year of the long depression, it was only £1.14. We have to see why this happened and what the results were.

Causes of Depression. English agriculture suffered because of the opening of the temperate grasslands of the world. These were found in Australia, New Zealand, the Argentine, but most of all in the U.S.A. and Canada. Here were vast areas of prairie, ideal for growing wheat. At first the settlers could do little more than shoot buffalo, as well as any redskins who objected to losing their only source of food. The prairies were remote from the sea, and labour was short. A series of inventions solved these problems. One was the reaper-binder which not only cut the wheat, but tied the sheaves with string. This helped make up for the labour shortage. Next there was the railway, which could take grain in bulk to the coast. Finally there was the steamship; this could guarantee regular crossings of the Atlantic, with large cargoes. Cheap grain threatened to flood into all the ports of Europe.

Nor did wheat come alone. In 1880 the *Dunedin* docked in London with the first cargo of refrigerated New Zealand lamb. The Prince of Wales was given a joint and pronounced it excellent, but farmers thought otherwise.

Most governments took alarm. The American competition would have meant the ruin of their peasantry, and the peasants were the stolid, dumb, conservative majorities that kept right wing governments and the old autocracies in power. Docile and healthy, they also made ideal soldiers. Not surprisingly practically every European country put such heavy tariffs on imported wheat that the Americans found no sale. The exception was Britain.

By 1850 half our population was urban, and each year the towns became more important in relation to the countryside. We had become an industrial nation, and we needed cheap food for our workers and markets for our finished goods. The developing countries provided both, and manufacturers were determined to take advantage of them.

Results. Obviously, farmers who grew wheat were the ones to suffer most. Those who had persisted in growing it on sticky clays quickly went out of business, but even those who had farmed intelligently and efficiently on light soils soon had to give up the struggle as well.

Farming activities that had once been despised as women's work became, in some areas, the only way to make a living. They were such things as keeping poultry and growing fruit and vegetables. Market gardening became important in the Vale of Evesham and in Kent. Of the major farming activities, dairying was profitable and also the production of good quality fresh meat. Not surprisingly, much ploughed land was sown with grass to make permanent pasture.

Arable farmers gave up their leases and men, experienced in dairying, took over. West of England farmers moved into the Midlands and quite a number of Scots went to Essex where the clay soil, if not the climate, favoured milk production for the London market.

The depression meant the end of most of the expensive improvements of the golden age, though there were some hopeful changes in dairying. Cheese factories were built; cows were bred to give higher yields; milking machines and cream separators were invented; very important from the customer's point of view, milking was done under more hygienic conditions.

Landlords had problems, too. Land values slumped, and so did rents. All that had been spent during the golden age turned out to be, literally, money down the drain. There was no longer any hope of return from more capital invested in land, so they no longer improved their farms in order to keep up the rents.

The close control which landlords had once had over their tenants now vanished. A man was lucky to find a tenant so he was unlikely to try and tie him down with a lot of restrictive covenants requiring, for example, a certain crop rotation, or specifying the amounts of manure that should be spread. Tenants farmed as they pleased.

119

The landed-gentry lost much of their political influence, too. Power lay in the hands of the men who controlled the industry and commerce of the country. In 1884 they delivered to their rivals what must have seemed the ultimate insult by giving the despised farm labourers the right to vote.

The most important fact about the labourers themselves is that between 1875 and 1900 one third of them left the land, either to work in the towns, or to emigrate. The main reason was that fewer men were needed for grass farming than for arable.

For those that remained, life became more bearable. Many had better houses; the Education Acts kept the children from work, at least some of the time; dairying gave more regular employment than arable farming. There was also an improvement in wages. In 1870 the average was about 62p a week and in 1890 it was 68p. In the meantime prices had fallen considerably.

There were even some Trade Unions to protect the labourers. At the end of the golden age, in 1872, Joseph Arch had formed the National Agricultural Labourers' Union. It was short lived, collapsing in 1874 after a strike had failed. In 1906, though, trade unionism revived with the formation of the National Union of Agricultural Workers. However, the movement has never been strong in the countryside.

There were well-meaning attempts to improve the labourer's lot by turning him into a peasant farmer. This was the Small Holdings Movement led by men like Jesse Collins. They had the vision of a contented rural society, each man with his "three acres and a cow". Actually, it is hard to imagine a tougher, more miserable existence than this. None the less in 1908 Parliament passed the Small Holdings Act that enabled County Councils, if they so wished, to buy land and let it off in lots of not more than 50 acres (about 20 hectares) each. It was not a success and only 13 000 such holdings had been established by 1914.

For the country as a whole the depression in agriculture seemed a necessary evil, and farming was sacrificed to industry. However, there was a price to pay, and this was dependence on imported food. On the eve of the Great War 40% of our meat and 80% of our wheat came from overseas.

A clandestine meeting of agricultural labourers

Questions
1. Where was this picture drawn?
2. What machines are at work?
3. How were they different from earlier machines of the same type?
4. Why were they especially valuable for these farmers?
5. Why is wheat growing easier in country like this, than in many parts of Britain?
6. Much of this wheat might have gone to Britain. How would it have been transported?
7. What problems did its arrival create for British farmers?
8. Why did most British people welcome it?

IMPROVEMENTS IN DAIRY FARMING
1. Cattle breeders who had been devoting their attention to the production of beef, awoke to the fact that milking qualifications of cows were worth consideration. Cheese and butter factories were established. Model dairies, elegant fittings, milk conveyances resplendent with all the colours of the rainbow, new churns and butter-workers, appliances for the manufacture of butter and cheese and apparatus for testing and analysing milk, were made in greater variety year after year. The centrifugal cream separator was introduced. Before long, agricultural societies began to offer prizes for milch cows and dairy produce, and to exhibit a working dairy in the showyard. More milk was drunk by children, and "soda and

milk" became a fashionable beverage. In short, there was a boom in dairying which has lasted to the present day.
2. The introduction of the cream separator marks an era in dairying. The milk is conveyed into a cylinder which is made to revolve very rapidly. The gravity of the skim milk being greater than that of the cream, the former is thrown to the circumference, while the latter collects in the centre, each being caused to flow out by a separate tube. Colonel Hayward who uses a Laval separator, says it gives him 25% more cream than skimming and that he gets 1lb. of butter more per cow per week. If we assume one third of the milk in the country goes to make butter, the gain by the universal use of the separator would be 53 000 000lb. of butter per annum.
(Bear—British Farmer and His Competitors. 1888.)

Questions
1. Why were many farmers compelled to go dairying?
2. How did the following help dairy farmers:

    (a) Cattle breeders (b) Manufacturers
    (c) Agricultural Societies (d) Social habits?
3. How does the cream separator work?
4. How did it help one farmer?
5. How could it help the entire country?

WEEKLY BUDGETS OF TWO FAMILIES OF SEVEN—1795 and 1906

1795	p.	1906	p.
Bread, flour	57½	Bread, flour, oats	19
Potatoes	7½	Bacon, beef	9½
Bacon, pork	19	Fish	1½
Cheese	4	Cheese	4
Milk	2	Milk	3
Tea, Sugar, Butter	9	Tea, Sugar, Butter	13
Soap	3	Lard, Suet	1½
Beer	3	Currants	½
Clothing	14	Sweets, Biscuits	1
Candles	1½	Oranges	1
Fuel	7½	Soap	½
Rent	2½	Papers, Beer, Tobacco	3½
Births and Burials	2½	Clothing	15
Total	£1.33p	Paraffin	1
		Fuel	6
Earnings		House Rent	7½
Man	47	Allotment rent	½
Woman	7½	Total	88p
Children	2½	Earnings	
Total	57	(man only)	75
Deficiency	76	Deficiency	13
(Eden—*State of the Poor.*)		(Davies—*English Village.*)	

Some Prices	1795	1906
Tea	13½	6½
Sugar	4	1
Butter	5	5
Wheat (per quarter)	£3.76	£1.41

Questions

1. Arrange the items in suitable groups (cereal foods, animal foods, groceries etc). and draw diagrams to compare them.
2. Draw up menus the two families could have used. (Don't forget the allotment for the 1906 family.)
3. What proportion of money went on food? Compare these proportions with your own family.
4. What had happened to prices and wages? What was the biggest single change this made?

5. How would the deficiency in income be made up? (see chapter 12).

Questions—Chapter Nineteen

1. What happened to wheat prices after 1875? Why?
2. What three inventions helped prairie farmers?
3. Why is 1880 an important date for the meat trade?
4. How did most governments react to foreign competition?
5. Why did Britain not do the same?
6. Which farmers suffered most from the depression?
7. What alternatives did they find? Which were the only two main farming activities to be profitable?
8. What happened to ploughed land?
9. What farmers migrated? Where? Why?
10. What happened about improvements?
11. How did landlords treat (a) their farms (b) tenants?
12. What political changes took place?
13. Why did many labourers leave the land?
14. Give five reasons why life was better for those who remained.
15. Who formed the first trade union for farm workers? When?
16. When did it collapse? Why?
17. When did trade unionism revive among farm workers?
18. What was the Small Holdings Movement? Who led it?
19. What Act was passed to encourage it? What success did it have?
20. What national problem did the depression in agriculture create?

Further Work

1. Read more about wheat growing on the prairies.
2. Find pictures of 19th century dairy equipment.
3. Read more about Joseph Arch.
4. You are a farmer in 1885. Explain why you are turning to dairying. What equipment will you use?
5. You are a landowner in 1888. Describe your problems. What are you doing about them?

123

SECTION SIX
Transport
1830-1914

CHAPTER 20

Railways

Following the success of the Liverpool to Manchester line, the railway soon became the most important method of transport. A complex system was built up, and there were many technical improvements. The railways had a profound effect on the life of the country, both economic and social.

The Railway System. The first stage, down to 1848, was to build the basic network. This was done, mainly, in two boom periods, 1836-1837 and, far more important, 1844-1847. The second boom was known as the "railway mania", so frantic were people to invest their money. Some lines did fail, but most were a success. When it was over the country had 8 000 kilometres of track, consisting of lines radiating from London and others serving the coalfields of Lancashire, the West Riding and the North-East of England.

There was a good deal of opposition, largely because of the noise and appearance. Landowners objected, and so did some towns, for example, Northampton, Oxford and Cambridge. Much of this died away when people realised the advantages of having railways. Organisations whose fears were more justified were turnpike trusts, coaching companies and canals.

Railways had also to solve a problem of organisation. Many of them were only about sixteen to twenty kilometres long which made it difficult for anyone travelling or sending goods on a long journey. George Hudson, known as the "railway king" showed the advantages of amalgamating lines when he built up the North-Eastern Railway in the 1840's. Unfortunately some of his methods were illegal and he had to escape abroad.

One of the many important lines built at this time was the Great Western Railway opened in 1841. It was engineered by Brunel. He gave it a gauge of seven feet (2.1 metres) which had many advantages, being, for example, safer and faster than the standard gauge. It ran from London to Bristol and was later extended to Cornwall. Because early locomotives were none too powerful, Brunel, like every other engineer, made his gradients as easy as possible. He was so successful with the G.W.R. that they called it his "billiard table". Important works on the line were the Box Tunnel, near Bath, and the Tamar Bridge.

After 1850, they added to the basic network. Lines were extended into remote areas, like the Highlands, branch lines were built and so were the suburban lines around London. By 1913 there was a total of 30 000 kilometres of track.

1863 saw the beginning of the London underground railway, with the opening of the Metropolitan line, joining the stations of Liverpool Street, Euston and St. Pancras.

Technical Changes. Locomotives were improved. Bogie wheels and automatic brakes made them safer, while superheated steam gave them more power and speed.

The block system of signalling introduced in 1840 cut down accidents. Under it a line is divided into sections and only one train at a time is allowed in any section.

Probably the most important changes came when cheap steel began to be produced in the 1870's. This helped with the manufacture of locomotives and rolling stock, while rails, too, were made of steel. Much longer bridges were also built, for example the Severn Bridge, the Forth Bridge, and the unlucky Tay Bridge that collapsed in 1879.

Much was done for passengers, especially when it was realised how important they were. By 1850 revenue from fares was higher than that from freight. Stations were built with every comfort, and completely covered in with structures of iron and glass. Carriages were improved, particularly towards the end of the century when they had corridors and heating. There were restaurant and sleeping cars as well.

At first, third class passengers were despised and had to travel in open trucks, but the companies came to value their fares and gave them seats and cover. Parliament intervened too. The Railways Act of 1844 stated that every company must run at least one train each way every day, stopping at every station and charging no more than a penny a mile. Although they had a bad reputation, these "Parliamentary trains" were a great help to poorer people going to and from work.

One change was not for the better, and this was the decision to make the "standard" gauge of 4 feet 8½ inches (1.43 metres) universal. Brunel showed clearly that travel was faster and safer on his wider gauge, but only the G.W.R. had adopted it. To fall in with the others, all 126 the G.W.R. had to do was put down a third line between the other two.

Victoria Station, Manchester

To have widened the lines of the other companies would have been an enormous task with work not only on the track, but at every cutting, embankment, tunnel and station. In 1846 Parliament refused to allow any more broad gauge lines and by 1892 the G.W.R. had adopted the standard gauge.

Effects of Railways. It is difficult to find any aspect of life in Britain that was not affected, directly or indirectly, by the coming of the railways.

In the first place they were, themselves, a major industry. Building them, then running them, gave employment to thousands. There were many industries that served the railways directly, and they grew considerably as a result. These included; coal, iron and steel, engineering and building. Moreover, practically all industries benefited from having a quick, easy way to transport their raw materials and finished goods. For agriculture, the coming of the railways was one of the main reasons for the so-called Golden Age after 1850. Fisheries gained too, so that by the middle of the century 70 tonnes of fish were coming daily to London from the east coast ports.

For some, though, the railways meant ruin. Coach companies and turnpike trusts collapsed quickly; canals put up a longer fight and sometimes railway companies had to resort to buying them up. However, where they survived they did so with difficulty. 127

Easy travel made big differences to social life. For the first time in history working class people could go where they wanted. The railways provided day trips and in 1841 Thomas Cook organised his first excursion, which took some Leicester people to a Temperance meeting. Annual holidays away from home became normal, and holiday towns became important. Bournemouth practically owes its existence to the railways.

There were some developments no one could have foreseen. For example, it was easier to keep law and order because of the speed with which troops could be moved. The Chartists who rioted in Birmingham in 1839 were soon put down by some of the Metropolitan Police. Robert Stephenson's London to Birmingham railway had been opened the year before.

Questions
1. What kind of carriage is shown here?
2. How had such carriages improved since 1830?
3. What are the passengers?
4. What time of day is this likely to be?
5. What Act of Parliament required companies to run trains like this?
6. What conditions did the Act make?
7. What nickname was given to these trains?
8. What reputation did they have?
9. Why were they useful?
10. Read the song about "making the punishment fit the crime" from Act Two of the Mikado by Gilbert and Sullivan.

RAILWAYS AND THE CLEVELAND IRON INDUSTRY

The discovery of the Cleveland ironstone took place in 1850. Its immediate result was a complete change in the position and prospects of the district served by the Stockton and Darlington Railway. New works for the manufacture of iron sprang up on the banks of the Tees with mushroom-like rapidity. The trade of the ports of Stockton, Middlesborough and Hartlepool became enormously developed. The Middlesborough and Guisborough Railway, which was projected to meet the needs of the Cleveland iron trade, was opened in 1853, and soon became one of the most valuable feeders of the Stockton and Darlington system.

From 1856 to the present time the iron trade of Cleveland has pursued a career of unparalleled prosperity. In 1874 the pig iron made there was 2 000 000 tons. The total quantity of pig iron produced in the United Kingdom was 6 600 000 tons, so that Cleveland contributed nearly one third of the total. The growth of the wrought iron trade generally follows that of the pig-iron trade in districts suitable for its development, and Cleveland has formed no exception to this rule. We find that within 20 years, nearly 2000 puddling furnaces have been built. Together they produce more than a million tons of wrought iron per annum and furnish employment to nearly 20 000 hands. (Jeans—*Stockton and Darlington Railway.* 1875.)

Questions

1. Find on a map: *Stockton, Darlington, Middlesborough, Guisborough, Cleveland Hills.*
2. When was the Stockton to Darlington line opened? Who engineered it? Why was it originally built?
3. What extension to the line is mentioned here? Why was it built?
4. Describe the growth of the Cleveland iron industry.
5. How did the local railways help it to grow? How would the iron industry, in its turn, have helped this and other railways?

A RAILWAY TOWN (Crewe, which grew up round the works of the London & North-Western Railway).

There are baths erected by the Company for which the charge is 1½d. If the Hercules who works the steam hammer can be scrubbed clean and white for 1½d he can have no reason to complain. To a doctor the Company gives a house and surgery. A clergyman with a salary from the Company superintends three day-schools for 300 children. There is a library and a mechanics' institute where a number of men whose education was neglected, attend at night to learn reading, writing and arithmetic. There is likewise a music class. The town contains 514 houses, one church, three schools and one town-hall all belonging to the Company. Although the new houses were built for railway servants, yet it was found necessary to construct a considerable number for the shopkeepers and others who wanted to join the new settlement, and accordingly, of the population of 8000, one half are strangers. The workmen began by having a cheap dancing master of their own, but we found a more elegant artist teaching in the town-hall—a splendid room able to hold 1000 persons. As 8000 people cannot live without occasionally biting and tickling each other with the sharp teeth and talons of the law, we saw on a door "Griffin, Attorney". The town is lighted with gas from the Company's works, the foot paths being of asphalt. The town is governed by a council of fifteen, two-thirds of whom are nominated by the inhabitants, one-third by the Company.

(Head—*Stokers and Pokers.*)

Questions

1. What buildings has the Company provided?
2. What does it do for education?
3. How else does it care for its employees?
4. How do the workmen enjoy themselves?
5. How is the town governed?
6. What people have come to Crewe, apart from the employees of the Company? How many are there?

129

Questions—Chapter Twenty

1. When was the "railway mania"?
2. Describe the basic network built as a result.
3. What opposition did railways face?
4. What problem of organisation did they have?
5. Who was the "railway king"? What did he do?
6. Who built the Great Western Railway?
7. Say where it ran and describe the way it was made—gauge, gradients, major engineering works.
8. How was the basic network extended after 1850?
9. What was the first London Underground line?
10. Describe improvements to locomotives.
11. What was the block system of signalling?
12. Give four ways in which steel was used.
13. How was passenger comfort improved?
14. What were "Parliamentary Trains"?
15. Describe the "battle of the gauges".
16. How did railways help employment?
17. How did railways help (a) other industries (b) agriculture (c) fisheries?
18. Who suffered as a result of railways?
19. How did railways affect social life?
20. Show how railways helped law and order.

Further Work

1. Find maps which show the railway network at various stages of growth.
2. Find out which company built the first railway in your area, and where the line ran. It is quite likely someone has written a history of the line. If so, find it and read it.
3. Read more about Brunel's Great Western Railway.
4. Find pictures of 19th century locomotives, rolling stock, equipment, stations, bridges etc.
5. Read about the railway navvies.
6. Who was Thomas Brassey and why was he famous?
7. Imagine you are a railway driver in 1900 and you have just retired. Describe the improvements to railways you have seen in your life.
8. You are living in a small country town in 1840. Describe your feelings when you learn your town is to have a railway.

CHAPTER 21

Shipping

Transport at sea and transport on land had to improve together. The development of the railway was linked to the development of the ship. First of all the sailing ship became more efficient than it had ever been, and later there was the growth of the steam ship.

Clipper Ships. When the East India Company enjoyed a monopoly of the trade with the Far East it built its ships to carry the maximum cargo. They had full, rounded lines and were broad in proportion to their length. They were slow as a result, but it did not matter because there was no competition. In 1833, though, the Company lost its monopoly and there was every point in having fast ships because the first ones home with the tea harvest had by far the best prices for their cargo. English ship builders began to copy, and improve, the American clippers, and they reached their peak in the 1850's and 1860's.

A clipper was narrow in proportion to its length, with fine lines, so that the hull offered the minimum resistance to the water. In addition it had a huge spread of sail. The two things together meant higher speeds. In 1854 the *Lightning* sailed a record 697 kilometres in one day; an East Indiaman could never have managed more than 240 kilometres.

Other improvements involved the use of iron. The hulls were composite, which meant that while the planks were of wood, the ribs were of wrought iron, which made for extra strength and lightness. Rigging was of wire, which was stronger than hemp and needed less crew to manage it.

Clippers first of all brought tea from China, and later wool and grain from Australia.

Early Steamships. Steamships began on inland waterways. In 1802 William Symington's *Charlotte Dundas* steamed thirty kilometres along the Forth-Clyde Canal. Four years later, Robert Fulton was operating the *Clermont* on the River Hudson in the United States, and in 1812 Henry Bell's *Comet* began a regular service on the Clyde. It soon became obvious that steamers were ideal for work in estuaries, like the Clyde and Thames, where towing barges by horse was out of the question and where sailing ships could not manoeuvre easily.

The next step was to venture cautiously into the open sea, first of all hugging the coast, and then making the comparatively short crossings to Ireland and France. By 1830, the year the Liverpool to Manchester railway line opened, there were 200 steamships in Britain, many of them on service in the English Channel and the Irish Sea.

The biggest achievement was the crossing of the Atlantic. Several sailing ships with steam engines in them made the voyage, then, in 1838, Brunel's *Great Western* went from Bristol to New York in 15 days. This showed it was possible to have a regular service across the Atlantic. For Brunel it was the logical extension of his Great Western Railway.

It is true that a small steamer the *Sirius* arrived in New York a few hours before the *Great Western*, but she was designed for the Irish sea and could never have kept up an Atlantic service. She had been sent by a rival company, just to beat the *Great Western*.

The Great Western

Later Steamships. Steamships grew rapidly in importance during the second half of the nineteenth century, and for a variety of reasons.

In the 1840's, the government, impressed by the regularity of the new
132 services, offered contracts to several steamship companies for carrying

mail. For example, Cunard obtained a contract to carry mail to America, and the Peninsular and Oriental to India. The companies were particularly glad to have the extra revenue because, at that time, steamers were still exceedingly expensive to build and run, compared with sailing ships. There was another piece of good fortune when the Suez Canal opened in 1869. It gave the steamship a great advantage over the sailing ship on the Far Eastern runs.

There were many improvements to the ships themselves. Screw propulsion was developed in the 1840's. It was shown to be better than paddles during a tug-of-war organised by the Admiralty in 1845. The screw came into general use in the 1850's and 1860's.

Early steamers burnt a lot of fuel. It was calculated that if one of them went to Australia it would need every scrap of space for fuel and could carry no cargo at all. It was most important to have more efficiency and this came about in 1854 when John Elder invented the compound engine. It had two cylinders and they used the same steam one after the other. Later, more cylinders were added and by 1900 fuel consumption had been cut by 80%.

In 1897 Sir Charles Parsons showed the value of the steam turbine by his antics at the Naval Review at Spithead. He raced in and out of the lines of battle ships and the Admiralty launches sent to head him off were left far behind.

There were also changes in the construction of hulls. "Iron Mad" Wilkinson had made an iron boat in 1787, and we have seen how the clippers had composite hulls. There were other experiments but Brunel has the credit for designing the first ocean going, all iron, screw driven ship. This was his *Great Britain*, launched in 1843. Brunel tried to push iron construction to its limits by building the *Great Eastern* in 1854. She was a magnificent failure, but other inventors were soon to succeed.

By the 1870's cheap steel was available in large quantities. Steel hulls were more efficient than iron, as they were lighter and stronger. Along with the compound engine they ensured the supremacy of the steam ship, as this table shows:

Comparative Tonnages	
Steam	*Sail*
1873	1 700 000	4 100 000
1913	11 300 000	800 000

Effects of Steamships. In the first place shipbuilding became a major industry, and this is discussed in Chapter 25.

Other activities had to keep pace with shipbuilding. Steel and engineering both grew, as did coal, especially the mining of steam coal in South Wales. There were major dock building programmes in many places, especially London. Southampton was particularly fortunate. It had been difficult for sailing vessels to approach this town, but with its double tides, its long, sheltered estuary and its railway link with London, it was a good port for steamers.

It was not only the allied industries that grew. With the exception of farming the whole economy benefited. Steamships provided cheap, easy transport for goods of all kinds, both small and bulky; they also carried passengers and mail. Brunel's vision had come true for the railway network had been extended, as it were, across the oceans of the world.

Questions

1. Who built the Great Britain? When?
2. What material was used in her hull? Why? (Her length was 322 ft—see next document).
3. How is the ship driven?
4. Why does she have sails?
5. In what ways was this ship different from earlier steamers?
6. One of the statistics given of the ship is:

"Stows 1200 tons of coals and 1000 tons of cargo."

What conclusion would you draw from this?

7. Find out what happened to the Great Britain in 1846.
8. Find out how she ended her working life.
9. Where can she be seen today?

CONSTRUCTION OF HULLS

After the introduction of steam came the use of iron and more recently of steel for the construction of ships; but even apart from the question of steam, the increase in length and speed showed that the requisite strength could not be maintained in wooden ships. The difficulties were insurmountable when the length reached about 300 feet. Vessels of this length when built of wood, showed serious signs of weakness. The height of trees must always be an important factor in the size of a wooden ship. The great alteration, however, did not take place without opposition, and no one more strenuously opposed it than the Government. It was a long time before the Post Office would give consent to iron ships being used for mail; and a still longer time elapsed before the Admiralty consented to the change for the Royal Navy, it being alleged that whilst in action a shot-hole in a wooden vessel could be at once repaired, a hole in an iron plate could not.

No wooden ship could be built sufficiently strong to resist the vibration of the powerful engines that are used in the larger ships of the present day; and then, besides its strength, another advantage of iron is its greater lightness, an iron ship not weighing one half of the same sized wooden ship. One advantage, however, the wooden ships possessed was that their bottoms, when sheathed with metal, never became foul as quickly as the iron ships' bottoms do from marine growths. Serious loss of speed results from much fouling of the bottom. Soon after the building of ships with iron was commenced the composite system was adopted, and some fine China tea-clippers were so built. The iron framing and wood skin planking produced a vessel that had the strength of an iron ship, whilst at the same time obtaining the freedom from fouling of a wooden one. However, the galvanic action set up between the copper sheathing and the iron frames of the ship tended to deteriorate the ironwork and sooner or later to involve the destruction of the ship.

The sides of the iron ship, including the frames, often do not exceed four inches in thickness, whilst the sides of the wooden ship will be some twelve inches at the least. The iron ship is also far less liable to destruction by fire. Not long since an iron ship, the *Colombo*, laden with cotton, jute, and hemp, took fire soon after leaving Calcutta, and the cargo continued to burn until she arrived in the Thames. At times the ship's sides were so hot it was

impossible to touch them. A wooden ship would have been burnt at sea.

The demand for larger vessels and greater speed led to the manufacture of mild steel. In 1859, £40 a ton was paid for steel; at the present time it can be obtained for £5 a ton. In 1882 Dr. Siemens said: "Steel has enabled ship-builders to save one fifth of the weight of the hull, and to increase to that extent its carrying capacity. It combines with a strength 30% more than iron, such toughness, that in a collision the side of a vessel has bulged several feet without rupture."
(Cornewall-Jones—*British Merchant Service*.1898.)

Questions
1. *Why were iron and steel used instead of wood?*
2. *What limits the size of wooden ships?*
3. *Who opposed the use of iron at first? Why?*
4. *Why must steam engines be in iron ships?*
5. *How do wood and iron ships compare in weight?*
6. *Why is it important for a ship to be light?*
7. *What advantage does a wooden ship have?*
8. *What is a composite ship?*
9. *What vessels were built in this way?*
10. *What advantages did they have?*
11. *What went wrong with them?*
12. *Why is it an advantage to have thin sides?*
13. *What did the story of the* Colombo *prove?*
14. *Why did steel fall in price? (Chapter 23].*
15. *Why was Siemens famous? (Chapter 23).*
16. *He gives three reasons why steel is better than iron. What are they?*

Questions—Chapter Twenty-One
1. *How did the East India Company build its ships?*
2. *When and why did it become important to have fast ships?*
3. *Why were clippers fast?*

4. How was iron used in their construction?
5. What cargoes did they carry?
6. Name three of the first steamships and their inventors.
7. Where were they first used?
8. What steamship proved it was possible to have a regular service across the Atlantic? Who built her?
9. What government contracts helped steamers?
10. What event of 1869 helped them? How?
11. What was shown to be the best method of propulsion? How?
12. What was the importance of the compound engine?
13. Who invented the steam turbine?
14. Name three important things about the Great Britain. Who built her?
15. Which was the largest all-iron ship? Who built her?
16. When was steel generally used? Why was it better than iron?

17. What happened to sailing ships?
18. What industries grew along with shipbuilding?
19. Why did Southampton grow in importance?
20. How was the whole economy helped by steam ships? What activity was the exception?

Further Work
1. Collect pictures of 19th century ships.
2. Find out what it was like to work in a sailing ship e.g. in Dana's book Two Years Before the Mast.
3. Read more about clipper ships. Visit the Cutty Sark at Greenwich.
4. Read the story of Brunel's Great Eastern.
5. You are a ship owner of the 1880's. Explain why you are giving up wooden sailing ships in favour of steel steamships.
6. Discuss the view that there has been a lot of romantic nonsense talked about sailing ships.

SECTION SEVEN
Industry
1815-1914

CHAPTER 22

Coal Mining

We have seen that in the eighteenth century coal output increased from 2½ to ten million tonnes a year. However, this was insignificant compared with the growth of the industry in the nineteenth century. From the ten million tonnes of 1800, output reached a record 287 million tonnes in 1913. None the less the basic reasons for the increase were the same—greater demand, improved mining techniques, and better transport.

Demand. In the early part of the nineteenth century demand for coal was stimulated by falling prices. In 1800 coal was about £2 a tonne, but by 1835 it had fallen to 80p. This was due to competition between mines, lower transport costs and the removal of government duties.

At the same time that prices were falling, the need for coal was growing. One of its most important uses was in the home. In the early years of the century, it is likely that between one half and two thirds of our coal was burnt on domestic hearths. The population was increasing, and for most people there was no alternative fuel for cooking and heating. Also there were a good many domestic industries which used coal, like the metal trades of the Black Country.

It was not long, however, before industry was taking more than the home.

We have already seen how the manufacture of iron had come to depend on coke and now, with the industrial revolution in full swing, iron was needed in quantity. Later, towards 1860, it became possible to make cheap steel, thus increasing demand even further. By 1870 iron and steel manufacturers were buying one third of all the coal that was produced.

Demand also came from the increased use of the steam engine. The textile manufacturers were pioneers, steam being used for spinning by the 1830's and for weaving by the 1840's. After 1850 steam power was common in many major industries.

From 1800 onwards, gas was being manufactured, and the first electricity generating stations opened in the 1870's. By 1913 gas and electricity were using considerable amounts of coal.

In transport, first railways, and then steamships were important. They burnt coal themselves and a great deal was also used for the iron and steel that built them.

Finally, exports increased. Other countries developed their industries and bought coal from Britain. South Wales benefited in particular because of its large resources of steam coal and because of the easy transport down the river valleys to the sea. Exports were especially important in the early twentieth century and of the record 287 million tonnes mined in 1913, nearly one third went abroad.

During the nineteenth century the economy of Great Britain changed completely and, not surprisingly, the proportion of coal going to different users changed as well. In the early years of the century, most of it went to private householders; in the 1860's the iron and steel industry was the best customer; after 1900, exports came first. However, during this time, all the markets for coal grew and some of them grew considerably.

Improved Techniques. A way to increase the output of coal was to employ more miners. In the 1840's there were 200 000, whereas in the early twentieth century there were one million. However, while the labour force increased fivefold, output increased tenfold, so it is obvious that mining techniques had improved.

One thing did not change, and that was the work at the face. Even when coal cutting machinery was invented, few mine owners installed any. They had plenty of cheap labour, so there was no incentive. However, every other aspect of mining was made more efficient.

Transport underground had been the work of women and children, but they could never have coped with the amount that was being hewn in the nineteenth century. Anyway, it was illegal to employ them underground after 1842. Increasingly, coal owners made use of trucks on iron rails, drawn by pit ponies.

Transport above ground continued to develop. Coal owners had pioneered the use of the iron rail and the steam locomotive and before long every coal mine of importance was served by its own railway, running either to the public network, or to water transport.

Winding gear had to be improved, as by the 1860's some pits were producing as much as 800 tonnes of coal a day. The horse-driven 139 capstan gave way to the steam engine, and instead of a basket dangling on the end of a hemp rope, there was a metal cage with guides to stop it swinging, and a wire rope to raise it.

Deeper mining had increased the danger from gas in some fields. To overcome it, Sir Humphrey Davy and George Stephenson both invented safety lamps in 1815. Also, from 1830 onwards, mines began to have power driven exhaust fans for ventilation. Many seams that had been too full of gas to be mined, could now be exploited.

All this is not to say that mining became safe. Many coal owners and miners were too careless, so men lost their lives regularly and from time to time there were major disasters.

Improvements in Public Transport. The railways were first developed on the coal fields and when, in the 1840's, a public network was built, lines which were not serving London were serving the coal producing areas of Lancashire, the West Riding, the Midlands and the North East. Much coal had been carried by sea, river and canal, but only the railways were able to take it quickly, easily and cheaply to wherever it was needed. We have seen how demand grew in the homes and in industry, and we have seen how output increased to meet it. The railways were the link between the mines and their customers.

By the early twentieth century, the steamship was equally important. There were bunkering stations all over the world that had to be filled and there were foreign railways and factories that wanted coal. It was because of the steamship that these needs were met. Great Britain was in much the same position as many oil producing countries are today.

Just before the first world war, then, coal mining was at its peak. Unfortunately this did not mean that all was well for its future.

In the first place, labour relations were bad. There were strikes that were so savage that the government had to call in troops. Secondly, there was growing competition from abroad, particularly America and Germany. While British mines still used men to hew coal, they were using machinery. Their competition was especially unfortunate as British coal owners were selling a third of their output abroad. Finally, and perhaps most important, a new fuel, oil, was already showing that it was better than coal in many ways.

The coal industry was torn by strife, it was becoming out of date, and it faced the double threat from foreign mines and oil. Clearly, there were troubled times ahead. Moreover, these troubles would be bound to upset the entire country. Coal made up ten per cent of Britain's exports, so much of her prosperity depended on an industry that was insecure.

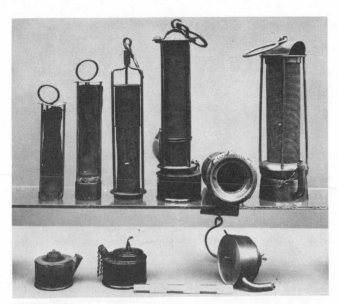

Early types of safety lamp

Questions

1. What is the use of the steam engine shown here? Name some of the things it might have replaced.

2. Identify: boiler, engine house, engine beam, crank, fly-wheel.

3. Name two ways in which coal will be carried from the pit.

141

4. What, most probably, was the material used to make the ropes?

5. Why is the man on the left pushing a cover over the pit mouth?

6. What other improvements, not shown here, were made to the winding gear?

7. Which part of the engine is inside the house?

8. What different uses for iron can you see in the picture?

TESTING FOR GAS WITH CANDLE AND SAFETY LAMP

The hand is placed before the naked candle, so as to make the top of the flame more distinct, which presents a vapour that shows the presence of caburetted hydrogen or other gases. The viewer commences at the floor and cautiously raises his candle till he ascertains that the upper region of the air be either safe or unsafe. "Trying" the candle is both tedious and dangerous, as gas may be concealed in the cavities of the roof whereas the Davy lamp may be thrust up into those places with perfect safety. Under some extreme cases the upper part of the lamp becomes quite red, a continued rushing noise and crackling of the gauze is heard, and the smoke and smell emitted from the lamp shew the immense combustion that is going on. From the observation of the flame a pretty good judgement may be formed of the quality of the surrounding air.

The advantage of the safety lamp in a financial point of view is incalculable, as in many mines the pillars, constituting two-thirds of the entire mine were enveloped in explosive gas. The invention, therefore, of the safety lamp led to the reopening of the wastes of many valuable collieries.

(Dunn—*Winning and Working of Collieries*. 1848.)

Questions

1. What does Dunn call the explosive gas found in mines? Give two other names for it.

2. How can the viewer tell from a candle flame that it is present?

3. Why does he work from the ground upwards?

4. Why is his work both "tedious and dangerous"?

5. Why was the Davy lamp so called?

6. When was it invented?

7. How can it be used to test for gas?

8. In what two ways is it better than a candle?

9. How much coal had been left unworked in some collieries? Why?

10. How did the safety lamp make mining more profitable?

THE TRANSPORT OF COAL

If you take your station on Tynemouth Priory, you may see many hundred vessels, mostly colliers, put to sea together. On one occasion some three hundred vessels, all laden with coal, were observed making sail together in a single tide. These dingy and crawling craft are, or were, the "nursery of British seamen" for being constantly at sea, winter and summer, they train up a race of hardy and practised mariners. But the naval nursery is in danger of abolition. A new line of screw-steamers has been started, designed to sail three feet to one of the lumbering collier brigs, and at once to reduce the time and cost of transit. These again have to contend with serious rivals—the railways—which convey coals at one farthing per ton per mile.

The first steam collier entered the Thames in September 1852, having run the distance from Newcastle in 48 hours. She consumed eight tons of coal on the voyage, and brought 600 tons as cargo, the whole of which was discharged in the day and the vessel went back for more.

(Leifchild—*Our Coal Fields and Coal Pits*. 1853.)

Questions

1. Which coalfield is the writer discussing?

2. Why was it able to transport its coal by sea?

3. Where would most of the coal be taken?

4. When did this trade begin?

5. How many ships might sail at one time?

6. How long might the voyage take?

7. How does the writer describe the sailing ships?

8. Why were they called a "nursery" of seamen?

9. What two new forms of transport are mentioned?

10. Why did they become increasingly important for the coal industry?

11. Describe the voyage of the first steam collier.

12. Why were steamships that burnt coal, more profitable than sailing ships that burnt none?

13. What advantage is given for railways?

14. What others can you think of?

Questions—Chapter Twenty-Two

1. What was coal output in 1800 and in 1913?

2. Give the three main reasons for the increase.

3. Give three reasons for falling prices.

4. What happened to most coal (a) in the early 19th century (b) in the 1860's (c) in the early 20th century.

5. Which manufacturing industry first used a lot of steampower?

6. When did steam power become general?

7. When did (a) the gas and (b) the electricity industries begin?

8. Give two reasons why coal was important for railways and steam ships.

9. How many men were employed in mining in 1840 and in about 1900?

10. Which mining operation did not change? Why?

11. How was transport improved underground and at the pit head?

12. Why were changes essential after 1842?

13. How was winding gear improved? Why?

14. Name two ways they tried to cope with gas.

15. What advantages did railways have?

16. How had coal been transported before railways?

17. Which areas did the railway network serve?

18. What other form of transport helped coal? How?

19. Name three problems of the coal industry in the early 20th century.

20. Why were they bound to affect the whole country?

Further Work

1. Explain why coal was more important in the home in the 19th century than in the 18th century.

2. Find out more about the beginnings of the gas and electricity industries.

3. Read about the coal strikes of the early 20th century.

4. Write a dialogue between a miner of the 18th century and one of the 19th, comparing and contrasting their mines.

5. Imagine you are a mine owner of the 19th century and you wish to make your mine a safe place to work. What will you do?

CHAPTER 23

Iron and Steel

In the early nineteenth century, Great Britain was producing a quarter of a million tonnes of pig iron a year; a hundred years later the figure was nearly ten million tonnes. This growth was due to improved techniques which were developed to meet increasing demand.

Iron. The Darbys, Henry Cort and other pioneers had solved the main problems in the manufacture of iron, well before 1800, but none the less there were important changes in the nineteenth century.

In the first place, blast furnaces grew in size. They had been as small as six metres high, with tiny hearths less than half a metre square. By 1900 there were monsters, thirty metres high, with hearths ten metres square, and capable of producing 2500 tonnes of iron a day.

They were much more efficient, too. The most important discovery was the value of having a hot air blast, which was invented by James Neilson in 1828. He showed that unheated air blasted into the furnace not only made the fire burn well as was wanted, but also had the unfortunate effect of cooling it. By heating the air to no more than 150°C he made a tonne of iron with just over five tonnes of coke, instead of eight. With higher temperatures came still greater economies.

In 1832 John Gibbons found that by having the furnace circular instead of square, output went up by a third.

In 1845 George Barry invented the bell and hopper to charge the furnace when the top was closed. Furnace gas no longer burnt to waste, but could be collected to heat the blast and to make steam.

All these ideas saved fuel and then, in the early twentieth century, British industry began to adopt American ideas for saving manpower. These included mechanical devices for feeding the furnace and for taking away the pig iron.

Blast furnaces, Middlesbrough. c. 1881

Steel. In its simplest form, steel is an alloy of iron and carbon. Pig iron also contains carbon, but 4% carbon is a large amount and makes it brittle. In steel, the carbon content varies from 0.25% to 1.4%. It will be remembered that wrought iron also has a low carbon content. However, with wrought iron not all the impurities are removed and remain in it in the form of fine threads. The impurities are known as "slag" and it is the slag in the wrought iron which makes it different from the milder forms of steel.

The problem, then, is to have the correct amount of carbon and to remove all the slag.

In the early eighteenth century they used a process called "cementation". They took bars of nearly pure iron, packed them between layers of carbon and heated them for a long time. The product was known as 145 "blister steel", because the bars came out blistered. They had absorbed carbon but, of course, there was more of it on the outside so they were hard there, but soft in the middle. Then, in about 1750, Benjamin Huntsman invented a furnace that would melt blister steel. This gave a good "mix" and Huntsman's steel was uniform all the way through. In its day it was called "crucible steel" because Huntsman melted it in small clay crucibles. We would call it "carbon steel" because it contained a high proportion of carbon. It was of excellent quality, but as the process was slow, it was expensive. Huntsman wanted it for clock springs, and it found other uses in the cutting edges of tools, but it could not be made in quantity. Until well after 1850, wrought iron was supreme.

The break-through began in 1856 when Henry Bessemer invented his "converter". It was the time of the Crimean War and he wanted to speed up the production of wrought iron and carbon steel. He put molten pig iron into a container and then blew air through it from holes in the bottom. There was an alarming reaction like a display of fireworks as the oxygen in the air burnt out the carbon in the iron. When it subsided, Bessemer found he had neither wrought iron nor carbon steel, but an entirely new product we know as mild steel. It contains about 0.25% carbon, which is about the same as wrought iron. However, as we have seen, wrought iron also contains minute quantities of slag and in Bessemer's converter most of this had been removed along with the carbon.

Several firms were eager to try the new process, but at once they ran into difficulty. By sheer good luck, Bessemer had experimented with an iron containing no phosphorus, but it is present in most British ores and it makes steel brittle and virtually useless. Manufacturers found they could only use the Bessemer process with non-phosphoric ores, most of which had to be imported.

The next step forward came in 1866 when William Siemens developed the open hearth furnace. His idea was to remove carbon from pig iron with the help of materials like limestone and fluorspar. In the furnace they form a slag which combines with the carbon. To melt the iron, Siemens used hot gases, played on to it from above. His process was a good deal slower than Bessemer's, taking up to fifteen hours, as opposed to thirty minutes. However, it is much easier to control. The steel maker can tap the furnace when the carbon content is just right. Another feature of Siemens' furnace was that it wasted little heat. However, it did have the same disadvantage as the Bessemer Converter. It could not use phosphoric ores.

The answer to this problem came from a young police court clerk called Sidney Gilchrist Thomas. He heard there was a fortune waiting 146 for anyone who could make steel from phosphoric ores, and he determined to try. He found that the phosphoric acid in the molten iron could be neutralised by lining the furnace with a basic material, like dolomite. Thomas had a cousin called P. C. Gilchrist to help him. He was a chemist employed by Blenaevon iron works. In 1878 they launched what we know as the Gilchrist-Thomas process. The vast supplies of phosphoric ores in Britain were now available for steel making. Unfortunately British steel makers were by then equipped for the "acid" process and went on using expensive, imported ores for some time to come. Other countries were not so slow.

Results. Steel output grew because of demand from other industries, and in its turn it helped them to develop.

Engineering prospered, as steel was used in machinery of all kinds. It replaced wrought iron which was not as strong and did not wear as well.

Railways now had steel rails and it was possible to build massive structures like the Forth Bridge. Locomotives and rolling stock were also made of steel. For shipping, steel was probably even more important. If they were to be strong, iron hulls had to be heavy. Steel hulls, however, could be much lighter without a loss of strength. This meant they could carry extra cargo thus becoming much more profitable to run.

In building there had already been experiments with iron frames, but with steel, much larger structures were possible. The most spectacular were the New York skyscrapers.

Later, there was the motor car industry, which could never have developed without steel.

A less likely result was some help for farmers, and not only in the matter of machinery and equipment. The slag that comes from a Bessemer converter is rich in phosphorus, which is an essential plant food. "Basic slag" proved to be a valuable fertiliser.

Other results were less fortunate. It was unlucky for Britain that her chief rivals in the late nineteenth century, the U.S.A. and Germany, also had large supplies of phosphoric ores. Their industries now leapt ahead of our own. Of all the great steel producing countries, Britain was the slowest to go over to the basic process.

However, what was unfortunate for everyone was the stimulus given to the armaments industry. Having vast supplies of steel at their disposal, the major producing countries could not resist building up their armed forces. They were able to wage war on a much more dreadful scale than ever before.

Questions

1. These blast furnaces were at Barrow-in-Furness. Find it on a map.
2. How many furnaces are there in the picture?
3. How much iron might they produce in a day?
4. What form of transport was essential for a works like this?
5. What three raw materials would be brought to the works?
6. What type of iron does a blast furnace make? What else comes out of one?
7. Locate the girder-like structure that took raw materials to the tops of the furnaces. Where was this device invented? What advantage did it have?
8. What other improvements were made to the blast furnace in the nineteenth century?

HOW BESSEMER CAST HIS FIRST INGOT, 1856

I well remember how anxiously I awaited the blowing of the first charge of pig iron. The furnace-man said, "Where be going to put the metal, maister?" I said, "I want you to run it into that little furnace, and then I shall blow cold air through it to make it hot." The man said in surprise and pity, "It will soon be all of a lump." The first element attacked by the atmospheric oxygen is the silicon. Its burning gives a great deal of heat, but only a few sparks indicate that something is going on. But after ten minutes, when the carbon is seized on by the oxygen, a large white flame rushes out of the openings and brilliantly illuminates the whole space around. On the cessation of the flame the furnace was tapped and out rushed a liquid stream of iron, almost too brilliant for the eye to rest upon. After ten minutes the ingot was removed. It is impossible for me to give any adequate idea of what my feelings were when I saw it rise slowly from the mould. In one compact mass we had as much metal as could be produced by two puddlers and two assistants, working arduously for hours and burning much fuel. We had obtained a pure 10in. ingot as the result of 30 minutes blowing, unaccompanied by skilled labour or fuel, while the puddlers would have made a dozen impure, shapeless puddle-balls, saturated with impurities. No wonder, then, that I gazed with delight on the first-born of the many thousands of ingots that now come into existence every day.

Questions

1. What was Bessemer hoping to make?
2. What, in fact, did he produce?
3. What material was he using?
4. What impurities did it contain?
5. How did he surprise the furnace-man?
6. What happened during the "blow"?

7. Why was no fuel needed?
8. In what three ways was Bessemer's process better than puddling?

STEEL AND WROUGHT IRON IN THE CLEVELAND DISTRICT

Manufacturing wrought iron is much decayed. The explanation is that steel has come into favour by leaps and bounds. In 1873 the make of iron rails in the north-east was 324 000 tons; in 1879 it had sunk to 6769—truly a terrible displacement. The make of iron plates for shipbuilding was 440 000 tons in 1883, and has hence fallen to the humble figure of 53 000 in 1895. There were in 1871 more than 1860 puddling furnaces; at the present time there are not more than 300, and the outlay represented by each one is £1000. Further the rolling mills in the old iron works were not strong enough for steel ingots from the Bessemer converter or the Siemens-Martin furnace. Only wealthy manufacturers could grapple with the situation and more than 40 firms succumbed, causing much distress among workmen who lost their employment. In great establishments where there was capital enough to substitute Siemens-Martin plant for the puddling furnaces the process was gradual. Although it was necessary to import new foremen with experience of open-hearth work, some of the puddlers, after being trained as second and third hands at the first of the new furnaces, proved able to take the leading places as more of the Siemens-Martin plant was introduced, and many of the rest were absorbed in other departments as output increased. But the great changes involved many occasions for disputes between employers and workmen. (Talbot Baines—The Industrial North.)

Questions

1. Find the Cleveland district on a map.
2. What were the new ways of making steel?
3. What happened to the production of wrought iron goods and the equipment that made them?
4. Which firms survived and which failed? Why?
5. What problems did the technical changes bring? Comment on investment, employment, industrial retraining and labour relations.

Questions—Chapter Twenty-Three

1. How did pig iron production increase in the 19th century?
2. Name three men who improved the blast furnace and describe how they did so.
3. Give other ways in which the blast furnace was improved.
4. Explain the differences between steel, cast iron and wrought iron.
5. How was "blister steel" made?
6. Who discovered an improved method of making steel in the 18th century?
7. Describe it. What disadvantages did it have?
8. Who first found a quick method?
9. Describe how it worked.
10. What problem did steel makers find with it?
11. Who found another method of making steel?
12. Describe how it worked.
13. In what way was it an improvement?
14. What was the Gilchrist-Thomas process?
15. Why was it important for Britain?
16. Why were British steel makers slow to adopt it?
17. How did steel help (a) engineering (b) transport (c) building (d) farming?
18. What modern industry was able to develop?
19. Which of Britain's rivals benefitted from the new steel making processes? Why?
20. Which less desirable industry was encouraged?

Further Work

1. Find out more about the Cleveland iron industry.
2. Read about "black band" iron ore in Scotland.
3. What processes are used to make steel today? Where are the most important steel works and the most important deposits of iron ore?

149

4. How do the steel industry's problems today compare with those of the late 19th century?

5. It is 1900. A steel worker, a coal miner and a railway man meet. Each thinks his own industry is the most important. Write what they say.

6. You are the ghost of Henry Bessemer. Say what you think of your invention after over 100 years.

CHAPTER 24

Engineering

Engineering is a varied industry whose products range from structures like the Forth Bridge to the nuts and bolts in a bicycle. Here we will use it in a rather narrow sense to mean making machines and machine tools. The latter are machines that make machines, a lathe being a common example. On it a craftsman could turn many of the parts needed for, say, a power loom or a steam engine.

We have already seen how the coal and steel industries grew but they were only useful because much of the steel was made into reliable, accurate machines.

First, we must discover what engineering was like in its early days; next we must look at the work of three inventors, Joseph Bramah, Henry Maudslay and Joseph Whitworth; finally we must see how the engineering industry grew as a result of their work, and of men like them.

Machine Making in the Eighteenth and Early Nineteenth Centuries.
About the year 1800 industrial machines, as we know them, were rare. There were horse gins, water mills and windmills, but most of their working parts were of wood, with as little iron as possible. Making them or repairing them was the work of wheelwrights and blacksmiths, and not of engineers.

It is true that cotton factories had, for example, mules and carding engines, that some iron works had rolling mills and that there was a certain number of steam engines. All these were machines, and had to be made by engineers using machine tools, but two things must be said about them.

In the first place there was little enough precision in their manufacture. As late as 1833 Joseph Whitworth caused a sensation when he used a rule marked in 32nds of an inch. No-one else tried to be as accurate. 151

The second thing was, that there were no standard parts. Every machine was made separately, and so were all its pieces. Of course, it took a long time, the finished job was expensive and then, if something broke, it would be no use to send to the manufacturer for a spare part from stock. Even nuts and bolts were made individually, each bolt with its own nut. Two bolts of the same size might be side by side in a machine, but it would be no use trying to change their nuts because they would not fit. As the demand for machines grew, there had to be changes.

Three Inventors. Joseph Bramah (1749-1814), Henry Maudslay (1771-1831), Joseph Whitworth (1803-1887). Bramah began work as an apprentice joiner. He came to London in 1770 and as part of his job was installing W.C.'s, he invented an improved model. It was a success and the money he made from it allowed him to go on and invent other things. They included a woodplaning machine, a machine for dating and numbering banknotes, and a hydraulic press. However, what was perhaps most important for future developments was his patent lock. It was so ingenious that it was almost impossible to pick, but was no good unless the parts were accurate. This was difficult to achieve with the equipment they had then, so Bramah, with his assistant Henry Maudslay, improved the lathe and other machine tools. They could then be used, of course, to make many things besides locks.

Henry Maudslay was trained as a blacksmith, and was such a good craftsman that Joseph Bramah was glad to employ him. Unfortunately for Bramah he did not value Maudslay enough to give him a rise so in 1797 he set up his own business near Oxford Street.

Maudslay's chance came when Marc Isambard Brunel brought him a set of drawings from which to make blocks by machine. It was during the Napoleonic wars and the Admiralty needed thousands of blocks for ships' rigging. Making them by hand was too slow and they asked Brunel to design machines for the work. Brunel could produce the designs, but he had to turn to Maudslay to produce the machines, which he did with great success. They can still be seen today in the Science Museum. Set up in their correct sequence in Portsmouth dockyard, they were one of the first production lines, a form of organisation that was to change industry completely.

Maudslay also invented a micrometer that he called his "Lord Chancellor", because of the true verdicts that it gave! Moreover he suggested, and tried to introduce, standard threads for nuts and bolts.

Joseph Whitworth began his working life in his uncle's spinning mill, where he was a mechanic. Later he worked for Maudslay and then, in 1833, he started his own business as a tool maker. His work can be summarised under the headings of organisation, accuracy and stan-

152

dardisation. None of these ideas was new, but Whitworth carried them further than anyone else had done.

Whitworth's organisation is shown by the way he laid out his factory at Chorlton Street in London. The machines followed each other in a logical order; there was a travelling crane to move heavy jobs from stage to stage; there were lifts to carry men and materials from floor to floor.

Whitworth was much more accurate than anyone before him. By 1865 he was working to one ten thousandth of an inch and could measure to one millionth.

Perhaps Whitworth's most important contribution, though, was in standardising parts and in particular, screw threads. Thanks to him there was an end to the chaos of each manufacturer making his own style of nuts and bolts, and from the 1880's any nut would fit any bolt, provided, of course, it was of the same diameter.

By the 1870's engineering was an efficient industry. A single example will give an idea of how much progress it had made. In 1840 it took a man one day to produce 10 000 bolts. This might seem a lot, but in 1875 a girl could make 120 000 in the same time.

An engineering workshop at Woolwich Arsenal. c. 1860

Engineering 1870-1914. Now that machines could be made in large numbers, more and more industries used them. In the first half of the nineteenth century cotton was the only large industry that was at all highly mechanised; by 1900 most manufacturing industries were. To give a few examples, the change came in hosiery with power driven stocking frames; in clothing with power driven sewing machines; in the boot and shoe industry, again with sewing machines and all sorts of other devices as well. In flour milling the old-fashioned grindstones powered by wind or water gave way to steel rollers, driven by steam. There were even machines to help brewers.

At the same time, British manufacturers began to sell machines abroad in increasing numbers. In 1850 they had made up 0.8% of our exports, and in 1910, 6.8%.

However, in the twentieth century progress began to slow down. Mechanisation had gone a long way, but a great deal still depended on skilled workmen. There were plenty of these in Britain so employers saw no need to replace them with even more complex machines. They also scorned trained scientists, preferring men who had learnt their trade on the "shop-floor". In Germany and the U.S.A., however, things were different. The Germans valued their scientists and learned from them, while the Americans turned a handicap into an advantage. They had few skilled craftsmen, so they invented machines to do their work. Soon both countries had left Britain behind. By 1913 the world production of machinery was:

U.S.A.	50%
Germany	21%
Great Britain	12%
Others	17%

However, engineering was not in the same uncertain position as other staple industries, like cotton and shipbuilding. In the first place there was a growing demand for bicycles and motor cars, and their factories needed machinery. Secondly, electricity was becoming an important source of power, so an entirely new branch of the industry, electrical engineering, had to develop. Engineering continued to prosper in the twentieth century because it was closely linked to growing industries.

Questions

The pictures show pit winding gear of about 1820 and pit pumping machinery of 1910.

1. *Name the machine of 1820.*

2. *From what materials is it made?*
3. *What craftsmen would have made it?*
4. *What horse power is it?*
5. *What material is used in the 1910 machinery?*

155

6. *How might it be powered? (Look at the piece of dismantled machinery in the foreground).*
7. *What craftsmen would have made it?*
8. *Why would the 1910 machinery have to be made much more accurately?*
9. *How do these machines show the progress made in engineering during the 19th century?*

AMERICAN ENGINEERING FACTORY, RHODE ISLAND

Many hundreds of kinds of milling, grinding, screw and gear cutting machines, lathes, drills, gauges, scales, rules and other tools are made of the finest workmanship. The automatic screw and gear-cutting machines are marvels of ingenuity. The number employed is about 2300 and include many skilled British mechanics, but a large part are unskilled men. Many are working automatic machines and are incapable of doing anything else; they are making things which they do not understand. The work requires neither intelligence nor skill; but the employers do not want them to know too much. The brains of the establishment are in the drawing office. Nevertheless the workmen are a superior looking set; they earn from 8s to 12s a day. The best paid British workers earn 8s a day.
(Shadwell—*Industrial Efficiency*. 1906.)

FORGE WORK IN A YORKSHIRE ENGINEERING FACTORY

Mechanical forging has much increased of late. But for a long time to come, if not always, the part played by individual workers must continue to be not only important, but very interesting. No visitor can fail to observe the promptness, alertness and accuracy required of the smith in the adjustment of his white-hot bars on the anvil, and in the delivery of blows from his hammer exactly where they are required, to produce the best effect. It is an old trade, which has never lost its romance.
(Talbot Baines—*The Industrial North*. 1896.)

Questions
1. *What is the standard of the American work?*
2. *Where do they find their skilled men?*
3. *Why can they use many unskilled workers?*
4. *Describe their work and wages.*
5. *How has forging been improved in Britain?*
6. *How is much of the work still done?*
7. *How do the men find their work?*
8. *What are the disadvantages of the British system of working?*

ENGINEERING AT DUSSELDORF

The firms here, I regret to say, send a great deal of their manufactures to England, and often to the very towns where the same things are made. I have seen heavy machine tools going to Glasgow, steel ingots and hydraulic presses to Sheffield, crank shafts for electrical machinery to Manchester, shaft linings to Kent, pumps to Middlesborough, forgings to the Tyne, and many other things. And do not suppose that these things are "cheap and nasty". That phrase is absolutely out of date in regard to German products. The work is first-rate. Nor is the export trade all "dumping" of surplus products. I found Haniel and Lueg executing more orders for England than for Germany, although they only entered the English market four years ago.
(Shadwell—*Industrial Efficiency*. 1906.)

ELECTRICAL ENGINEERING IN LANCASHIRE AND YORKSHIRE

In the construction of machinery for the use of electricity there is, both abroad and at home, an almost limitless sphere for the application of British resources. In Manchester, Newcastle and Leeds large works have devoted special departments to the construction of dynamos and motors. An extensive trade is done in these products with Russia. In Sweden an electric railway has been equipped from Manchester, and even in Germany, in spite of the fact that her engineers have paid special attention to the subject, a firm from the same city had obtained a contract

for a plant for the manufacture of chemicals by electrolysis.
(Talbot Baines—*The Industrial North.* 1896.)

Questions

1. Why does Shadwell regret German exports to England?
2. What quality are they? What reputation did they once have?
3. What proves that dumping is not happening?
4. What branch of English engineering is thriving?
5. What is remarkable about its exports to Germany?

Questions—Chapter Twenty-Four

1. What goods do engineers make?
2. What machines were there in 1800?
3. What were they made from?
4. Who made and repaired them?
5. What two industries had more up-to-date machinery?
6. Give two defects these machines had.
7. How did Joseph Bramah first make money?
8. What was the importance of his patent lock?
9. Who first employed Henry Maudslay?
10. What work did he do for Marc Isambard Brunel?
11. What was his "Lord Chancellor"?

12. *What three things were typical of Whitworth?*
13. *Describe his works at Chorlton Street, London.*
14. *How accurately did he work?*
15. *What was the most important thing he standardised?*
16. *Name some of the industries that were mechanised in the late 19th century.*
17. *What percentage of British exports was machinery, in 1910?*
18. *In what ways was British engineering old fashioned by 1914?*
19. *Explain why German and American engineering made more progress than British.*
20. *Why did British engineering remain prosperous?*

Further Work

1. *Find pictures of machinery of the 18th century and of different periods of the 19th and 20th.*
2. *Read more about Bramah, Maudslay and Whitworth.*
3. *How accurately is it possible to work on the machines in a school metalwork room?*
4. *What standard threads are in use today? How are they different?*
5. *Find out what machinery is in use in one of your local factories and, if you can, where it was made and how old it is.*
6. *It is 1900. Write a letter to a newspaper saying why you are concerned about the British engineering industry.*

CHAPTER 25

Cotton and Shipbuilding

Cotton and shipbuilding had a good deal in common. They both made rapid strides in the nineteenth century, so that by 1914 Britain produced more cotton goods and ships than any other nation. However, these industries were not in a strong position as they were letting themselves become out of date. This was doubly unfortunate because they relied heavily on exports so that foreign competition, when it came, would be bound to hit them hard.

Cotton. At the end of the Napoleonic Wars, the cotton industry was ready to make big strides. There had been a series of inventions, which meant that every process could be done by machines. Moreover, some of the leading manufacturers had already built integrated factories. In them, they not only used the new machines and steam power, but their organisation was much improved. They had finished with the inefficient domestic system and instead had all their employees working in their factories, closely under their control.

What happened in the thirty or so years after 1815 was that the use of new methods became general. Little mills using water power and doing nothing but spinning went out of business. Also, when the power loom was perfected, the handloom weavers found themselves, as one said, "in competition with fire and water". They had to work up to sixteen hours a day even to earn a bare living and, one by one, they gave up their trade. After 1850 there were hardly any left.

However, if small mills and handloom weavers suffered, the large manufacturers and their customers did well. An important result of the new methods was that labour costs fell, so prices could fall, too. They were cut by one third during the twenty years from 1830 to 1850. This did not mean that manufacturers lost money. Their profit on each individual item was less, but they more than made up for it by extra production. In 1820 they made sixty million kilogrammes of raw cotton into cloth, while in 1850 the figure was 280 million. Keeping up profits by increasing production is only possible if people will buy the extra goods. Fortunately demand was growing, because the population of Britain was increasing in numbers and in wealth, and, even more, because there were plenty of good markets abroad. By 1850 over 60% of cottons produced in this country were exported. They made up 40% of our exports and paid for all the raw cotton, and most of our imported timber, sugar and tea as well.

From 1850 the industry went on growing, but like a man who has reached middle age, its rate of progress was slower. Labour costs began to creep up, partly because it was made illegal to employ children, and the cost of raw materials increased as well. There were so few technical changes that by the early twentieth century productivity was lower in cotton than in many other industries. Moreover, the industry was making five times as much as could be sold at home, so it had to export 80% of its products. This might not have mattered if Britain had still been the only country making cottons on a large scale, but foreign competition was growing.

Continental countries now had their own factories, especially Germany. Moreover, producing countries wanted to spin and weave their own raw cotton instead of allowing the British to do so. The U.S.A. had had their own industry for some time, and now India was building her own. They found that setting up factories was not difficult, especially as they had help. The British engineering firms that supplied Lancashire and Scotland with textile machinery had no scruples about taking orders from abroad. They equipped many of the foreign firms that were later to put our own out of business.

By the early twentieth century, then, the position was the opposite of a hundred years before. Cotton was no longer the most progressive industry in the country with no competition from abroad. Instead it was relatively backward and its foreign rivals were already dangerous. None the less, this ageing, threatened industry was still vital for the economy of the country since nearly a quarter of our exports were cotton goods. It was high time to find alternatives, but cottons went on selling, so British manufacturers went on increasing production right up to the First World War.

Shipbuilding. Shipbuilding has to be done on river estuaries and close to its source of materials. In the early part of the nineteenth century the most important material was wood, so shipbuilding took place near oak forests. The Thames estuary was ideal because it was not far from the Weald. Yards were usually quite small, and often temporary. The 159 builders would find a firm piece of shore called a "hard", would work there until they had used all the timber in the area, and then move on.

During the nineteenth century the industry was transformed. It began with the use of iron in sailing ships, but the really important development was the coming of the steam ship in the second half of the century. At the same time there was growth in world trade that created a demand for ships far greater than there had been before.

In the first place ships increased in size. The *Cutty Sark*, launched in 1869, weighed less than 1000 tonnes. The *Mauretania*, launched in 1906, weighed 31 000 tonnes. Secondly, wood and iron gave place to steel. Thirdly, sails gave place to steam engines and these became bigger and more complicated as time went on. Towards the end of the century the steam turbine was replacing the piston engine.

For such changes to take place firms had to become much bigger. By the 1860's some were employing more than 1000 men, which was a great many for those days. Shipbuilders also tended to take over factories making components, and then they became larger still. In the 1860's there were combines made up of firms producing steel and armaments, as well as ships.

Obviously the industry had to change its position. The ideal places were now the Clyde and Tyne estuaries. They had the sheltered deep water channels that the larger vessels needed, while in the hinterland were the steel and heavy engineering industries that supplied the components.

160 *Shipbuilding in a British Yard—1910*

By 1914 British shipbuilding was ahead of any other power, over 60% of the world's vessels being built in Britain. It was indeed fortunate that the industry had grown so much, because during the war we needed all the ships we could build. However, the long-term outlook was not good.

In the first place, technical progress was already slowing. Britain's success depended on the skill of her craftsmen and other countries did not have men of such quality. As in engineering, though, this worked to the foreign nations' advantage. They found machines that would do the work of men, and do it better and more cheaply. The British industry was becoming out of date compared with the U.S.A. and Germany. Secondly, shipbuilding depended on world trade. A good quarter of the ships built in Britain were sold abroad, and many of those we kept for ourselves made their money by carrying goods for foreigners. The industry would be in trouble if world trade declined, and particularly if there was an economic depression.

Conclusion—Nineteenth Century Industry. During the nineteenth century Britain became a prosperous industrial nation by building up what we now call the "old staple industries". We have seen the progress of the most important, which were coal, iron and steel, engineering, cotton and shipbuilding. Their products were varied, ranging from trans-atlantic liners to cotton socks, and from raw coal to complicated machines. None the less, all these industries had much in common.

In the first place, they progressed well in the nineteenth century, some early on, like cotton, and some later, like steel. On average they gave the country as a whole an economic growth rate of perhaps 2% a year, which was quite exceptional for a hundred years ago.

Secondly, they reached a peak in the early years of the twentieth century, and between them they were responsible for well over a half of our industrial output.

Thirdly, they were all of them producing far more goods than could be used at home, cotton being the outstanding example, exporting as it did, 80% of its products. These industries prospered because they were able to export. Between them, moreover, they accounted for almost all of Britain's exports, so it was not only their own prosperity, but that of the entire country which depended on their sales abroad. It was, of course, essential that such industries should be strong and progressive. Unhappily, they were not. We have seen how, in all of them, technical changes were beginning to slow down, while other countries, notably the U.S.A. and Germany, began to pull ahead. Great Britain was like a family whose breadwinner is growing old, and who is likely to lose his job to an up and coming young competitor.

Until 1914 world trade boomed and foreign competition was only beginning to bite, so things seemed much better than they really were. 161

However, if world trade ever declined, and if foreign competition grew, there would be economic disaster for Britain. This was what happened after the First World War.

Questions

The picture shows the shipyard of John Brown & Co on the Clyde in 1910.

1. *From the size of the men, estimate the length, width and height of this ship.*
2. *What was the tonnage of the largest ships of this period?*
3. *How, probably, will this ship be powered?*
4. *What material is being used?*
5. *What older materials did it replace and what advantages does it have over them?*
6. *Which parts have been practically completed?*
7. *Which parts are now being added?*
8. *Why is the Clyde a suitable place for shipbuilding?*
9. *What other industries, connected with shipbuilding, will be found near at hand?*

SHIP BUILDING ON THE TYNE, WEAR AND TEES

Probably 4/5ths of the tonnage of new shipping is the produce of British shipyards. And of that large proportion a full half is provided by the builders of the north-east. This is not surprising. The presence of great steelworks and an excellent railway system and the proximity of the sea make it easy to bring together all the materials required. Immense sums have been spent making the rivers navigable. At one point near Newcastle there is 24ft of water where 30 years ago there was an island. In this district not fewer than 313 vessels of various kinds were built last year, from the first class battleship and ocean liner to the steam trawler. And side by side with its yards, sometimes under distinct but frequently under the same ownership, are great works devoted to marine engines and boilers suited for every variety of vessel. The combination of industries is at once vast in scale and remarkably complete. This spirit of progress has survived great fluctuations in prosperity. Times were when the shipyards were beset by eager shipowners, ready to pay any prices the builders named. But those times are not now. Last year there was a great spurt in shipbuilding caused by the "boom" in freights, but the boom died away and there seems to be no reason to expect any such revival in the rates for sea carriage as would create a large and steady demand for new ships of any kind. (Talbot Baines—*The Industrial North.* 1896.)

Questions
1. What proportion of the world's ships are built on the north-east coast?
2. What advantages has the area for shipbuilding?
3. How have the rivers been improved?
4. How many ships were built in one year?
5. What kinds were they?
6. What other industries have grown up?
7. What makes shipowners order new ships?
8. What was happening in 1896?

THE COTTON INDUSTRY IN OLDHAM, LANCASHIRE
There are in this town 12 500 000 spindles, which is nearly as many as in the whole of the New England States of America, half as many again as in the whole of Germany and twice as many as in France. With such an enormous activity the Oldham mills are largely dependent on foreign markets. They have for many years been feeding the growing cotton weaving industries of other countries and their "cops" went everywhere. Germany and France were among their best customers, but these markets have fallen off. All the indications point to growing competition. They have good reason to watch with concern the rapid increase of mills in the Southern United States.

The other great industry of the town—the manufacture of textile machinery—is even more flourishing. The machinery of Platt and Co. goes all over the world, to America, China, India, Japan and the continent of Europe. These works can turn out 30 000 mule spindles a week, 12 000 ring spindles, 250 looms and the other machinery to match. Some deplore the export trade of textile machinery from England, which gives other countries the means of competing with home manufactures, but that is a narrow view. Any restriction of export is unthinkable. The only effect would be to stimulate the manufacture of machinery in other countries, which are already coming up fast. (Shadwell—*Industrial Efficiency.* 1906.)

Questions
1. In which branch of the textile industry does Oldham specialise?
2. Draw a diagram to compare the size of Oldham's industry with those of foreign countries.
3. Why does Oldham depend on exports?
4. What markets are being lost?
5. What is the latest competitor?
6. What machinery does Oldham export? Where?
7. Why has this trade been criticised?
8. What is Shadwell's opinion on preventing it?

Questions—Chapter Twenty-Five
1. Why was the cotton industry in a strong position in 1815?
2. What kind of mill went out of business?
3. What happened to the handloom weavers? Why?
4. Which mills prospered?
5. What happened to labour costs down to 1850?
6. How did manufacturers cope with falling prices?
7. What proportion of exports were cotton by 1850?
8. Why did costs increase after 1850?
9. Why did productivity fall?
10. Which countries built up their own industries?

11. Why did they find it easy to do so?
12. What was the position of the cotton industry in the early 20th century?
13. Why was this unfortunate for the whole economy?
14. Where must ships be built?
15. How was the shipbuilding industry organised in the early 19th century?
16. How did ships change—size, materials, engines?
17. How did firms change?
18. Name two new shipbuilding areas and give their advantages.
19. What proportion of the world's ships were built in Britain in 1914?
20. Give two reasons why the industry had an uncertain future.

Further Work
1. Read about the decline of the handloom weavers.
2. Find out about "ring spinning".
3. What is the condition of the British cotton industry today?
4. From Geography books copy maps of the Clyde and Tynes areas, showing the shipyards, the related industries and coal and iron deposits.
5. You are a cotton manufacturer in 1900. Say how prosperous your industry is, but explain why you are worried about the future.
6. Suppose a shipbuilder of 1800 could have visited a shipyard in 1900. What differences would he have seen?

SECTION EIGHT
Social Changes 1815-1900

CHAPTER 26

Care of the Poor

In 1834 the Old Poor Law was reformed, though more with a view to efficiency and economy, than to helping people in need. However, the new Poor Law was, in its own way, as big a failure as the old, a fact that was at last recognised towards the end of the century.

The Poor Law Commission of 1834. After the Reform Act of 1832 there was a strong Whig government that felt able to tackle the problem of poor relief. They appointed a Royal Commission to investigate it.

A member of the Commission was a man called Edwin Chadwick. He was keen on social reform and was, moreover, able and hard-working. He busied himself so much that the Report issued by the Commission was virtually all his work.

Chadwick was appalled at all the inefficiency and waste of the old system, but what disturbed him most was that there were men who, though quite able to work, chose instead to live in idleness and draw relief from the parish. This was true, but in fact most people "on the parish" were either elderly, or were orphan children. Only a small proportion were able-bodied adults, and many of these were in need of help because they could not find work. Those malingering were few, yet the problem of dealing with them was the one that Chadwick, and indeed everyone else, thought the most important.

There were parishes where the idlers had been cured. Chadwick was impressed by Southwell in Nottinghamshire, which had been "depauperised" by a man called George Nicholls. What he had done was to refuse to give "outdoor relief", which was money the paupers could take away and spend as they pleased. All relief had to be "indoor", which meant living in the workhouse. Here the paupers were fed and 166 clothed but apart from that, everything was done to make life disagreeable. Men were separated from women; there was no drinking or smoking; discipline was strict; food was plain and dull. There was also plenty of hard work, like smashing bones with sledge hammers.

The aim was to make life in the workhouse less pleasant than the meanest existence outside it. Having done this, they could apply what they called the "workhouse test". A man asking for relief was offered a place in the workhouse; if he chose to take it, it was clear proof that he was in dire need.

Chadwick thought the Southwell system would be the answer for the entire country and the Report of the Poor Law Commission recommended an administrative system that would make it possible.

The Poor Law Amendment Act 1834. This Act followed the main ideas of the Poor Law Commission.

As most parishes were too poor to build workhouses they were ordered to join together, and form what were known as Poor Law Unions. In each Union the ratepayers were to elect a Board of Guardians and they in turn had to appoint salaried officials such as a workhouse master, relieving officer and a medical officer.

Supervising the Guardians there was to be a central organisation called the Poor Law Board. It was to consist of three men, helped by a Secretary with a staff of civil servants.

In 1834, then, they had seen one problem—the able-bodied pauper who refused to work for his living. They had also seen one simple solution—offer such a man life in a well-regulated workhouse, or nothing. To carry out these ideas there were to be more powerful local authorities, the Boards of Guardians, and, in case they should neglect their duties, there was a Government department, the Poor Law Board, to keep them in order. We must now see how much success they had.

The Working of the Poor Law. In one unfortunate way the new system worked very well. It stopped the poor from living on the rates. Working class people looked on the Poor Law authorities with a mixture of fear, hatred and contempt, so that rather than turn to them they would live on credit and charity, steal, or even starve. Here, however, the success of the new system ended.

In the first place the administration of the poor law was inefficient. The Poor Law Board did not start well, partly because the one man with the energy and ability to make it work, Edwin Chadwick, was pushed into the subordinate post of Secretary, and none of his superiors would listen to him. The main problem, though, was that they found it impossible to bend the Guardians to their will, and this difficulty was never solved. Even after the Ministry of Health took over in 1919, the Guardians went on much as they pleased.   167

The Guardians had their difficulties, too, the main one being finance. Although the parishes in a Union put their money into a common fund, they paid, not in proportion to their wealth, but according to the number of paupers they had. A rich parish with no paupers would pay nothing to the Union; a poor parish with many, would pay a great deal. An Act of Parliament of 1865 put this right, but there were still big differences between Unions.

Secondly, and mainly because of the poor administration, few workhouses were as the reformers of 1834 would have wished. Some, like one in Manchester, were fine buildings, well-kept, clean, comfortable and well-organised. The worst was perhaps Andover, where the paupers fought over the scraps of meat that clung to the bones they had to smash. Most of them came between the two, the problem being not so much that they were foul buildings, run by inhuman people, but that they were too small and poor to do their job properly. They were "general mixed workhouses" in which paupers of all kinds lived together. This meant that the authorities could not give the special, separate treatment required by children, lunatics, the elderly, the chronic sick and idle vagabonds.

Thirdly the "workhouse test" for the able bodied was no use. It would deal with a handful of malingerers in a country village, which was all they had in mind in 1834, but the problem was to be mass unemployment in the industrial towns. The vast majority who were out of work were not lazy, but were just unable to find jobs, so there was no point in condemning them to the workhouse. The Poor Law guardians in the cities understood quite well, and when there was a trade depression in the early 1840's they insisted on giving out-door relief. Indeed, it was clear until the end, that the Poor Law could do next to nothing about unemployment.

Finally, there was the most serious failure of all. The Poor Law left the problem of poverty almost untouched. During the nineteenth century the total wealth of the country grew considerably, but in the 1890's one third of the people in the large cities still did not have the money to buy enough food and clothing to keep themselves in good health. Faced with a problem of this size, the Poor Laws were useless.

New Attitudes. Towards the end of the nineteenth century, many people began to think differently about the poor.

Even the authorities became less stony-hearted and many Guardians made special arrangements. The elderly, the chronic sick and the insane had their own special buildings, while children went into cottage homes. They lived there, much as they would have done in ordinary families, and went to ordinary schools.

168   Next, there were serious attempts to find the causes and extent of

poverty. Two surveys were particularly important. One was by a shipowner, Charles Booth, who investigated London, and the other was by a chocolate manufacturer, Benjamin Rowntree, who did his work in York. In both cities they found thirty per cent of the population below the "poverty line" as they called it, and they analysed the reasons as low wages, death of one or both parents, illness and unemployment. Idleness had almost nothing to do with it, though perhaps stupidity did. One curious fact that emerged was that the poorest families added to their difficulties by having large families. This meant that the majority living below the poverty line were children. They were the victims of their parents and of an economic system which gave great wealth to a few, while leaving millions on the verge of starvation.

A poor family sleeping out

At last the government decided it should act and appointed a Royal Commission to look into the Poor Laws. It reported in 1905, suggesting important changes, but it was completely ignored. The government did do a good many other things, but the Poor Law itself was left almost unaltered until abolished in 1948.

CBBSEH—M

Questions
1. Why are there no men or older children in the picture?
2. What do you notice about the women's clothing?
3. What conclusions do you draw about their food?
4. What different things do the women seem to be thinking and doing?
5. On the tall building is the word "Union". Why is it there?
6. What idea do you have of the order and discipline in this workhouse?
7. What general impression is the artist trying to give of life in the workhouse?

EXTRACT FROM POOR LAW COMMISSIONERS' REPORT 1834
A universal principle is that the pauper's situation shall not be so eligible as that of a labourer of the lowest class. It is shown that in proportion as the condition of any of the pauper class is elevated above the condition of the independent labourers, the condition of the independent class is depressed. Such persons, therefore, are under the strongest inducements to quit the less eligible class of labourers and enter the more eligible class of paupers. Every penny bestowed, that tends to render the condition of the pauper more eligible than that of the independent labourer is a bounty on indolence and vice. As the poor rates are at present administered, they act as bounties of this kind to the amount of several millions of pounds annually.

Questions
1. What is meant by "eligible"?
2. What tends to make a labourer become a pauper?
3. How have the poor rates been spent unwisely?

STATEMENT BY THE KEEPER OF SOUTHWELL WORKHOUSE
The orders were: 1. To separate males and females. 2. To prevent any visitors, and to make them keep regular hours. 3. To prevent smoking. 4. To disallow beer. 5. To find them work. 6. To treat and feed them well.
To the violent young paupers who came in, swearing they would beat the parish, I gave bones to break in the yard—had a hammer made on purpose.
(*Poor Law Commissioners Report. 1834.*)

Questions
1. Why was life unpleasant in Southwell Workhouse?
2. Was there any deliberate cruelty?
3. How were unruly paupers controlled?
4. Who, probably, made up the workhouse rules?
5. What problem had they solved at Southwell?
6. Who admired this system? What did he recommend?

A PAUPER IN ANDOVER WORKHOUSE
I was employed at bone-breaking. We looked out for the fresh bones and then we used to be like a parcel of dogs after them. The marrow was as good as the meat; it was all covered over by bone and no filth could get to it. Sometimes I have had one that was stale and stunk, and I ate it even

then, because I was hungered, I suppose. A pint and a half of gruel is not much for a man's breakfast. The food we got in the workhouse was very good, all I wanted was a little more.

I have seen a man named Reeves eat horse flesh off the bones. I told him it was horse flesh, but he did not care. It went down as sweet as a nut.

(*Report of Select Committee on Andover Union. 1846.*)

Questions
1. What were the Andover authorities doing to make life unpleasant for their paupers? Why?
2. What did the men eat? Why?
3. What was wrong with the food they were given?
4. What is gruel?

EXTRACTS FROM BAXTER'S "BOOK OF THE BASTILLES".
A little boy having been separated from his mother in Nottingham Union raged in all the agony of despair and tore off his own hair by the handful.

At Iddesham a little girl was heard crying in violent grief, "Let me out, let me out; I want to see my daddy; I must go to my daddy".

At Bourne a poor man applied to the Guardians for relief. They offered him a place in a workhouse, but he refused. A week later he was found dead in a field, having chosen death by starvation rather than enter a workhouse under the present system.

Questions
1. Which of the workhouse rules caused the boy and the girl such distress?
2. What relief did the man at Bourne hope to have?
3. Why was he offered the workhouse?
4. How did "less eligibility" work in his case?

Questions—Chapter Twenty-Six
1. When was the Poor Law Commission appointed? Why?
2. Why did Chadwick have so much to do with it?

3. What seemed to him the most serious fault with the old poor law? How far was he right?
4. Who had reformed Southwell Workhouse? How?
5. What Act was passed in 1834?
6. What were Poor Law Unions?
7. Who was elected to run them? Whom did they appoint?
8. Who made up the Poor Law Board? What were their duties?
9. What success did the new system have? How did the poor feel?
10. What was the Poor Law Board's main problem?
11. Why did some Unions have money problems?
12. Name a badly kept workhouse. What happened there?
13. What were most workhouses like?
14. Why was the "workhouse test" ineffective in towns? What happened in the early 1840's?
15. What major problem did the Poor Law not solve?
16. How did the care of some paupers improve?
17. What two men examined the problem of poverty?
18. What did they discover?
19. What happened in 1905?
20. When was the poor law finally abolished?

Further Work
1. Find out more about Chadwick's career at the Poor Law Board.
2. What did George Nicolls become after 1834?
3. Who was Thomas Frankland Lewis?
4. Was there a workhouse in your area? Where was it? It may still be in use e.g. as a hospital.
5. Your father has lost his job and your family will have to go to the workhouse. Describe your feelings.
6. Write two articles, one imagining it is 1834 and the other that it is 1850. In the first say why you like the new Poor Law, and in the second why you have doubts about it.

CHAPTER 27

Public Health

During the industrial revolution the towns grew quickly and some places which had been little more than villages became large cities. All this happened without any proper controls so that public health was a serious problem.

We must first of all look at this problem, and then at the measures taken to solve it.

The Problem of Public Health. Perhaps the most serious lack was pure water. The traditional sources were wells and rivers, with more fortunate places having leats or conduits. Leats were artificial streams, for example the New River which brought water to London from Hertfordshire, over sixty kilometres away. A conduit was a large pipe running from a spring. The water poured out at a conduit head in the town where people could come and fill buckets. Then, in the eighteenth century, numbers of water companies were set up. They pumped water along wooden mains and piped it into private houses for the rich, and to stand pipes in the streets for the poor. Some companies were efficient, like the Trent Water Company that supplied Nottingham, but the London ones were more typical. Most of them took their water from the Thames, which also acted as the main sewer for the town. Moreover they only supplied water for a few hours a day at the most.

Coupled with inadequate water supplies was bad sanitation. Where there were sewers, they were brick tunnels, large enough for a man to go along, but in spite of their size they often blocked. They discharged their contents, untreated, into the nearest river. Most houses though, particularly the poor ones, had no sewers and made do with cess pits. A cess pit was simply a brick-lined pit with a lavatory seat over it. When full, it was supposed to be emptied and its contents carted away.

172

Twenty families might have to share one of these places.

Houses were poor. The new ones, built as the industrial towns grew, were made for cheapness. A typical one consisted of a cellar, a living room and a bedroom above that. They were not only side by side, but also back to back. Another type was the tenement, which was usually a big, old house that had fallen into decay.

Most working class homes were overcrowded. A family with a house would not only sub-let the cellar, but might even have lodgers along with them in the remaining two rooms. In the tenements there was usually at least one family to every room.

The shortage of water and sanitation, the bad houses and the overcrowding meant that poor people were dirty and disease was rife.

Interior of a working man's home

The Public Health Movement. Not surprisingly, the first people to take alarm at the state of the towns were doctors. There were the medical officers of the new Poor Law Unions set up in 1834, who saw a great deal of the working classes, but there were prominent medical men as well, like Doctors Arnott, Kay and Southwood-Smith. However, the most active and determined reformer of all was Edwin Chadwick. As Secretary of the Poor Law Board it was easy for him to collect 173 information about public health, and in 1842 he published his findings in his "Report on the Sanitary Condition of the Labouring Population of Great Britain". The conditions it described were so bad that Parliament appointed a Royal Commission on the "State of the Large Towns and Populous Districts". When it reported in 1844 it endorsed everything Chadwick had said.

In spite of pressure from an organisation called the Health of Towns Association, which was under Lord Shaftesbury's leadership, Parliament did nothing until 1848 when it was obvious there was a cholera epidemic on the way. They then moved quickly enough and passed a Public Health Act.

The Act made it possible for any town to have its own Local Board of Health. This was compulsory if the death rate was above 23 per 1000, but otherwise it was voluntary. The task of a Local Board was to see that its town had proper water supplies and sewerage. To pay its expenses it had to levy a rate, which explains why many places did not like the idea of having such a Board.

To supervise the Local Boards there was a General Board of Health that met in London. It was made up of three Commissioners and the men appointed were Lord Morpeth, who had sponsored the Public Health Act, Lord Shaftesbury and Edwin Chadwick. Dr. Southwood-Smith was Chief Medical Inspector to the Board.

Their first task was to fight the cholera epidemic of 1848 and here they had little success because no-one understood the disease. However, the cholera was of some help to the Board, because its very presence discredited the opponents of the public health movement, or the "dirty party" as they were called.

Following the epidemic, the Board settled down to its more routine task of encouraging towns to adopt the Public Health Act and provide themselves with proper water supplies and sanitation. Chadwick was anxious to show that this could be done cheaply, calculating that a house could have piped water, sewers, and a water closet for as little as 1½p a week. As he said, this was a fraction of what the average working class family spent on beer and tobacco. One important economy the Board urged was the use of small tubular sewers in place of large brick tunnels. They were much cheaper, but had to be laid properly and would only work if there was plenty of water to flush them.

By 1854, 284 towns had asked for Local Boards of Health and in many places the new systems for water supplies and sewage were almost finished. Sometimes there were dramatic results, the death rate falling considerably.

Unfortunately there were dramatic failures as well. In the first place London remained outside the scope of the Act. Chadwick busily produced schemes for its water supplies, its sewage and its graveyards, but they came to nothing because the opposition was too great. Secondly in places where his plans were carried out, they sometimes failed. Where the Local Boards did not supply enough water, tubular sewers often blocked, but the worst disaster was in Croydon. Here a typhoid epidemic broke out in the houses that had been connected to the new sewers. The contractors had laid them badly, alongside a water main, so that sewage had seeped into the drinking water. Their faulty workmanship brought the whole system into disrepute.

The Board also made itself powerful enemies. It threatened such bodies as Commissioners of Sewers and private water companies, while its attempts to interfere with London caused a good deal of anger. In 1854 the Board's term of office was over and although it could have been renewed, its enemies in Parliament voted that it should only continue with new members and less power. Chadwick, whom they considered the arch-villain, was driven into retirement at the early age of 54.

The Public Health Movement in the Late Nineteenth Century. After 1854 the public health movement went forward more slowly for a time. Then, in 1869, another Royal Commission reported on the state of the towns, as a result of which the Local Government Board was set up with responsibility for public health.

There was important legislation when Disraeli was Prime Minister. In 1875 the Artisans' Dwellings Act allowed local authorities, if they so wished, to clear slums and build decent houses.

Also in 1875 there was another Public Health Act. It consolidated a lot of earlier laws and gave them more force. Each local authority was to have a Medical Officer of Health and an Inspector of Nuisances. It had also to provide efficient sewage works and proper water supplies. These were much the same measures that had been passed in 1848, but now they were compulsory for the whole country. There were permissive clauses, too, allowing rates to be spent on such things as parks, hospitals and public lavatories.

Numbers of local authorities were active. Leeds did away with many of its back-to-back houses. Liverpool emptied its insanitary cellar dwellings of their inhabitants. In Birmingham, Joseph Chamberlain started an important scheme that involved clearing acres of slums and building Corporation Street. In London the Metropolitan Board of Works pulled down slums, opened the Embankment and gave the city a comprehensive system of main drainage.

At last all these measures started to have results. The death rate which had been stationary since 1815 began to fall again in the last quarter of the century.

house drains, and the construction of a dust bin, has been a penny a week, being a total average cost of one halfpenny a day. We have endeavoured to complete a new system of sewerage, substituting for brick sewers in every street large enough for men to go up, a system of sewers graduated in size, impermeable and therefore preventing the escape of sewer fluid, self cleansing, instead of accumulating deposit. With a new system of sewerage we have endeavoured to combine improved water supplies. In general the water is led into a reservoir at the head of the main so as to adjust the 24 hours flow to the 12 hours delivery, which is constant and direct, the water never being stagnant, but fresh, cool and fit for immediate drinking. We have attempted to connect the system with the application of sewer manure to agriculture. We look forward to important results from this new use of refuse which will afford an increased stimulus to town drainage, and exercise an important influence on the agriculture of the country.

Questions
1. *Estimate the width of the street and its height.*
2. *Estimate how many hours in the day the sun would shine in this street.*
3. *How is the street paved? How would this affect cleaning it?*
4. *What is the condition of the houses?*
5. *What traffic is there? Does much come this way?*
6. *What animals are there?*
7. *What are the people doing?*
8. *What would be the use of the tubs on the left?*
9. *What sounds and smells would come from this street?*
10. *What dangers to health can you see here?*

Questions
1. *What improvements to houses has the Board encouraged?*
2. *What is their total cost likely to be?*
3. *Why is the Board anxious to show it was cheap?*
4. *How were sewers once built?*
5. *In what two ways are the new ones better?*
6. *How do the new water works ensure a regular supply of water to the houses?*
7. *In what condition is the water?*
8. *What use can the Board see for sewerage?*
9. *Was this idea ever adopted generally?*

REPORT OF THE GENERAL BOARD OF HEALTH 1854
The cost for water supply is an average of a penny halfpenny a house per week, and for main drainage a penny per house per week. The average expense for introducing a service pipe, putting down a sink, filling up the cesspool, and substituting a W.C. and self cleansing

EXTRACT FROM *THE TIMES* **OF AUGUST 1st 1854**
The Board of Health has fallen. Mr. Chadwick and Dr. Southwood Smith have been deposed and we prefer to take our chance of cholera than be bullied into health. Everywhere the Board's inspectors were arbitrary, insulting and expensive. They entered houses and factories,

insisting on changes revolting to the habits or pride of the masters and occupants. There is nothing a man so much hates as being cleaned against his will, or having his floors swept, his walls whitewashed, his pet dungheaps cleaned away, or his thatch forced to give place to slate, all at the command of a sort of sanitary bombailiff. It is a positive fact that many have died of a good washing, as much from the irritation of the nerves as from the exposure of the skin no longer protected by dirt. All this shows the extreme tenderness with which the work of purification should advance. Not so thought Mr. Chadwick. New mops wash clean, thought he, and he set to work, everywhere washing and splashing and twirling and rinsing, and sponging and sopping, and soaping and mopping, till mankind began to fear a deluge of soap and water. It was a perpetual Saturday night and Master John Bull was scrubbed and rubbed, and small-tooth-combed, till the tears came into his eyes, his teeth chattered, and his fists clenched themselves with worry and pain.

Questions
1. What event is The Times reporting?
2. Who were Chadwick and Dr. Southwood Smith?
3. What complaints are made about inspectors?
4. What reforms does the article mention?
5. Compare them with those in the Board's report. Which list seems more likely?
6. How, says the article, can washing cause death?
7. How is Chadwick said to have done his work?
8. Explain: "It was a perpetual Saturday night."
9. What is the use of a small-tooth-comb?
10. What does the article tell you about the opposition the Board of Health had to face?

Questions—Chapter Twenty-Seven
1. When and why did public health become a problem?

2. Give four traditional sources of water.
3. Describe the first water companies.
4. What was wrong with sewers? How did houses manage that had none?
5. Describe two typical houses in a large town.
6. Describe the problem of overcrowding.
7. What were the results of bad living conditions?
8. Which doctors were alarmed at the state of the towns?
9. Why was Chadwick able to find out a great deal? What book did he write?
10. What action did Parliament take in (a) 1844 (b) 1848? Give reasons for both.
11. Name the new local public health authorities and give their duties. What towns had them?
12. What government department was set up? Name its members.
13. What success did it have with its first problem?
14. What reforms were encouraged?
15. Why did Chadwick have no success in London?
16. What went wrong in Croydon?
17. Why did Chadwick retire early?
18. Name and describe two Acts passed by Disraeli.
19. Describe improvements in four large cities.
20. What proves the success of all these measures?

Further Work
1. Are there any remains of old fashioned water supplies in your area?
2. Find out when your town had its first park.
3. Find what you can of the history of your local hospital.
4. Read about the cholera epidemics in this country. How was the disease conquered?
5. Find out what you can about the following: typhoid, typhus, smallpox, tuberculosis.
6. Imagine you are Edwin Chadwick in 1854. Say why you became involved with the public health movement, describe your work and explain why you were driven to retire early.

CHAPTER 28

The Police

As the Industrial Revolution progressed, crime became more profitable, just like most other ways of making a living. People were richer, and there was much to be made by robbing and stealing. Furthermore, in the large towns that had grown up, it was easy to be anonymous and to hide away, thus criminals were better able to do their work. Constables, watchmen and the like, who had rarely been effective, were now even less so. The answer was to reform the police system, and this was done, first of all in London and then in the rest of the country.

The Origins of the New Police. Although there was a crying need for efficient police, people hesitated to have them. They knew that in Europe policemen had acted as government secret agents, arresting men for their political views as much as for crime. Furthermore, the way our own government had used spies, seemed to show that the same could happen here. So it was, that although Parliament appointed a number of committees to look into the possibility of having a police force, they all turned down the idea, mainly because they thought it would threaten the freedom of the people.

The position changed when Wellington became Prime Minister in 1828. He was anxious to check crime, and so was his Home Secretary, Sir Robert Peel. When Peel had been Chief Secretary for Ireland, he had set up a police force there, and he wanted to do the same in England. Parliament appointed yet another committee of enquiry, and this one was persuaded to report in favour of a new police force at least for part of London. Armed with the report, Peel presented his Metropolitan Police Bill to Parliament. It became law in 1829.

178

The Metropolitan Police Act of 1829. Although this Act brought into being the famous "Peelers" and was the beginning of our modern police system it was really quite a cautious measure.

In the first place it only affected a part of London, and this was the area covered by the Bow Street Foot Patrol. The New Police could not go into the City and they could not go into outer London. Secondly, their duties were limited. They were to be uniformed foot police, patrolling their beats and nothing more. The Bow Street Horse Patrol remained, and so did the Marine Police that had been established for the Thames shipping in 1800. Any detective work would be done by the Bow Street Runners, or by the officers attached to the Police Offices set up by the Middlesex Justices Act of 1792.

None the less there were changes. These amounted to dismissing all other foot police within the Metropolitan area: The Bow Street Foot Patrol was abolished, and so also were the old parochial police—constables, headboroughs and watchmen. As the magistrates had no-one left to supervise they lost their police duties, much to their annoyance.

The new force was to consist of 3000 men, under the control of two Commissioners of Police, responsible to the Home Secretary.

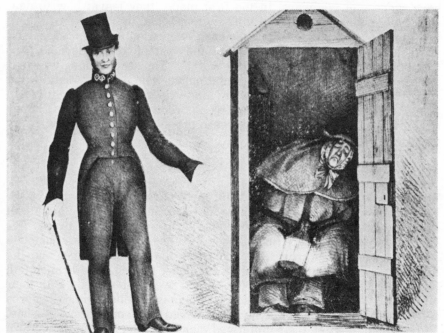

The Peeler replaces the Charlie

The Organisation and Work of the New Police. The two Commissioners appointed were a soldier, Colonel Sir Charles Rowan, and a young lawyer, Edward Mayne. They set up their office in 4, Whitehall Place, a house that had a doorway into Scotland Yard. They divided their area into seventeen divisions, each one with a company of police under the charge of a Superintendent. He was assisted by four Inspectors. Each Inspector had four Sergeants, and each sergeant commanded a section of nine constables. That meant there were 144 constables in a company.

Rowan and Mayne had clear ideas about the work their men should do. They were to prevent crime by patrolling regularly and keeping an eye on known and possible criminals. There was to be no detective work of any consequence. If detection was necessary, it meant a crime had taken place and that the police had failed.

The new force ran into trouble at first. Pay was £1.05p a week and as a skilled man could earn £1.50p in industry, good recruits were hard to find. The public were hostile including educated people and even magistrates. As we have seen, they had lost some of their authority and quite often showed their displeasure by taking the side of the criminals that were brought to trial.

How far the New Police reduced crime is difficult to say, but they did have success in two ways. In the first place, they learnt how to deal with rioters. Here they had an unlikely teacher in the Radical politician Francis Place. He saw that violence was ruining his cause and suggested to the Commissioners that they should treat the mob to a baton charge. This was tried and it worked. The second thing was that public opinion turned in favour of the police. The ordinary man in the street became used to the "Peeler" and recognised he was there to protect life and property, not to act as a government agent. This change of heart allowed Parliament to increase the authority of the New Police considerably, which it did in 1839.

The Metropolitan Police Act of 1839. In the first place the area of the New Police was extended to include all the ground that the Bow Street Horse Patrol had covered. Its boundary ran within about twenty-five kilometres of Charing Cross. Secondly they were given complete authority within this area. They took over the Marine Police, and the Bow Street Horse Patrol, the latter becoming the mounted branch. All the Police Offices, including Bow Street, were abolished, and their officers dismissed. A curious result was to leave London without a force of detectives. Rowan and Mayne still believed they could prevent crime, and it was only after their uniformed men had bungled the arrest of a 180 murderer that they could be persuaded to appoint a few detectives.

The Police Outside London. The New Police were, apparently, effective in London, and the public accepted them, so the next step was to have similar forces all over the country. This was done by two Acts of Parliament.

In 1839 the County Police Act allowed magistrates to organise police forces in their counties, and use the ratepayers' money to pay for them. However, the Act was permissive, which meant that magistrates could please themselves, and many places went on as before, rather than spend the money. Then, in 1856, Parliament passed the Rural Police Act, which made it compulsory to have proper police forces everywhere. The Home Secretary was to appoint Inspectors to see that it was done. In order to encourage efficiency, and soften the blow to the ratepayers, the Government was to pay one quarter of the cost of every force that earned a satisfactory report from the Inspectors.

A THUNDERING PEEL TO THIEVES PICKPOCKETS WATCHMEN, &c. &c.

Questions

1. Who is the statesman shown here? How is he dressed?

2. Which is the proper way to spell his name? Why has it changed?

3. What early experience had he in organising a police force?

4. What is he saying he will do?

5. Has the cartoonist given his aim correctly?

6. What is the date of the cartoon and why was it drawn in that year?

7. Why are watchmen included with thieves and pickpockets?

181

8. Who suffered the same fate as the watchmen?
9. How does the cartoonist think that criminals will feel about the new police?
10. Do you think the cartoonist is in favour of the new ideas? What was the general opinion at the time?

of which they must feel to be beneath their notice.
If a Cabdriver is spoken to by the Police, he is to be called "Cabdriver" and the vulgar, offensive word "Cabby" is never to be used.
(*General Instructions to the New Police.*)

Questions for picture on page 183.
1. What was the purpose of this poster?
2. The first three questions are objecting that anyone who has a complaint about the police has to take it to the Commissioner of Police. Why should the writer object?
3. What does the writer mean by saying the British Magistrate is "stripped of his powers"?
4. Who is the "Military Man" mentioned in the fifth question?
5. What was the objection to the government having charge of the police?
6. Whom does the writer think should appoint the police?
7. Had they ever done so?
8. What does the writer say should be done to bring about the change?

Questions
1. How is a policeman to speak to: (a) Wealthy or important people (b) Ordinary people?
2. What must he do if he sees something unimportant happening?
3. How must he act if some crime is likely?
4. What are members of the public likely to do to try and upset him?
5. How should he react?
6. What does the instruction with regard to cabdrivers show?
7. Who would have drawn up these instructions?
8. Why were they anxious the police should behave properly?
9. How is the tone of this document different from the poster?

THE DUTIES OF A CONSTABLE
He will be civil and attentive to all persons of every rank and class; insolence and incivility will not be passed over.
He must be particularly cautious not to interfere idly; when required to act he will do so with decision and boldness.
He must remember that there is no qualification more indispensable to a Police Officer than a perfect command of temper, never suffering himself to be moved in the slightest degree, by any language or threats that may be used; if he does his duty in a quiet and determined manner, such conduct will probably induce well-disposed bystanders to assist him should he require it.
Police Constables are particularly cautioned not to pay attention to any ignorant or silly expressions that may be made use of towards them personally, all

Questions—Chapter Twenty-Eight
1. Why did crime increase in the early 19th century?
2. Why did people not want a proper police force?
3. What Prime Minister wanted to check crime?
4. What position did Peel hold in his government? What experience had he of organising police?
5. Name the Act passed in 1829. What area did the new police have to cover?
6. Which of the former police remained?
7. Which were abolished?
8. How big was the new force?
9. Name the two first Commissioners. Where did they have their office?
10. How did they organise their force?
11. What did they see as the main duty of the police?
12. What two problems did the new police meet?

13. Name one crime they managed to control. Who suggested the method? Why?
14. What happened to public opinion? Why?
15. What Act was passed in 1839? What area did it give the new police?
16. Which of the existing police forces did they absorb?
17. Which were abolished?
18. What important branch did the force lack for some years?
19. What Act made it compulsory to have police forces all over the country?
20. How did the Government help?

Further Work
1. Find out about: the Daniel Good case, Jack the Ripper, garrotting, the history of finger printing, some of the 19th century detectives.
2. Read more about Sir Robert Peel.
3. Read the following by Dickens: Reprinted Pieces, The Detective Police, Down With the Tide, The Uncommercial Traveller, Chs. 5 and 30.
4. You are living in London in 1829. Say what misgivings you have about the new police.

The New Police.

PARISHIONERS.---Ask yourselves the following *Questions*:

Why is an Englishman, if he complains of an outrage or an insult, referred for redress to a Commissioner of Police?

Why is a Commissioner of Police delegated to administer Justice?

Why are the proceedings of this new POLICE COURT *unpublished* and *unknown*? and by what Law of the Land is it recognized?

Why is the British Magistrate stripped of his power? and why is Justice transferred from the Justice Bench?

Why is the Sword of Justice placed in the hands of a MILITARY Man?

Consider these constitutional questions: consider the additional burthen saddled on you---consider all these points, then UNITE in removing such a powerful force from the hands of Government, and let us institute a Police System in the hands of the PEOPLE under *parochial* appointments---

UNITY IS STRENGTH;

THEREFORE,

I.---Let each Parish convene a Meeting.

II.---Let a Committee be chosen, instructed to communicate with other Parishes.

III.---Let Delegates be elected from each Committe to form a

CENTRAL COMMITTEE,

To join your Brother Londoners in one heart, one hand, for the

Abolition of the New Police

These Bills may be had at the Printer's, at 4d. per Dozen; 2s. per Hundred; or, 17s. 6d. per Thousand; and the enemies of oppression requested to aid its circulation.　　ELLIOT, Printer, 14, Holywell St. Strand

CHAPTER 29

Prisons

In the eighteenth century prisons were the property of the local authorities, and were in a deplorable condition. In the nineteenth century, the central government gradually increased its control over them, and they were reformed. There were also serious attempts to discover ways of reforming criminals as well.

The State and Local Authority Prisons. Largely as a result of Howard's work there were a number of new laws passed in the late eighteenth century that attempted to make prisons better places. However, the only effective one was an Act of 1774 sponsored by an M.P. called Popham. It said that prisoners found innocent at their trials must be set free in the open court. Formerly they had been dragged back to prison where the gaolers held them until they paid the fees they were supposed to owe.

Parliament went on tackling the problem piecemeal until 1823, when an Act sponsored by Sir Robert Peel consolidated all the earlier measures. It said that gaolers were to have salaries and were not to make money from prisoners. Buildings were to be clean. A chaplain and a doctor were to visit the prisoners regularly, and those who needed education were to be taught. All these were valuable reforms, but Peel's Act had a weakness in that there was no way of seeing it was obeyed. Increasingly, though, local authorities wanted to reform their prisons, and they now had the authority of Parliament to do so. The result was that some prisons were improved, while others remained as bad as they ever had been.

In 1835, Parliament decided to tackle the problem of the unwilling local authorities by passing a Prisons Act which allowed the Home
184 Secretary to appoint Inspectors. The Inspectors' duties were to see that

the laws for the management of prisons were obeyed. To encourage efficiency the Government would make a grant towards the upkeep of any prison that had a good report from its Inspector.

Conditions now improved everywhere, but even so, there were still considerable differences which the Inspectors lacked the power to iron out. Some prisons were comfortable, by the standards of those days, but others, like Leicester, had a dreadful reputation for cruelty. So as to have more uniformity, Parliament passed another Prisons Act in 1877. It made all prisons the property of the Government and put them under the control of the Home Secretary.

Government Prisons and Transportation. At the same time that the government was increasing its control over local authority prisons, it was creating a system of its own.

An Act of Parliament of 1717 had allowed judges to give a sentence of transportation instead of hanging, where they saw fit. Criminals sentenced to transportation were the responsibility of the government. At first they caused few problems. They were simply handed over to

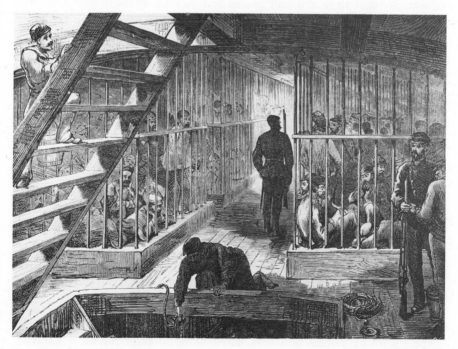

Convicts bound for Botany Bay

traders who shipped them to North America and sold them to planters. The traffic came to an end, though, with the outbreak of the American War of Independence in 1776, so the government hurriedly converted hulks into prisons. Hulks are old ships that have been stripped of their masts and equipment. Such were the first government prisons, for ordinary criminals, in this country.

Soon it was found that the Australians would welcome convict workers, simply because they could not find any others. The first ship-load went out in 1787 and others followed in large numbers. The traffic went on until the middle of the nineteenth century, when the Australians decided they wanted no more convicts. Transportation had to stop and the government had to build more prisons in this country.

Indeed, it had already begun to supply its own. Not counting the hulks, the first was Millbank, which was on a site now occupied by the Tate Gallery. It opened in 1841. Next was Pentonville in 1842. Dartmoor, which had been built for French prisoners during the Napoleonic Wars, was re-opened for convicts in 1850.

Prison Buildings and Staff. Some nineteenth century prisons were built so soundly that they are still in use today. One of these is Pentonville, which was a model for many others. The building was clean, warm and healthy. It was also secure, so that there was no need to load prisoners with irons. The cell blocks were built on the radial wing plan, that is, laid out like the spokes of a wheel. A warder standing at the centre could look along all of them. Other buildings included a hospital, a chapel and exercise yards. The prisoners had ample food.

The governor and warders were salaried. They were efficient men who organised the prison well, and according to a strict routine. All the abuses of John Howard's day had gone.

The Treatment of Prisoners. In the nineteenth century, society began to take a more humane attitude towards criminals.

The movement started with the reform of the Criminal Law. We have seen that about two hundred offences had been made punishable by death, which, on the face of it, was quite barbarous. One of the early reformers was Sir Samuel Romilly who won his first success in 1808 when he persuaded Parliament to abolish the death penalty for picking pockets. Progress was slow at first, but in 1823 Sir Robert Peel had the death penalty abolished for one hundred offences. By 1838 only high treason and murder were capital crimes.

The even more common eighteenth century punishment, transportation, went on a good deal longer. It was indeed a convenient way of disposing of criminals and was more humane than hanging. Convicts had a long and uncomfortable journey, and many died, but for those who arrived, life might not be too bad. They were "assigned" to settlers who gave them their keep and, usually, a small amount of spending money. Skilled men were sought out eagerly, and were well treated by their employers. Much depended on the convict. If he behaved, life might not be too bad. If, on the other hand, he committed another crime, then he could be sent to a penal settlement like Botany Bay, or Norfolk Island. These places were like concentration camps.

As we have seen, transportation had to end, so Parliament found an alternative in Penal Servitude, introduced in 1853. Under this a convict started his sentence in a prison like Pentonville, usually in solitary confinement. Next he went on to public works, such as helping to build a naval dockyard. Finally, if his conduct had been good, he finished his time with a "ticket of leave", which meant he was free to lead his own life, apart from having to report regularly to a police station.

As hanging and even transportation were going out of favour, it became increasingly important to find ways of turning criminals into worthy citizens. There were two systems in favour, both of which had been developed in America.

One was the Silent System. As the name suggests, prisoners were not allowed to speak, and this stopped them exchanging evil thoughts and corrupting each other. However, the main idea behind the Silent System was to make prison life so unbearable that a criminal would be frightened into good behaviour. He was in prison not as punishment, but for punishment, and the punishment was hard, unpleasant work. The least disagreeable was oakum picking, which was unravelling old rope. They found it much harder on the treadwheel or even worse, the crank. Introduced in 1846, this machine had a stiff handle which the convict had to turn several thousand times a day, entirely unproductively, before he could eat.

The other method was the Separate System. Prisoners were together only for brief periods, at exercise and in chapel, and even then they had to wear masks so they could not recognise each other. Most of the time, moreover, they were in solitary confinement. This, if kept up long enough, will break all but the toughest of characters, at which point the prison chaplain would try the influence of religion. The theory was that he would help the criminal build a new character so that when he left prison he would lead a good life of his own free will. It was like "brain washing", though done with good motives. However, what happened too often was that the solitary confinement drove a man, not to a good life, but to insanity or suicide.

None the less all this was an advance on the eighteenth century when the main idea had been to be rid of criminals, either by hanging them, or shipping them out of the country. By the nineteenth century the state recognised that it had a duty not just to punish, but also to reform.   187

There should be no tea and sugar, no assemblage of female felons round the washing tub—nothing but beating hemp, pulling oakum and pounding bricks. (Quoted in Webb—*English Prisons*.)

Questions
1. Which prison system does Smith favour?
2. What does he suggest prisoners should do?
3. What things would he stop?
4. What effect would he hope to have on criminals?

SHOT DRILL (The men stand three yards apart and pass 24lb cannon balls to each other).
"One!" shouted the officer and all the men, stooping, took up the heavy shot. "Two!" was scarcely uttered when the entire column moved sideways, three yards, until each man had taken the place where his neighbour stood before. On "Three!" every one bent down and placed the iron ball on the earth, and at "Four!" they shifted back, empty-handed, to their original stations. They grew hot and breathed hard. Some, who at the beginning had been as yellow as goose-skin, had bright spots appear, almost like dabs of rouge on their prominent cheek bones. The warder said, "It tries them most taking up, because there is nothing to lay hold of, and the hands get slippery with perspiration so the ball is greasy." (Mayhew and Binny—*Criminal Prisons of London*.)

Questions
1. What prison system is in use here?
2. Describe shot drill in your own words.
3. What was the point in doing shot drill?
4. Who would favour it, Clay or Smith? Why?
5. Why would the men have prominent cheek bones?

Questions
1. Under which prison system was the treadwheel used?
2. Why were prisoners made to do this work?
3. Prisoners called the treadwheel the "everlasting staircase." Can you see why?
4. Each prisoner on the wheel has a bar in front of him at chest height. Why does he need it?
5. What are the men doing who are sitting down? Why are they not speaking to each other? What do you suppose they are waiting for?
6. Describe the prison uniform.

THE REV. SIDNEY SMITH ON WAYS TO CURE CRIMINALS
I would banish all the looms of Preston Gaol and substitute nothing but the treadwheel or capstan, or some species of labour where the labourer could not see the results of his toil—where it is as monotonous, irksome and dull as possible.

A CHAPLAIN'S IDEAS ON THE TREATMENT OF CRIMINALS
In his cell the prisoner has no temptations from without, and many salutary admonitions from within. His memory

collects and brings before him everything that ever happened to him since he was a child; reflection traces painful consequences back to their sinful causes; the sense of sin and sorrow for it follow; he is directed to Him who bore our sorrows and atoned for sin. Then rises up a prayer for pardon and he says, "By God's help I'll be a different man for the future."

As a general rule, a few months in the separate cell render a prisoner strangely impressible. The chaplain can then make the brawny navvy cry like a child; he can work on his feelings in almost any way he pleases; he can, so to speak, photograph his own thoughts, wishes and opinions on his patient's mind and fill his mouth with his own phrases and language.
(Clay—The Prison Chaplain.)

Questions

1. Does Clay prefer the Silent or the Separate System?
2. What does he imagine a prisoner in solitary confinement thinks about his past?
3. What good resolution does the prisoner make?
4. How will the prisoner's personality change?
5. What will this allow the chaplain to do?
6. Is this the same as "brain washing"?

SOLITARY CONFINEMENT—COLERIDGE

As he passed by the Coldbath Fields he saw
    A solitary cell,
And the Devil was pleased for it gave him a hint
    For improving his prisons in Hell.

Questions

1. What was the Coldbath Fields?
2. What does Coleridge feel about solitary cells?
3. Would he agree with Clay on their value?

Questions—Chapter Twenty-Nine

1. Who owned the prisons in the 18th century? Who took them over in the 19th?
2. What was attempted for criminals?
3. What did Popham's Act say?

4. Describe Peel's Prisons Act. What weakness did it have? What good results?
5. In what two ways was the Government able to control the prisons after the Act of 1835?
6. Why did Parliament pass the Prisons Act of 1877? What did it say?
7. Where were criminals first transported?
8. Why did the government begin to use hulks?
9. Why did Australians welcome convicts at first?
10. When and why did transportation stop?
11. Name the first government prison.
12. Describe Pentonville Prison.
13. Why were its governor and warders efficient?
14. Who first persuaded Parliament to abolish the death penalty for some offences?
15. What politician took up this work?
16. What happened to criminals sent to Australia?
17. What replaced transportation? How did it work?
18. How did the Silent System work?
19. What was the idea behind the Separate System?
20. What often went wrong?

Further Work

1. Find out more about (a) Transportation (b) The hulks (c) Pentonville Prison (d) Dartmoor Prison.
2. Read the chapters in the following books by Dickens: David Copperfield 61 (What does Dickens think of the Separate System?); Pickwick Papers 6; Great Expectations 5, 32, 39.
3. You have finished a sentence under the Silent System. Write a conversation you have had with someone who has come from the Separate System.
4. Write the thoughts of a prisoner in solitary confinement (a) as Clay might have imagined them (b) as you think they really were.
5. Write an essay on how you think prisons should be run. Look at some books on prisons for ideas.

189

CHAPTER 30

Elementary Education

It has been estimated that at the beginning of the nineteenth century only one child in twenty went to school. A hundred years later, almost all of them did. This was the result of a good deal of work by voluntary organisations, mainly the Church of England, and also by the state. The state began to play its part in the 1830's by helping the voluntary schools; next, after 1870, it built its own schools in places where there were not enough voluntary ones; finally, in 1902, it began to draw the voluntary schools into the state system.

State Aid to Voluntary Schools. In 1833 Parliament made a grant of £20 000 for education. It was a paltry sum in comparison with what was needed, but the very fact that it had been given was important. It showed that the state had accepted some responsibility for the education of the poor.

Each year Parliament renewed the grant, usually increasing it, and the payment of a regular sum of money meant there had to be a government department to see it was spent properly. A committee of the Privy Council was given the task, with the title of the "Committee of Council for Education". It was the forerunner of the Board of Education established in 1899, which in turn became the Ministry of Education in 1944. It had a Secretary with a staff of civil servants and Inspectors who saw that the voluntary bodies that took the Government money spent it in the proper way.

The first Secretary to the Committee of Council was James Kay-Shuttleworth, a man of considerable energy and ability. He saw that the chief need was for qualified teachers, and to provide them he started the Pupil Teacher system. A pupil teacher was like an 190 apprentice in industry. He was given indentures at the age of twelve or thirteen, and under these he was bound to teach in his school during the day. In return he received a small wage but, even more important, he went on with his own education in the evenings, with the help of his head teacher. If at the end of five years he had been successful, he could go to a Training College and become fully qualified.

It took a long time, but by the end of the century, Kay-Shuttleworth's system was producing a reasonable supply of teachers. At first only heads were qualified and they had to run their schools with just monitors and pupil teachers to help them. Finally, though, there were qualified assistant teachers as well.

Government money helped pay the pupil teachers, and more of it was given for buildings, equipment and salaries. By 1860 the annual grant was half a million pounds and the Government appointed a Royal Commission under the Duke of Newcastle to see if they were getting value for money. The Newcastle Commission reported in 1861, and found cause for concern. In the first place most children only went to school for a short while, perhaps no more than a year or two. Moreover, even during this time, they attended badly. Secondly, teachers were concentrating on their older, brighter pupils and neglecting those who found it difficult to learn. Finally, there were not enough schools. Wealthy parishes had them, but then, as now, educational problems were worse in the depressed areas of the big cities where, quite often, there were no schools at all.

In 1862 the minister responsible for education, Robert Lowe, determined to do what he could to put matters right. He introduced a new set of regulations called the Revised Code which made the government grants to schools depend on the efficiency of their teaching. Each year an Inspector would examine the children in the 3 R's—reading, writing and arithmetic. For every pass there was a grant of 40p. In addition there was a grant of 20p for good attendance, so that a child who came to school regularly and learnt his work could earn his school 60p a year, or about one half of the cost of his education. Teachers now did all they could to make children attend school and learn their basic subjects. Education became, to quite an extent, a hard grind at the 3 R's. This meant that the Revised Code was unpopular with members of the Church of England who had built their schools in order that they might teach religion, a subject which now tended to take second place.

The Education Act of 1870. Gladstone came to office in 1868 and his Government decided there should be a school place for every child in the country. The churches had done well, but, as the Newcastle Commission had shown, voluntary effort was never going to be enough. Accordingly, in 1870, the minister responsible for education, W. E. Forster, drafted a most important Act which aimed, as he put it, to "fill 191 in the gaps left by the voluntary system". If any town or village did not have enough schools, then its ratepayers had to elect a School Board. The duty of a School Board was to take money out of the rates and use it to provide schools.

The problem was religion. Ratepayers belonged to all religions so it was felt that Board Schools could not teach any particular creed. The answer was provided by an M.P. called Cowper-Temple who suggested they should give non-denominational religion, that is the general ideas of Christianity, accepted by most people. On the face of it this was fair, but while Noncomformists agreed, it did not please members of the Church of England who attached great importance to their own special beliefs.

The religious rivalry led to a lot of building. In any town where there were not enough schools, the Nonconformists spurred the School Board to "fill the gaps". At the same time members of the Church of England would be raising money as fast as they could to provide their own schools and make sure, if possible, that there were no gaps to fill.

It was not long before there were virtually enough schools for everyone, and in 1876 education was made compulsory.

The Education Act of 1902. In the later years of the nineteenth century there were problems with School Boards, and with voluntary schools.

The Act of 1870 meant that there were, eventually, over 2500 School Boards. Some of them, like London School Board, were powerful, efficient bodies. Many a Board, though, served a small village and was responsible for just one school. This made the administration of education difficult.

As for the voluntary schools, they were having money problems. In common with the Board Schools they could earn grants from the Government, but these were not enough to meet all expenses. For a Board School there was no problem, as they could have anything else they needed out of the rates. The managers of a voluntary school, however, had to appeal to its subscribers who might or might not be generous. Voluntary schools, most of which now belonged to the Church of England, began to lose the race with the Board Schools. Their buildings and equipment were poorer, and their teachers had lower salaries.

In 1902 the Conservative government of A. J. Balfour decided to pass an Education Act to solve these and other problems.

The Act abolished School Boards and transferred their schools to the County and County Borough Councils that had been created in 1888. Board Schools were now known as Council Schools. There were only 330 of these new Local Education Authorities, so the administration of

A village school

education was much simpler. The new Authorities were also big enough to develop Secondary Education as is described in a later chapter.

Since the Church of England supported the Conservatives, Balfour's Act was generous to the voluntary schools. The new Local Education Authorities had to pay the salaries of their teachers, which was by far their largest expense. In return, the Local Education Authority had the right to nominate one third of the managers. It was the start of a process which has brought nearly all voluntary schools into the state system, but at the time it seemed a small price to pay.

Nonconformists were furious with this part of the Act which was quite against the ideas of 1870. They had to help support schools that taught a religion in which they did not believe, and for a time many of them preferred to break the law and refused to pay their rates. However, the money was of great benefit to the voluntary schools because they could now give as good an education as the council schools. Not only was an elementary education available for everyone, but all schools had at least the opportunity of reaching the same standards.

193

Questions

1. How many children are there in the school?

2. Who are the young people, aged about 16 or 18 standing at the sides?

3. The children at the back are in a gallery. What is the point of this arrangement?

4. What lesson is the headmaster giving to the children bending down?

5. What must the rest of the school do meantime?

6. Why is the room so high?

7. Describe the floor.

8. How is the room heated? (Look at the left of the picture).

9. Locate the gas jets used for lighting.

10. How is the window different from one in a modern school?

11. *What furniture and equipment is there?*

12. *What would be the disadvantages of teaching in this school? Remember for one thing, there would be no other class rooms.*

EDUCATION OF PUPIL TEACHERS

After a hard day's work in school the headmaster has to teach his pupil teachers; perhaps he has three or four, all in different years, all needing a certain amount of help. And what have they to work at? Dry, elementary subjects, important to learn, but very dull to grind at year after year, on top of an equally dull grind at still more dry and elementary work in the day school; and remember that these subjects have to be most carefully taught, not got through, not shirked, but beaten inch by inch, a scrap of grammar, a scrap of geography, a scrap of history, a scrap of Euclid, and all to be taught in a high and dry way.

(*Article in Bath newspaper by clergyman.*)

Questions

1. *When do pupil teachers have their own lessons?*

2. *Where will they go, if they do well?*

3. *What subjects do they learn?*

4. *Why do they find their studies tedious?*

REPORTS ON PUPIL TEACHERS

E. Bishop has failed her examination badly. If she fails to the same extent next year, the Grant will have to be reduced by £10. Lesson by A. Hudson on the "Apple". The lesson was too advanced and not given in a way that would interest anyone. He lost control of the children.

I find Culley and Berry quite useless. This afternoon I went into the classroom where they were engaged with the First Standard at 2.40 (Lesson began at 2.15). Not a stroke of work had been done and the two teachers were playing round the desks.

(*Headteacher's Log Book.*)

Questions

1. *What may happen when a Pupil Teacher fails an examination?*

2. *What was wrong with Hudson's lesson?*

3. *How were Culley and Berry misbehaving?*

4. *Summarise the problems Pupil Teachers caused.*

HISTORY LESSON IN A TRAINING COLLEGE 1902

We had got to the last page of the text-book of dates and one after another we were repeating what we had learnt by heart. The book ended "May 1st 1870, Outbreak of Franco-German War." The man who had successfully recited this very last date upon this very last page had barely sat down when up sprang his next neighbour with, "Printed and Published by Smith and Son, Stamford St., London." (*New Liberal Review.* September 1903)

Questions

1. *What had these students been told to learn?*

2. *How were they being tested?*

3. *What does this extract tell you about the education they were receiving?*

DESCRIPTION OF A HEADMASTER

Mr. Wadsworth had a fine head and a handsome profile, which, terminating in a long beard and surmounted by his skull-cap, made his figure one not easily forgotten. He was a very fair disciplinarian, but he punished in two ways which were unwise. First, he would flick a scholar's ear with his second finger smartly released from the thumb, which inflicts more suffering than might be supposed. Secondly he would seize two boys by the right and left ears respectively and bump their heads together with considerable violence. It never paid to avoid his canings, and the boy who withdrew his hand always lived to regret it. Mr. Wadsworth would hold his fingers in a vice-like grip and add substantial interest to the contemplated punishment. (Records of Bathforum School, Bath.)

Questions

1. *Describe this teacher's appearance.*

2. *What effect would it have on the children?*

195

3. What punishments are mentioned?
4. What does this extract tell you about the discipline at Bathforum School?

Questions—Chapter Thirty

1. What proportion of children was in school at the start of the nineteenth century and at the end?
2. What were the three stages by which the state became involved in education?
3. When did Parliament make the first grant for education? How much was it?
4. What Department administered the grant?
5. Who was its first Secretary?
6. How did he solve the shortage of teachers?
7. Why did the Government appoint a Royal Commission in 1860? Who was its Chairman?
8. Name the three weaknesses the Commission found.
9. Who introduced the Revised Code? How did schools earn their grant under the Code?
10. How did the Code affect teaching?
11. Who was responsible for the 1870 Education Act?
12. How did he describe his aim?
13. Which places were to have School Boards? What were their duties?
14. What was done about the religious problem?
15. Why were many schools built after the Act?
16. What did the Act of 1876 do?
17. By the end of the 19th century, what problem was there with many School Boards?
18. What trouble did voluntary schools have?
19. Who was responsible for the Act of 1902? How did it solve both these problems?
20. Why were Nonconformists annoyed?

Further Work

1. Read more about James Kay-Shuttleworth, Robert Lowe, W. E. Forster and A. J. Balfour.
2. Read about the beginnings of Secondary Education from 1889 to 1902. (Chapter 48).
3. You are a child at an elementary school in the late 19th century. Write a description of it.
4. It is 1870 and you are a wealthy member of the Church of England. Say what you think of the Education Act. What are you doing about it?
5. A Nonconformist and an Anglican argue about the Education Act of 1902. Write what they say.

CHAPTER 31

Child Labour

Children had always been put to work, but what was new in the nineteenth century was their mass employment in factories and mines. Here they attracted the attention of social reformers.

Children in the Textile Factories. In the textile factories much of the work was so easy that children could do it quite well. Typical child workers were "piecers" who joined any threads that broke, and "scavengers" who cleaned the floors under and around the machines.

Enemies of the factories complained that the buildings were over-heated, stuffy and unhealthy. There were also tales of dangerous machinery causing dreadful accidents, and accusations of hideous brutality. Supporters of the factories said that they were healthier than the children's own homes, that the work was easy, and that there was little or no cruelty. The truth was that there were good mills and bad ones, but at least two evils were clear. One was the length of the working day, and the other was the employment of pauper apprentices.

At the height of a boom, mills could work for sixteen hours a day and children had to keep the adults company. Twelve hours was not uncommon and ten hours or less was reckoned short time. However good the mill, hours like these were bound to damage health.

The employment of pauper apprentices came about in the early days of cotton spinning when water was the only source of power. Many mills were in remote valleys and it was impossible to persuade people to live there. Employers took orphan children from the workhouses in big cities, undertaking to feed, clothe and house them. In return the children had to work without wages until they were 21. They learnt no skills so the term "apprenticeship" was just a polite word for "slavery." 197

Children in Coal Mines. Children, and indeed women, were responsible for bringing the coal to the surface. They tugged and pushed it along galleries to the bottom of the shaft and in some mines even carried it up ladders. In larger mines with ventilation systems children as young as five worked as "trappers". Doors were needed to make sure the air circulated through all the workings and trappers opened and closed them as the coal came through.

Young miners were usually healthy enough, but frequently suffered injuries. However, what shocked Victorians just as much were the moral dangers. Hewers found their work hot and used to strip, so that women and girls were working with naked men.

198 *Children carrying coal from the mines*

Children in Other Industries. There was work for children in almost every industry and most of these were carried on in the home or in workshops. In so far as one can judge children were worse off with their parents or a small employer than they were in the cotton mills. There are distressing stories in the report of the Royal Commission 1842 which investigated, amongst other things, the metal trades of the Black Country. Here children helped to make nails, chains and locks. They slaved away in abominable little workshops, badly fed, badly clothed and subjected to every sort of cruelty.

Parliament and Child Labour in the Textile Factories. The Ten Hours Movement. In the early nineteenth century most people believed in the economic theory of "laissez-faire", or "leaving alone". They thought that trade and industry would only develop properly if the government made as few rules and regulations as possible, leaving both employers and workmen in freedom. On the question of working hours, they held that if any adult chose to work himself into ill health, that was his own affair. They did recognise, though, that children were not free agents and Parliament was not unwilling to make laws for their protection. The first of these laws was passed in 1802 when Sir Robert Peel the elder sponsored the "Health and Morals of Apprentices Act". It should have done a lot for the unhappy pauper apprentices, but in fact it did little, because there was no way to see that it was obeyed.

There were further attempts to protect children until, in the 1830's, people doing this work were caught up in the "Ten Hours Movement". Its leaders were philanthropists, like Lord Ashley (later Lord Shaftesbury), and even some factory owners like John Fielden. One of the most outspoken was an estate bailiff called Richard Oastler. The ordinary men who joined the movement wanted a ten hour day for themselves. They knew Parliament would not give them this directly, but the factories could not work without children. Their tactics, then, were to make a great deal of the sufferings of the children because if their hours could be limited, so too would those of the adults.

The first step forward came in 1833 when Parliament passed the Factories Regulation Act. It is sometimes known as Althorp's Act because he was Home Secretary at the time.

The main terms of the Act were:

1 No child under the age of nine was to work in a textile factory.
2 Children between the ages of nine and thirteen were to work no more than nine hours a day.
3 Factory children were to go to school twelve hours a week.
4 There were to be four Inspectors of Factories, with assistants, to see the law was obeyed.

The last point was most important because it meant there was now some chance that employers would obey the law.

Adults who hoped for shorter hours were soon disappointed. Employers simply took on extra children and ran a complicated system of shifts for them, so that the factories stayed open as long as before. Not only that, the shift, or relay system as they called it, was so complicated that Inspectors had great difficulty in finding how long individual children were working. The result was a further Factory Act in 1844 (Graham's Act) which said that children aged from nine to thirteen must work only 6½ hours a day, and this was to be entirely in the morning or in the afternoon. The Inspectors now found it easier to protect children, but the adults were still far from happy. Employers had two shifts for children, one in the morning and one in the afternoon, so keeping their factories going for thirteen hours a day.

The Ten Hours Movement finally succeeded as the result of a number of Acts of Parliament passed in the middle of the century. One of the most important of these was John Fielden's Act of 1847 which gave protection, not just to children, but also to young persons aged between thirteen and eighteen, and to women. Their hours were limited to ten a day. Nothing was said about men over eighteen, but they could not work on their own, so the machines had to stop.

Parliament and Children in Other Industries. An Act of Parliament of 1842 forbade the employment of boys under ten and all females in coal mines. However, other industries were difficult to regulate. It was easy to inspect large factories and mines, but impossible to supervise thousands of homes and small workshops. The only way was to provide enough schools for all children, and then make it compulsory for them to attend. By the end of the nineteenth century this had happened and most employers, parents and children were obeying the law.

Fork grinding at Sheffield

Questions
1. In what ways would this room be unpleasant and unhealthy?
2. Why was it difficult to regulate child labour in workshops like this one?
3. What was the only effective way to prevent it?
4. When did this happen? (See Chapter 30)

EVIDENCE GIVEN TO ROYAL COMMISSIONS

1. Robert Blincoe, a Mill Worker
I have had two hand-vices of a pound weight each, screwed to my ears. Then three or four of us have been hung on a cross-beam above the machinery, hanging on by our hands, without shirts or socks. Mind, we were apprentices, without father or mother to take care of us; I don't say they often do that now. Then we used to stand up, in a skip, without our shirts, and be beat with straps or sticks.

Questions
1. What children were these?
2. Where would they have come from?
3. How were they punished?
4. Why were they treated especially cruelly?

2. John Moss, Apprentice Master
What were the hours of work?—From 5 o'clock in the morning till 8 at night, all the year through.
What time was allowed for meals?—Half an hour for breakfast and half an hour for dinner.
Had they any refreshment in the afternoon?—Yes.

201

Did they work whilst they ate it?—Yes. They had no cessation after dinner 'til 8 o'clock at night.
Did any children work on Sundays as cleaners of the machine?—Yes, every Sunday from six to twelve.
Were there any seats in the Mill?—None.
Were they usually much fatigued at night?—Yes, some of them were very much fatigued.
Did they frequently lie down upon the mill floor when their work was done, and fall asleep before their supper?—I have found them frequently upon the mill floor after the time they should have been in bed.

Questions
1. What hours did the children work?
2. What arrangements were there for meals?
3. How did the children feel at the end of the day?
4. Which of the above are leading questions?
5. What is the point of asking such questions?

CHILD LABOUR—URE, PHILOSOPHY OF MANUFACTURES
I never saw a child in ill-humour. They seemed to be always cheerful and alert, taking pleasure in the light play of their muscles, enjoying the mobility natural to their age. The scene of industry, so far from exciting sad emotions in my mind, was always exhilarating. It was delightful to see the nimbleness with which they pieced the broken ends, and to see them at leisure, after a few seconds' exercise of their tiny fingers, to amuse themselves as they chose. The work of these lively elves seemed to resemble a sport, in which habit gave a pleasing dexterity. Conscious of their skill, they were delighted to show it off to a stranger. As to exhaustion by the day's work, they showed no trace of it on emerging from the mill in the evening; for they immediately began to skip about and to commence their little amusements the same as boys issuing from a school.

Questions
1. What work were these children doing?
2. In what mood did Ure find them?
3. Why were they pleased with themselves?
4. How did they feel at the end of the day?

REPORT FOR ROYAL COMMISSION OF 1823
If anything like abuse in respect to punishment now takes place, it is in the smaller mills, where a strap is sometimes in the possession of the overseer; but I doubt very much whether any such abuse exists, or has of late years existed in any degree worthy of notice. My impression is that country schoolmasters in Scotland are far more apt than mill owners to exert their authority by applying the strap with undue severity.

Questions
1. What punishment is mentioned here?
2. How common was it in factories?
3. Where were children likely to suffer more?

Questions—Chapter Thirty-One
1. Name two jobs done by children in factories.
2. What complaints were made about factories? What was said in their defence?
3. How many hours might a child work in a mill?
4. Why were pauper apprentices employed?
5. Where did they come from? Under what conditions did employers take them?
6. What work did children do in coal mines?
7. What was the main danger they faced? What shocked Victorians about their work?
8. Where were children probably worse off than in mines and factories?
9. Why was Parliament unwilling to control working hours of adults?
10. Why did they make laws to protect children?
11. Which was the first of these laws? Why was it a failure?
12. Name three leaders of the Ten Hours Movement.

13. How did they hope to bring about a shorter day for adults in textile factories?

14. Give the title and date of Althorp's Act. What were its four main provisions?

15. Why did it not shorten the adults' working day?

16. Why was it difficult to enforce? How did Graham's Act solve this problem?

17. Why did it not please adults?

18. Whose Act brought in the ten hour day in textile factories? How did it do this?

19. What did the Mines Act of 1842 say?

20. What was the only way to control child labour in small factories and workshops?

Further Work

1. What enemies did factory owners have? Why? (Read about the Corn Laws in Chapter 17).

2. Read more about the life of Lord Shaftesbury, especially his work for boy chimney sweeps.

3. Imagine you are a pauper apprentice in a spinning factory. Describe a day in your life.

4. Write a discussion between a factory owner and a critic of the factories. (Read Chapter 10).

CHAPTER 32

Trade Unions

Following the repeal of the Combination Acts in 1824, trade unions were free to develop. Down to about 1850 what attracted most attention was Robert Owen's Grand National Consolidated Trades Union. Its collapse in 1834 was a set-back to the trade union movement among the poorer workers. At the same time, however, the skilled workers were beginning to organise themselves. From 1850 to 1875 these men created what we call the New Model Unions and won important legal rights. Towards the end of the century the unskilled workers at last formed effective trade unions, a movement known as the New Unionism.

Robert Owen and the Grand National Consolidated Trades Union. Owen's idea was to reform society through the trade union movement. He planned to organise all the workers in one big union and paralyse the country with a general strike. The workers would then take over all the factories and firms to run them for their own benefit. In 1833 he took the first step by forming the Grand National Consolidated Trades Union and inviting all other unions to join. A great many did, but at once there were difficulties.

In the first place prosperous workers were not interested and important groups like the builders and spinners held aloof. Owen's movement only attracted men in depressed trades like handloom weavers. Organisation was difficult, too, and there were premature little strikes that failed.

On the other hand the employers were determined. They met strikes with lock-outs and would only employ men who had signed a declaration that they were not union members. This declaration was called the Document.

The workers were much discouraged, too, by what happened to the 204 so-called Tolpuddle Martyrs. In 1833 some Dorset farm labourers

A meeting of the Unions. Birmingham—1832

formed a trade union which was to join the G.N.C.T.U. Their employers determined to prosecute them. Trade unions were now lawful, but the Tolpuddle men had been taking oaths of loyalty. Accordingly, the employers were able to take advantage of an Act which had made certain kinds of oath illegal. It has nothing to do, originally, with trade unions, but had been passed in 1797 to help check a mutiny in the fleet. George Loveless and five others were given seven years transportation and hurried out of the country. They were pardoned as the result of a public outcry, but did not return to England for five years.

In 1834, after barely a year, the G.N.C.T.U. collapsed. However, Owen's failure only affected the unskilled and the poor. While he was carrying out his grandiose plans the prosperous workers were being much more practical. They moved on from having small, local trade clubs and built up unions that were organised nationally. They came into their own after 1850.

The New Model Unions. The first of the New Model Unions was the Amalgamated Society of Engineers, founded in 1851, and others, like the Amalgamated Society of Carpenters and Joiners soon followed. They were successful for several reasons. In the first place their members were skilled craftsmen and the key men in their industries. Secondly, since they were well paid they could afford high subscriptions. The A.S.E., for example, had £73 000 within ten years. Thirdly, they were well organised, each union having an elected Executive Council, with a salaried Secretary and a staff of clerks.

205

The New Model Unions used their strength wisely, and would only call a strike when all else had failed. They had no far-fetched schemes like Owen, but wanted simply to improve the wages and working conditions of their members by degrees. Because they were moderate the ruling classes were willing enough to accept them.

They also began to work together. It was not long before the Secretaries of the big unions were having regular meetings and in 1868 there was the first Trades Union Congress.

However, the unions did have problems. There were two unfortunate events. First there were the Sheffield outrages of 1866 when rival unions among the cutlers took to violence and even murder. The government appointed a Royal Commission on the Trade Unions to find out what was wrong with the movement.

Secondly, there was the case of Hornby v Close in 1867. Close, the treasurer of the Bradford branch of the Boiler Makers' Society, took £24 of the funds and the judges said he need not pay it back. They held the remarkable view that although Trade Unions were legal in fact, they were not legal in law, so their funds had no protection.

Fortunately for the unions the skilled workers had been given the vote in 1867 and both Liberals and Conservatives were anxious for their support. In 1871 the Liberals, under Gladstone, passed a Trade Union Act which made it illegal to take union funds. However, Parliament also remembered the Sheffield outrages and passed the Criminal-Law Amendment Act which made it almost impossible to picket without breaking the law. This offended the working classes and at the next election they voted Conservative. Disraeli rewarded them with the Conspiracy and Protection of Property Act of 1875, which said that any action that was legal for an individual was also legal for a group. This, in effect, made peaceful picketing legal.

The New Unionism. The spread of the trade union movement to the unskilled workers began with two successful strikes.

The first was the London match girls' strike of 1888. Women and girls were being paid starvation wages for work with dangerous chemicals. With the help of a Fabian Socialist, Annie Besant, they organised a strike and won higher wages with safer working conditions.

In 1889 there was the London dock strike. The dockers wanted 6d (2½p) an hour minimum wage, known as the "dockers' tanner". They paralysed the port of London for four weeks, when the employers gave way. The following reasons led to their success.

In the first place they had good leaders in John Burns, Tom Mann and Ben Tillett. Secondly they won public sympathy. Many people recognised that the docker's work was unpleasant and that he was often out of a job. As many of the dockers were Roman Catholic Irish, Cardinal

Manning acted as mediator and his intervention seemed to make the strike respectable. Also, other organisations gave money, including the Australian unions who sent £30 000. Thirdly, 1889 was a boom year for trade, so that the employers were anxious to have the docks working again.

Following the success of the dockers other unskilled and semi-skilled workers formed unions. From 1892 to 1900 alone, membership rose from 1 500 000 to 2 000 000.

There were important differences between the new unions and those of the 1850's. They were open to all workers in a trade and there was no attempt to limit membership to the skilled few. In order to make it easy for everyone to join, subscriptions were low, although this meant that the unions were slow to build up funds. Finally, socialist influence began to grow. Men like Keir Hardie, the miners' leader, saw the unions as a force in the class struggle. This was to have important results later on. Trade unionists began to revive some of Robert Owen's ideas.

To Thomas Wakely Esq. M.P. This plate representing the meeting of the Trade Unionists in Copenhagen Fields April 21st 1834, for the purpose of carrying a Petition to the King for a remission of the sentence passed on the Dorchester Labourers is respectfully dedicated by Isiah Saunders.

Questions
1. What is the name usually given the Dorchester Labourers?
2. What sentence had been passed on them, and why?
3. Why is the meeting being held?
4. What is in the carriage? Where is it going?

5. What impression is the artist trying to give of the trade union members? Consider their dress, how they are standing, the numbers present, and the absence of police.
6. How far do you think this picture is accurate?

MINERS' STRIKE—NORTHUMBERLAND AND DURHAM 1844
DURING THE STRIKE

1. Cowpen Colliery was eleven weeks on strike. A man called George Hunter was attacked and injured so severely that he died. Hunter was not a union man, and was disliked by the other men.
2. The mine owners got together enough men, of one sort or another, to set the mines going again. As soon as the strangers arrived they needed houses, and as the men on strike still occupied the cottages, the work of ejecting them now commenced. Bands of policemen, with low, mean, ragged fellows were ordered into the miners' houses and, "Will you go to work?" was asked of the pitman. The answer being "No!" orders were given to remove everything. The yelling and shouting and the pitiful cries of the children had no effect. The furniture was removed into the lanes. In one lane a complete new village was built, chests of drawers, beds, etc, forming the walls and the top covered with bedding.
3. Detachments of regular troops, horse and foot, assisted by Colonel Bell's Yeomanry, were stationed near Wallsend; sentries patrolled the pits for the protection of the engines and premises, and the men who were at work; each night the country was scoured by squadrons of cavalry.

Questions

1. What happened to George Hunter? Why?
2. Why was he unpopular?
3. What might he have done during the strike?
4. Why did the mine owners bring in strangers?
5. Why were the miners thrown out of their houses?

6. Who, do you suppose, owned the cottages?
7. Under what condition would a miner have been allowed to keep his cottage?
8. Where was the furniture taken?
9. What did the miners do with it?
10. Who would have ordered troops into the area?
11. What were Yeomanry?
12. Who and what were the strikers likely to attack?
13. What two tasks did the soldiers carry out?

AFTER THE STRIKE

Numbers were refused work, generally those who had taken a leading part in the strike. Mr. Haswell was one. He and his father travelled round a great number of collieries in the two counties, and in many places, though men were wanted, they would not give them employment. It was evident the name was on the "black books."

The men who had been on strike and those who had been at work during the strike as "blacklegs" never met on friendly terms, and the former gave indications that they would have a day of reckoning. On 15th August a great riot occurred. Hundreds of men had drawn together, including English, Welsh and Irish, and a pitched battle began. They tore off the garden railings, got pick shafts and anything that would deal a blow. Soon every lane was thronged with reinforcements from other collieries. The Welshmen finally fled, making their escape over the railway and into their houses. Rumours were raised that soldiers were coming and but for this the English would have followed and destroyed them and their houses. As it was, great numbers were wounded and severely injured on both sides.
(Fynes—Miners of Northumberland and Durham.)

Questions

1. What had Haswell done?
2. What problem did he have after the strike?
3. Who suffered along with him?

4. What agreement do the mine owners seem to have made among themselves?
5. What is a "blackleg?"
6. What did the miners mean by a "day of reckoning"?
7. Who took part in the riot?
8. How many were there?
9. What weapons did they use?
10. Why were the Welshmen defeated?
11. Why did the riot end?
12. What would have happened if it had gone on?

Questions—Chapter Thirty-Two
1. Why did Trade Unions develop after 1824?
2. What Union was formed by Robert Owen? What plans did he make for it?
3. Name two difficulties it had.
4. How did employers react?
5. Who were the Tolpuddle Martyrs?
6. For what offence were they prosecuted?
7. How did their sentences affect Owen's Union?
8. Name two of the early New Model Unions. Give three reasons for their success.
9. What were their aims? Why were they accepted?
10. What important meeting was there in 1868?
11. Why was there a Royal Commission on Trade Unions?
12. What problem was created by Hornby v Close?

13. Name and describe two Acts passed by Gladstone.
14. Name and describe an Act passed by Disraeli.
15. What was the New Unionism?
16. Describe the London Match Girls' Strike.
17. When was there a London Dock Strike? Why?
18. Give three reasons for its success.
19. What did unskilled workers do after the strike?
20. Give three differences between the new unions and those of the 1850's.

Further Work
1. Read about Robert Owen's Grand National Guild.
2. Who was Robert Applegarth?
3. What was the Junta? (In Trade Union history).
4. Why was the first Trades Union Congress called?
5. Find out more about the Sheffield outrages.
6. Read more about the London Dock Strike.
7. Why was Keir Hardi's cap famous?
8. Read Elizabeth Gaskell's Mary Barton, chs. 15 and 16 and North and South chs. 17, 19 and 22.
9. It is 1900 and you are a trade union leader, 70 years old. Describe what you think were the three most important events in the history of the movement during your life.

CHAPTER 33

Chartism
1838-1848

Although the working classes had taken part in politics before 1838 they had tended to follow middle class groups who seemed to favour them. Chartism, however, was the first large scale working class political movement. Its aim was to give ordinary people control over Parliament so that they could have laws which would improve their economic position. It was an alternative to the trade unions who tried to do the same thing more directly by putting pressure on employers.

Causes of Chartism. There were many reasons why Chartism came into being. One of the most important was poverty.

From time to time there were depressions in industry bringing short time working and unemployment. If a depression coincided with a bad harvest and high food prices then there was much distress. It was at times like these that there was most interest in Chartism. The whole problem of poverty was made worse by the Poor Law Amendment Act of 1834. As we have seen, a man who was unemployed through no fault of his own might have to choose between the workhouse and starvation.

Along with poverty, there was a feeling among the workers that others had failed them. These were the middle classes and, from time to time, the trade unions.

Many people had supported the agitation for the Reform Act of 1832. They did the dangerous work of rioting and throwing stones and, indeed, violence in the street did a good deal in forcing through the Act. When it was passed, however, the ordinary man found it did nothing for him. Only middle class men gained the vote and the government they put in power was even less sympathetic than the one before. The Poor Law Amendment Act was proof of that.

As for the trade unions, they did least when they were needed most. During a depression they could not wring money from employers since, trade being bad, they were not making any. The failure of Owen's Grand National Consolidated Trades Union was also a serious set-back.

Under these conditions it seemed good sense for the working classes to form a political party of their own.

The Charter. In 1838 three organisations sent representatives to a meeting in Birmingham. They were the London Working Men's Association, whose Secretary was William Lovett, the Birmingham Political Union, recently revived by a banker, Thomas Attwood, and some reform groups in Manchester where an Irishman called Feargus O'Connor had founded a newspaper called the "Northern Star" to speak for the workers in the industrial towns.

At Birmingham the delegates from these three groups adopted a programme of reform drawn up by Lovett, and called the Charter. This was the document which gave the movement its name. It made six demands which would have given ordinary people control of Parliament. They were:

1 Manhood suffrage, which meant every man having the vote.
2 Vote by secret ballot, to prevent intimidation and bribery at elections.
3 Annual Parliaments, which would mean a general election every year, and ensure Parliament represented the will of the people.
4 The abolition of property qualifications for M.P.s, so that anyone could be elected.
5 Salaries for M.P.s, again to enable men who were not rich to stand for Parliament.
6 Equal electoral divisions, so that all M.P.s represented roughly the same number of people.

The Charter was printed and circulated widely. In a great many towns people organised themselves to support it and the Chartist movement was born.

Chartist Activities. The Chartists tried to have their way by persuading Parliament that the majority of the people in the country supported them. When this failed some tried violence while others made idealistic plans for village settlements.

In 1839 Chartist groups all over the country sent delegates to a meeting in London, calling itself the Convention. The name was a deliberate reminder of the French Revolution. There were torch-light processions and public meetings with talk of revolution and a general strike. As 1839 was a year of depression and hardship it was easy 211 enough to make people angry. The Convention drew up a petition asking Parliament to accept the Charter. They claimed that 1 200 000 people had signed it.

The Government acted firmly. Some London police went to Birmingham and put down a riot, while troops were sent to other disturbed areas. Parliament rejected the Charter by a large majority.

The Convention now divided. The "moral force" men wanted to go on trying persuasion, but the "physical force" men wanted violence.

They managed to start a small rebellion in South Wales, but it was a fiasco and gave the Government the excuse to arrest a good many Chartist leaders.

In 1842 there was another petition to Parliament with, it was claimed, 3 750 000 signatures. Parliament rejected the petition and once again there were disorders including the so-called "plug plot". Rioters stole the plugs from the boilers of factory steam engines. Again the disorders were put down, and with the return of prosperity most workers lost interest in Chartism.

It was at this period that the idealists in the movement decided to reform society in another way. They felt that the perfect existence was cultivating one's own plot of land in a village where everyone was equal. In 1845 they formed their Co-operative Land Society. They bought estates and on them built villages, each house having a few acres of land. One of these was Heronsgate in Hertfordshire, renamed "O'Connorville" after the Chartist leader. Families moving into the settlements bought their plots on the instalment plan and in theory the Co-operative Land Society should have made a profit. In fact it made a loss and collapsed in 1851. Some of the settlements, though, continued, O'Connorville lasting for some 25 years.

In 1848 there came yet another industrial depression, and once again the ordinary worker was willing to listen to the Chartists. There was the Third National Petition which was supposed to have five million signatures. It had two million, and many of them were bogus. They planned a mass meeting on Kennington Common to be followed by a procession carrying the petition to Parliament. Once again the Government was firm, and called the Duke of Wellington out of retirement to organise the army. The procession found its way blocked by troops with artillery and it dispersed quietly. They were allowed to send their petition on its way in a cab, but Parliament, of course, rejected it.

Chartism lingered for a few years, but after 1848 it was never again important.

Reasons for Failure. It is significant that apart from the impractical idea of annual Parliaments, every point in the Charter has since become 212 law. The aims of the movement were sound enough, so why did it fail?

Chartist procession in London—1848

In the first place the government of the day was particularly strong. By 1832 the middle classes had gained power from the aristocracy and they were determined not to lose it to the workers. The authorities were willing to meet force with force and made effective use of troops and police.

On the other hand the Chartists were not particularly strong. It is easy to blame their leaders and certainly men like Lovett and O'Connor were ineffectual. Also, their aims were ahead of their times, and some of their ideas, like the Land Society, were unrealistic. However, the rank and file were even more wayward. There were counter-attractions, for example, the Ten Hours Movement which promised less work, and the Anti-Corn Law League which promised cheaper food. Both of these were more attractive than the right to vote. Even more important, the ordinary workers could not keep their interest. During a depression, when they were out of work and hungry, they would join processions, attend meetings, sign petitions or even risk life and limb in a riot. However, when their stomachs were full, all these things were too much trouble. Chartism failed because the British working man lacked the will to make it succeed.

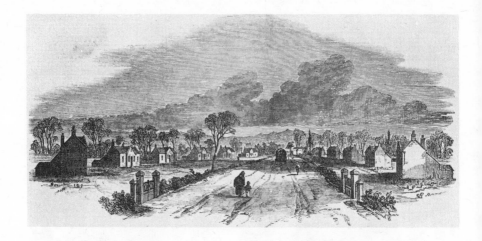

This picture is of a Chartist settlement, Snig's End in Gloucestershire.

Questions

1. At what period were Chartists interested in starting settlements of this kind?
2. How did they imagine life would be in these settlements?
3. Why are the houses alike and equally spaced?
4. Why are they so far apart?
5. Describe the business arrangements of the settlements—purchase of land etc.
6. How successful were these arrangements?
7. What settlement was named after a Chartist leader? Where was it?
8. How long did it last?

CHARTISTS AT BURNLEY, LANCASHIRE, 1842

Groups of idlers stood in the street, their faces haggard with famine, and their eyes rolling with that fierce and uneasy expression which I have often noticed in maniacs. Each man had his own tale of sorrow to tell; their stories were complicated details of misery and suffering, gradual in their approach and grinding in their result. "We want not charity, but employment" was their unanimous declaration. I found them all Chartists, but with this difference,—that the block printers and handloom weavers united to their Chartism a hatred of machinery, which was far from being shared by the factory operatives. The latter also deprecated anything like an appeal to physical force, while the former strenuously urged an appeal to arms. I heard some openly advocate the burning down of mills in order to compel the factory hands to join an insurrectionary movement.
(Cooke Taylor—Tour of Lancashire.)

Questions

1. Why have the men of Burnley become Chartists?
2. Which groups want violent action? Why?
3. Who wants more peaceful action? Why?
4. What names are normally given to these two divisions of the Chartist movement?

THE COLLAPSE OF THE CHARTIST MOVEMENT IN 1848

In the spring of 1848 the Chartist movement assumed an astonishing rapidity. Never was a time of greater power. The middle class were ready to make concessions; the governing faction were paralysed into inactivity, and yet the people were frustrated—not by the hands

of the Whig oligarchy but by their own. The movement stood in a proud position on the last day of the National Convention. It was strong and united, and no hostile power dared assail it. Well might the Attorney-General say at my trial that: "We had caused them many a sleepless night." But when division and discord had been seen among our ranks; when a separation had taken place between "moral force" and "physical force" men; when, out of 100 delegates summoned only 60 came to the Assembly; when even the money for its support became deficient; then the Whig faction saw it was the hour to strike: it said, "They are fighting among themselves; Now crush them". But, I ask you, had that assembly met in its full numbers; had the working classes poured up the voice of their sympathy from far and near; had they withheld from the gin-palace the money that would have given vigour to the Assembly; had the popular will been manifested day by day, from hundreds of gatherings; had every town marshalled its thousands from one end of Britain to the other, all lifting the same cry; then, I ask you, would the usurping faction have dared to strike? The failure of the Convention and the Assembly is more at the doors of the people who neglected to support them, than in any incapacity on their part. I believe that the less enlightened portions of the working classes feel little sympathy with political rights, unless they can be made to see the result in social benefits; I believe they do not yet fully understand the link between *Political Power and Social Reform*; there is little use in holding before them the Cap of Liberty, unless you hold *The Big Loaf* beside it.
(*Writings and Speeches of Ernest Jones, Chartist.*)

Questions

1. Why were the Chartists strong early in 1848?
2. How did the middle class and government feel, according to Jones?
3. What went wrong in the Chartist Assembly?
4. How should the workers have given support?
5. Who is most to blame for the failure?
6. Why did many workers not support the Chartists?
7. How could they be persuaded to do so?
8. What other movement of the 1840's seemed to offer "the big loaf"?
9. What were the main events of 1848?

Questions—Chapter Thirty-Three

1. What were the aims of the Chartist movement?
2. What two things, sometimes coming together, made the problem of poverty especially serious?
3. How did the Poor Law Amendment Act make it even worse?
4. Why did the working classes lose faith (a) in the middle classes (b) in the trade unions?
5. Name the three organisations that met in 1838. Who were their leaders?
6. Give the six points of the Charter.
7. What meeting gathered in London in 1839? What action did it take?
8. What did the government and Parliament do?
9. What division appeared in the Chartist movement? What did the more violent element do?
10. Describe what happened in 1842.
11. Why did many workers lose interest for a time?
12. What were the aims of the Co-operative Land Society?
13. What work did it do? With what success?
14. Why did Chartism revive in 1848?
15. What did the Chartists organise in that year?
16. How did the government deal with them?
17. How many points of the Charter have since become law?
18. What opposition did the Chartists face?
19. What was wrong with their leaders and their aims?
20. Why did working men not give them full support?

Further Work

1. Read about Lovett and Feargus O'Connor.
2. Read the full story of the Chartist riots in South Wales.
3. Find out what revolutions there were in Europe in 1848.
4. You are a working man who has joined the Chartists. Explain why you did so and say what you hope the movement will achieve.
5. It is 1850 and you are a government supporter. Give your opinion of the Chartist movement and say why you think it is a failure.

CHAPTER 34

The Co-operative Movement

The modern Co-operative movement is a large complex of shops, factories and commercial organisations. The idea behind it is that its profits should be given back to the people who use its services. The customers are the owners, and not any private individual or group of shareholders. It took some time to discover how to organise all this.

The Early Nineteenth Century. There were people who felt that in industry, the workers should have the profits, and that in a shop, the customers should have them. There were numbers of experiments to try and bring this about.

There were some co-operatives of producers. Craftsmen like handloom weavers who were threatened with competition from factories, joined together. They bought their own raw materials and they sold the finished goods, so that they kept the profits for themselves. Co-operatives of producers did not succeed. They could not compete either with experienced businessmen, or with factories.

There were also co-operatives of consumers. A number of people would open a shop, and then they would buy goods from it at cost price. This idea failed because without profits the shop could not build up capital. Also, it is not easy to work out the true cost price of goods in advance, and the shops did not always charge enough to cover expenses.

Finally there were some remarkable attempts by Robert Owen to use the co-operative movement to reform the whole of society. He set out his ideas in his book, "A New View of Society". He had a vision of everyone living in "villages of co-operation" where they worked for the common good, not for themselves.

217

A view of Owen's 'Village of Co-operation'

To prepare the way, Owen organised labour exchanges, that is, places where workers could exchange their labour. They brought their goods to a store and took tickets representing their hours of work. They then went round the store and exchanged the tickets for things into which other craftsmen had put the same amount of time. A weaver, for example, might bring in a piece of cloth and go away with a pair of shoes. He had exchanged his labour with the shoemaker's. The labour exchanges had some success, but they failed in the end, because unlike shops they could not refuse articles they would be unlikely to sell. Their shelves became piled with unwanted goods.

In 1839 Owen established what he hoped would be the first of many villages of co-operation. This was at Queenswood in Hampshire. By 1845 it had failed.

The Rochdale Pioneers. It was a little group of weavers in Rochdale who were the first to make a lasting success of a co-operative shop. Twenty-eight of them saved 2d a week until they had £1 each. In 1844 they hired the ground floor of a warehouse in Toad Lane, and opened a small retail shop. It was at this little shop that the modern co-operative movement began. There were several reasons for success.

In the first place they never gave credit, so they did not lose money through bad debts. Secondly, they gave value for money; for example there was no adulteration of food, with plaster in the flour and mahogany sawdust in the coffee. However, the main reason the Rochdale pioneers did well was that they sold their goods at the full retail price. The profits were indeed returned to the customers but they came later, as a dividend, when all the costs of running the shop had

218

been met. In this way there was no risk of being too generous, and going out of business as a result. The customers liked it, too. Keeping their dividend in the shop was a painless way of saving and they could draw a useful lump sum when they needed it. This in turn helped the shop. Since the customers kept in their dividend, it built up capital and was soon able to expand.

Co-operative shops began to appear in many northern towns. Private traders became worried and jealous and put pressure on the whole-salers, who, as a result, refused to supply the co-operatives. Their answer was to open their own wholesale business, which they did in 1863, calling it the "North of England Co-operative Wholesale Society". Ten years later they dropped the words "North of England" from the name, as by then they were covering the whole country.

Later Developments. The next step was to build factories to supply the wholesale warehouses. The first of these was the Crumpsall Biscuit Works near Manchester. Later there were factories for boots at Leicester, soap at Durham, tobacco at Manchester and cotton at Bolton.

The co-operative movement has since gone into commerce. It runs insurance, banking, travel agencies, and has its own fleet of tramp steamers.

There has been social activity as well. The movement has done good work for adult education, providing lectures and classes for its members. It has also played a part in politics. In 1917 the Co-operative Party was founded and it has had up to twenty M.P.s in Parliament. However, it usually helps the Labour Party with funds and moral support, rather than field candidates of its own.

Also a system of democratic control was developed for the shops. With a Co-operative the customers not only take the profits but, indirectly, run the shop as well. Shareholders meet to elect a committee of management and this in its turn appoints and supervises the staff.

The Importance of the Co-operative Movement. In 1970 the Co-operative movement controlled 8% of the retail trade of this country. This shows that it is certainly important, but that it is nowhere near taking over our capitalist system, as some people once thought it might. In recent years competition from highly efficient private firms has stopped it increasing its share of business. None the less it has done a good deal of useful work.

In the first place it helped to increase the standard of living of the working classes. Secondly, it helped by its competition to put down vicious trading practices, like adulterating food. Thirdly, through its system of elected management committees, it has given ordinary people practical lessons in the workings of democracy.

219

Questions

1. What is meant by "labour exchange"? (See top of note).
2. Whose idea was it to start such organisations? Find his signature on the note.
3. Which branch issued this note?
4. How much is it worth?
5. How was it possible to obtain a note like this?
6. What can be done with it?
7. What did the founder of labour exchanges hope would develop from them?
8. What happened to labour exhanges in the end and why?

FOUNDING A CO-OPERATIVE SHOP, 1865

The members held meetings and subscribed about £20. Two were sent to Newcastle to make the first purchases. They laid out the money to the best of their ability, buying a cask of herrings, a side of bacon, a firkin of butter, coffee, tea, sugar, tobacco etc., and not omitting lucifer matches into which they went largely. Their return was looked for anxiously. Cramlington being on a hill, with two roads leading from Newcastle, men were seen walking from one end to the other, like smugglers looking for a lugger. At last a little spring cart made its appearance, which caused some to come out and stand laughing at the madcaps. The cart having got to the little room, the shop was opened. The reader can imagine how the parcels would be made up by inexperienced men, but the purchasers had their weight. The stock was nearly sold out, except the matches, on the first Friday night and the two men went to buy more. They went on this way for the first three months, doubling and trebling their orders, till at last the dividend was declared. The number of members now rapidly increased. Men who had been fettered to a shop by the credit system all their lives began to look for themselves. Ladies, instead of running up ruinous accounts at ordinary shops became energetic supporters of the new movement. In the first quarter £450 was received, realising a profit of £39. The receipts of the quarter ending March 1873 amounted to £23 000 of which £2478 was profit. The members had increased from 80 to 1688.

(Fynes—*Miners of Northumberland and Durham*.)

Questions
1. How was capital raised to start the shop?
2. What goods did they buy? What mistake was made?
3. How did different people feel about the new shop?
4. What sort of service did it give?
5. When and why did numbers increase?
6. What good habits did the shop encourage?
7. Draw a table to show how the shop prospered.

Questions
1. Why does this shop sell so many different goods?
2. Should the owner have done well?
3. Why do her customers need credit?
4. Why does she let them have it?
5. What problem does it create for her and them?
6. How would a co-operative shop act differently?
7. What would happen if one opened near by?

A VILLAGE SHOP
At one end of the little street is the shop of Judith Kent, widow, "Licensed to vend tea, coffee, tobacco and snuff". These, however, form but a small part of the multifarious merchandise of Mrs. Kent, whose shop is the only one on the hamlet. In her window, candles, bacon, sugar, mustard and soap flourish amidst calicoes, oranges, dolls, ribands and gingerbread. Crockeryware was piled on one side of her door way, Dutch cheese and Irish butter encumbered the other; brooms and brushes rested against the wall; and ropes of onions and bunches of red herrings hung from the ceiling. She sold bread, meat and garden stuff, and engrossed the whole trade of Hilton Cross. Notwithstanding this monopoly, the world goes ill with poor Judith. She is a mild, pleasant-looking middle-aged woman, with a heart too soft for her calling. She cannot say No! to the poor creatures who come to her on a Saturday night, to seek bread for their children, however deep they may already be in her debt, or however certain it is that their husbands are, at that moment, spending, at the Four Horse Shoes, the money that should have supported their wives and families. She cannot say No! as a prudent woman might have said; and, accordingly, half the poor people in the parish may be found on her books, whilst she herself is gradually getting in arrears with her baker, her grocer and her landlord.
(Mitford—Our Village.)

Questions—Chapter Thirty-Four
1. What happens to the profits of a co-operative shop?
2. How were producers' co-operatives organised?
3. Why did they fail?
4. Why did the first co-operatives of consumers fail?
5. What was Robert Owen's aim for the co-operative movement?
6. How were his "labour exchanges" organised?
7. Why did they fail?
8. Where did he set up a "village of co-operation"?
9. Where did the modern co-operative movement begin? What name is given to the founders?
10. How did they return profits to the customers?
11. Why did customers like the method?
12. Why was it helpful to the shop?
13. Why did wholesalers refuse to supply co-operative shops?
14. How did co-operatives cope with the problem?
15. What factories were built?
16. What commercial work does the movement do?
17. Describe its social and political activities.
18. How are shops managed?
19. What has checked the growth of the movement?
20. Give three reasons for its importance. **221**

Further Work

1. Find out when your local co-operative society was founded.
2. What goods and services does it supply?
3. Read more about Robert Owen.
4. Read more about the Rochdale Pioneers.

5. A 19th century shopkeeper and a customer discuss the possibility of a co-operative being opened in their village. Write what they say.
6. You are helping to start one of the first co-operative shops. Explain why you are doing so, and how you propose to organise it. What mistakes will you try to avoid?

PART THREE

THE TWENTIETH CENTURY

SECTION NINE
Agriculture Since 1900

CHAPTER 35

Farming
1900-1939

By the early twentieth century the long depression in British farming was coming to an end. It is true that there was little improvement, but at least things were no longer becoming worse. An increase in world food prices had eased competition, while farmers had at last recognised that cereals were not profitable, except in the areas that favoured them most. Milk and quality meat made money, so their policy was "down corn, up horn". However, in the panic caused by the first world war a lot of grassland was ploughed to grow more food, and at the same time farmers began to make good money again. The prosperous times only lasted until 1921 and from then until 1939 there was a depression that was as bad as anything that had gone before. At the same time there was a social revolution in the countryside, as the landed aristocracy sold their land to their tenants.

The First World War. In 1914 British agriculture was in no condition to feed the country. There were farms that were simply neglected and while "down corn, up horn" had saved many from bankruptcy, it had cut total production drastically. While forty hectares of arable will feed 150 people, forty hectares of grass will only feed 15. The country was importing four-fifths of its cereals, two-fifths of its meat, three-quarters of its fruit, and all of its sugar.

On top of this, the war brought problems of its own. Farm labourers enlisted, and horses were commandeered for the army. There was a shortage of fertilisers, while machines were rusting in the barns and many of the craftsmen who could have repaired them were away in the forces.

In the face of all these problems, the Government, at first, did 224 surprisingly little. There was the Milner Report of 1915 on how to increase food production, and County War Agricultural Committees were set up to supervise farming in their areas. On the farms themselves, however, there were few changes. Then, towards the end of 1916 the Germans began unrestricted submarine warfare and the government was galvanised into action. The farmers would have to plough.

In the first place the Board of Agriculture set up a Food Production Department. It found a labour force of prisoners of war, women, and volunteers of all ages, including school children. It also supplied tractors. These had been quite rare in 1914, but were common enough by 1918. Next, farmers were promised a guaranteed price for their cereals and potatoes. Finally, a Cultivation of Lands Order gave the War Agricultural Committees powers to compel farmers to plough.

In farming, immediate results are impossible, but a good deal was done within the next two years. Almost half a million hectares extra were cropped in the 1917 harvest, and a further one million in 1918, just in time for the Armistice. The output of cereals and potatoes went up by about a half, though there was some decline in milk and meat because of the loss of grassland.

Boy Scouts helping with the harvest—1918   225

1918-1939. In the first few years of peace there was prosperity in most industries, including farming. Prices were high and Parliament felt it was safe enough to pass the Agricultural Act of 1920. It made farmers pay their workmen minimum wages, but at the same time guaranteed the prices for their cereals. In 1921, though, world prices fell alarmingly and the tax-payer was faced with a massive bill for farm subsidies. Parliament hurriedly repealed the Act of 1920.

The dismal story of the years before 1900 was now repeated, as our agriculture was once again exposed to the cold blast of foreign competition. Things were bad all the time, but worsened during the depression of the early 1930's.

Farmers reacted in various ways. The easiest was to neglect their holdings, and some of them did. Buildings, roads and enclosures went without repairs, and fields went without fertilisers. Other farmers went over to products that would sell at a better profit than cereals, and these were milk and meat. As a result, over one million hectares of arable went back to grass, which was as much as had been ploughed during the war. There were also attempts to increase productivity which, in the main, meant buying equipment. There were more tractors and milking machines, and the first combine harvesters appeared in this country.

The government also gave some help. Most of it came late, but as early as 1925 they decided to encourage the growing of sugar beet, and offered a subsidy for the crop. They hoped in this way to do something to check unemployment. They had some success, for by 1934 there were 160 000 hectares of beet and a new industry, beet sugar refining, had been created.

After the depression of 1931 the government was willing to do something for farming as a whole. In the first place there was direct financial help. Farms no longer had to pay rates and there were subsidies not only for sugar beet, but for cereals and cattle as well. Furthermore, the Agricultural Marketing Acts of 1931 and 1933 tried to secure fair prices. The idea was that there should be Marketing Boards for potatoes, hops, milk and pigs. The Boards were to limit the amounts that individual farmers could produce to avoid flooding the market, but in return would pay them guaranteed prices.

Finally, since the depression had killed faith in free trade, there was to be some protection from foreign competition. Here, though, there was a problem. As we were an industrial country, our prosperity depended more on our manufacturers than on our farmers. So that we could have a good market for our industrial products the government had made an agreement with the Commonwealth countries at the Ottawa Conference of 1932. They were to take our goods, without putting duties on them,
226 and we were to do the same for their foodstuffs. All that could be done

to protect farming was to tax food imports from countries outside the Commonwealth, and they were comparatively unimportant.

The government measures had little success. Their financial help was not enough; with the exception of the one for potatoes the Marketing Boards were failures; the import duties only succeeded in making the Danes unhappy, without doing anything significant for our own farmers.

Social Changes. The depression in farming affected the people whose lives depended on it.

In the first place there was the failure of the government to increase the number of small holdings. They had already attempted this before the war, and then in 1919 the Land Settlement Act aimed to provide ex-servicemen with little farms as part of the promise of "homes fit for heroes". There were indeed a number of small-holdings set up under the Act, but fortunately for the efficiency of the industry they were not enough to check the general trend. This was for large farms to grow at the expense of small ones.

Next, there was the continued flight of farm labourers to the towns, which went on in spite of the high level of industrial unemployment. In 1924 farm labourers could earn, on an average, £1.40 a week, while builders' labourers had £1.80 and bricklayers £2.65. Not surprisingly, they left the land at the rate of 10 000 a year.

Finally, there was an end to the old landed aristocracy. The great estate was no longer a status symbol, and all you needed was a nice house in the country. The land itself had become a liability so its owners were anxious to sell. Fortunately for them the post-war boom gave farmers the impression it was a good time to buy and in the four years from 1918 to 1921 there was a veritable flood of sales. Not since the dissolution of the monasteries under Henry VIII had so much land changed hands in so short a time—probably it amounted to one quarter of the country.

Farmers did not, as a rule, have the money to buy outright, so they borrowed from building societies. Their repayments were usually higher than their rents had been, and when the boom broke they were in trouble. Instead of considerate landlords who were willing to help in difficult times, there were impersonal institutions demanding their cash in full, whatever the consequences.

This problem, on top of all the others, meant that farmers, however intelligent and hard-working, could only scrape a living. It took the Second World War to save them.

Questions

1. What season of the year is this?
2. What work is the farm hand doing?
3. What device has he to help him?
4. How are the cows kept in place? Why is this method better than tying them with ropes?
5. What other equipment was there to help dairy farmers?
6. How would the policy of "three acres and a cow" have prevented the use of new equipment?
7. Why, between 1900 and 1939, did many farmers give up growing crops and go over to dairying?
8. At what time, during the same period, did the opposite happen?

CONDITION OF FARM LAND IN THE 1930's

There are great acreages of permanent pasture that have had no implement of any sort on them for thirty years, and many that have scarcely been trodden by man or beast during the same period.

Bracken has gained considerably on fields bordering on woodlands and rough grazings. I can give an example of 22 farms in Radnorshire, that stand between 800 and 1000 feet. Not many years ago wheat was grown; now the plough is not active, the pastures are outrun, and fences are broken down. As much as 18% of the acreage is in bracken. This shows how high land of much value is reverting to rough grazings.

The acreage under rushes on the permanent grasslands is large, and in recent years there has been an increase. Rushes may occur in great blocks of 50 or more acres together. On 18 farms in Cardiganshire they dominated 410 acres out of 1620. Here this was primarily due to periodic flooding, the trouble being increased because the farmers do not make an effort to keep all the waterways clear. The area under wheat in the 1870's

was 3½ million acres. By 1931 it had fallen to less than 1¼. When we think of the enormous advances that have been made with artificial fertilizers, mechanical aids and the science of crop production, to say nothing of the increase in population, this dwindling of our arable acreage seems incredible.
(Stapledon—The Land Today and Tomorrow.)

Questions
1. How long has some pasture been neglected?
2. What land is reverting to bracken?
3. How have the Radnorshire farms been neglected?
4. What use is land invaded by bracken?
5. What plant is giving trouble in Cardiganshire?
6. Why is it spreading?
7. What has happened to wheat farming?
8. Why does Stapledon find the change "incredible"?
9. What explanation would you give for the conditions described here?

Questions [see letter on next page]
1. What is the date of this letter?
2. Who sent it?
3. What is their authority for sending it?
4. What instruction does it contain?
5. What reason does it give for making the order?
6. What had caused the emergency?
7. What other measures were taken by the Government at this time?
8. What success did they have?

Questions—Chapter Thirty-Five
1. What was meant by "down corn, up horn"?
2. How did this policy cause problems after 1914?
3. What problems did the war cause farmers?

4. What Report was issued in 1915?
5. What organisations were set up to supervise farming?
6. What finally made the government take action?
7. What measures did it take?
8. How much extra land was ploughed in 1917—1918?
9. What products increased? What decreased, Why?
10. Why did Parliament repeal the Agricultural Act of 1920?
11. How did farmers react to the depression?
12. What new crop did the government encourage?
13. What else was subsidised after 1931?
14. What were the duties of the Marketing Boards?
15. Why did the government only give limited protection from competition from abroad?
16. What success did the government measures have?
17. What was the aim of the Land Settlement Act?
18. Why did labourers leave the land?
19. Why did the aristocracy sell their land?
20. Why did farmers buy it? How did this create problems for them?

Further Work
1. Find pictures of farms, farm equipment, villages, country people and the countryside generally before 1939. Old picture postcards can be valuable.
2. Talk to people who were in farming before 1939. Ask them to describe the problems they had.
3. Which of the big country houses in your area have been abandoned by their owners?
4. Read about the German submarine campaign during the First World War.
5. Find out more about the Ottawa Conference 1932.
6. You are an official in the Board of Agriculture in the 1930's. Explain what the problems of farming are and say how the Government is trying to help. What hope have you of success?

229

Bucks Agricultural Executive Committee.

Telephone
Aylesbury No. 158.
Telegrams
"Growmore, Aylesbury."
Executive Officer:
G. E. NEWTON.
Secretary
R. DAVEY

Hintlesham House,

29, New Street,

Aylesbury.

....10th April............1918.

To ...Mrs...Willatts...

District ....Eton............................. Parish ......Wraysbury..69...................

Farm ....Tithe.................................

Sir,

On behalf of the Executive Committee acting under the power conferred upon them by Regulation 2M (1) (e) of the Defence of the Realm (Consolidation) Regulations I have to require you to cultivate the land contained in the schedule hereunder in the manner therein indicated.

I may say for your information that the terms of the Regulation referred to are as follows:—

"2M.—(1) Where the Board of Agriculture and Fisheries, after such consultation with the Food Controller as may be arranged, are of opinion that, with a view to maintaining the food supply of the country, it is expedient that they should exercise the powers given to them under this regulation, the Board may (e) by notice served on the occupier of any land require him to cultivate the land in accordance with such requirements as the Board may think necessary or desirable for maintaining the food supply of the country and may prescribe in the notice."

Yours faithfully,

Leonard Herbert

Chairman of the Executive Committee

SCHEDULE.

Ordnance No.	Area.	
167.	8.029 acres	To be ploughed before 15th August, 1918, suitably prepared, and sown with wheat for the 1919 Harvest, the sowing to be completed by 1st December, 1918.

CHAPTER 36

Farming
Since 1939

During the Second World War, much the same sort of thing happened in farming, as during the First. Grassland was ploughed, food production increased, and the industry flourished. None the less there were differences, because in 1939 the government was better prepared and its organisation was efficient. Even more important for farming, prosperity did not end with the war, but has continued to the present day.

World War II. 1939-1945. The Second World War brought the same problem as the First. The country was not growing enough food. In 1939 we were importing, for example, nearly 90% of our wheat, and we urgently needed shipping space for war materials, especially as U-boats were soon sinking large numbers of merchant vessels. Once again, farmers had to plough their grassland so that they could increase their output.

To see that they did so, the government took the same measures as before. In the first place they gave guaranteed prices for crops. Secondly, they offered subsidies for ploughing grassland, for cultivating wastes and for improvements like liming, ditching and draining. Thirdly they saw to it that farmers had the means to do the work. Once again, men had left the land to join the services, so the government found a labour force of prisoners of war and women. Even more important, there were tractors. They had been increasing in numbers between the wars so that in 1939 there were already 56 000 of them; by 1945 there were over 200 000. There were more of other machines, too, like cultivators, disc harrows and combine harvesters. Finally, the government encouraged the use of fertilisers which, before the war, farmers had just not been able to afford.

To organise all these services there were once again County War Agricultural Committees. They gave help and advice, and allocated resources like labour, machinery and fertilisers. They also had considerable powers. In spite of all the encouragement the government was offering, there were a few farmers who refused to cooperate. They soon found that the County War Agricultural Committees could compel them.

To sum up so far, then, the government was encouraging farmers to plough more land and to improve their methods, while giving them the money, the labour, the machinery and the fertilisers to do so. At the same time the County War Agricultural Committees had powers to deal with the few who were reluctant.

However, most of them responded well. The amount of land under the plough went up from five million hectares to eight million hectares, an increase of over 50%, while output went up 70%. Farmers were not only working harder, they were working more efficiently.

So far this is much the same story as World War I, but there were differences, because the government had learnt its lesson and was better organised.

In the first place, there were no delays. Even before war broke out farmers had been offered a subsidy of £2 for every acre of land they ploughed. Also, there was a good supply of tractors in hand, and ready for use in the grassland areas where they were still rather scarce.

Secondly, they did not rely only on prisoners of war and voluntary labour. Women were conscripted as well as men, and many found their way into the properly organised Women's Land Army.

Thirdly, there was no loss of milk. With so much ploughing, grassland products would have to fall, but they cut down on meat, not milk. It was better to import meat than feeding stuffs, because it took up far less shipping space. Milk on the other hand, cannot be imported, and it is an essential food, so there was a subsidy for dairy cattle. Farmers used their dwindling pastures efficiently, so that by the end of the war they were producing more milk than at the beginning. This is in marked contrast with the First World War when they ploughed their grasslands without due thought, and milk production declined along with meat.

1945-1960. After the end of the war, British farming was not allowed to decline again. There were a number of reasons:

In the first place we had already gone into two World Wars quite unable to feed ourselves, and the folly of this was now clear. Secondly, there was a world shortage of food, that made it expensive. The third reason, though, was the most important and the most long-lasting. The country was desperately short of dollars, so it was important to buy as little as possible from the U.S.A. and Canada. Accordingly the government did a great deal to encourage our own farmers.

In 1947 Parliament passed an Agricultural Act which guaranteed prices. The Ministry of Agriculture fixes them every year, so that farmers have a fair profit. There were marketing boards which took the produce and saved the farmer the problem of finding customers. There were subsidies that have been so high that they have accounted for two thirds of the farmers' incomes. There was also a National Agricultural Advisory Service which gave scientific information and advice on such things as soils, crops, cattle and farm management.

Because of government help, farmers have had the money, and the encouragement, to improve their methods.

Any modern farm yard will contain machinery and equipment worth thousands of pounds, including such things as combine harvesters and grain driers. On dairy farms, the milking is done by machine, and there are the highest standards of cleanliness.

Breeds of animals have improved. Beef cattle, pigs, sheep and poultry all give more meat and at higher food ratios, which means they eat less for every pound that they increase in weight. Once it was rare to find a dairy cow that gave more than 4500 litres of milk a year, but now it is common and many will give over double that amount.

Out on the fields, hedges have been uprooted to gain land and give the big machines room to work. Fertilisers are always used, and in the correct quantity for the crop and the soil. There are sprays that will kill both weeds and pests, and they have done a lot to improve yields.

The result has been a still further increase in production. No new land has come into cultivation since the war, and indeed much has been lost for building and roads, but output has gone up by one third. The farmers themselves are more prosperous than they have been in time of peace since 1870. In 1960, for example, incomes were six times what they had been in 1939.

In one respect, though, farming has not recovered and that is in its relative importance for the economy of the country. Around 1800 30% of the national income came from farming, which was considerably more than from all the manufacturing and mining industries put together. By 1870, the figure had dropped to 15% and in 1935 it was 4%. Since the war it has crept up a few points, but even with forestry and fishing it is still under 5%. From being the only industry that really mattered, it is now one among many. Drink and tobacco count for nearly as much.

throughout the country by trained instructors. This is but one example of the efficiency drive which led to the greatest harvest on record—1943.

The 1943 harvest was spectacular, with an acreage not quite double that of 1939, but a yield increased by 110%. This is all the more remarkable since the increases came largely from the non-corn growing counties. Thus, Cumberland with 341 acres of wheat in 1939 had 19654 in 1943.

2. *Land Use*

(000's of Acres).	1937	1944
Permanent Grass	17338	10804
Temporary Grass	3668	4233
Arable	8357	13711

(Stamp—*The Land of Britain.*)

Questions
1. *What work are these girls doing?*
2. *Is it suitable for women? (Look at the size of the fork).*
3. *How might this job have been done later during the war?*
4. *How can you tell the girls are not used to farm work?*
5. *From what jobs might they have come?*
6. *Why are they needed on the farm?*
7. *Who has sent them here?*
8. *How else did farmers find labour?*

Questions
1. *Why was grassland ploughed during the war?*
2. *Why was ploughing not enough in itself?*
3. *Do more machines mean more efficiency?*
4. *Why did farmers need instruction?*
5. *How successful was the campaign? What was remarkable about its success?*
6. *Draw diagrams to show the changes in land use.*

THE PLOUGH-UP CAMPAIGN DURING THE SECOND WORLD WAR
1. The objective to put at first a million acres of old grassland under the plough and then a further million, and so on caught the imagination, and ploughing was almost regarded as an end in itself. But a 10% increase in yield on existing ploughed land, would have given as large an increase in production as ploughing another million acres. Accordingly, the second practical step was to increase yields by using the most suitable seeds, the provision of lime and in many other ways. The third step was the amazing mechanisation farming underwent. This does not necessarily indicate more efficiency. It depends on whether the implements are correctly used. A tractor can draw a properly set three-furrow plough with less consumption of fuel than it can draw a badly set two-furrow plough, so that plough setting was explained

CHANGES AT LEIGHTON-BROMSWOLD, HUNTINGDONSHIRE

234

Crops (Per cent of farmland).	1920	1970
Cereals	32	67
Fallow	10	—
Potatoes, sugar beet and other crops.	4.5	25
Grass	53.5	8

Hedges	1945	1972
Average Field Size in acres	19	45
Length of hedges per acre	95	58
Hedgerow trees per 100 acres	59	12

The number of holdings has been halved since 1920 resulting in an increase in the average size from 122 to 317 acres. Some farmers, however, farm several holdings and the average amount of land worked by farmers exceeds 1000 acres.

65% of the labour force is provided by the farmers and their families and today there is only one permanent worker to every 240 acres, compared with one to 74 acres in 1930.

(Westmacott—*New Agricultural Landscapes*.)

Questions

1. Draw diagrams to illustrate the tables.
2. Why has arable farming increased in modern times?
3. What are the advantages of increasing the sizes of (a) fields (b) farms?
4. What does the use of fallow tell you about a farm?
5. How has the labour force changed?
6. How has the landscape been changed?

Questions—Chapter Thirty-Six

1. How much of our wheat was imported in 1939?

2. In what ways did the government encourage farmers to plough?
3. What local authorities supervised them? What powers did they have?
4. How much did the amount of ploughed land increase?
5. How much did output increase?
6. In what ways had the government been ready?
7. How was the labour force organised?
8. What grassland product was increased?
9. Give three reasons why farming did not decline after the Second World War.
10. What did the Agricultural Act of 1947 say?
11. How can farm products be sold easily?
12. How much income have farmers sometimes had from subsidies?
13. What organisation gives farmers advice?
14. What machinery is found on modern farms?
15. What is meant by increasing food ratios?
16. How much milk will a good dairy cow give a year?
17. Why have hedges been uprooted?
18. Name two ways in which chemicals are used.
19. How much has output increased since the war?
20. How much of the nation's income is produced by farming today? What was the figure for 1800?

Further Work

1. Find pictures of the machines used on a modern farm and, if possible, see them at work.
2. Ask people who remember the Second World War about the food problem.
3. Ask people in farming what changes they have seen and what they think of government policies for agriculture.
4. How has the landscape changed in your area in recent years—new buildings, roads, uprooting of hedgerows etc.?
5. How has modern farming affected wild life, plants and animals?
6. Write the history of a farm since 1939, preferably a real one, but if not, an imaginary one.

235

SECTION TEN
Transport Since 1900

CHAPTER 37

Railways
and Shipping

Part 1   Railways

Since the First World War, railways have been fighting a losing battle with road transport. To meet it they have introduced technical improvements and changed their organisation, but in the end the only way to check their mounting losses was to close thousands of kilometres of track.

Competition with Road Transport. Motor transport on the new tarmacadam roads of the twentieth century has many advantages over rail transport. For passengers, a car is more convenient because it can go everywhere. Over any but the longest distances it is quicker, since although a train will travel faster, its passengers have the tedious problem of making their way to and from the station. Buses have fewer advantages than cars, but they are much cheaper than trains. For example, in 1939 the average fare by road was under 1p per kilometre and by rail 6p.

When it comes to freight, there is much to be said for the railways. However, they have even lost a lot of that traffic. Before the war, road haulage firms realised they had a decided advantage, because they knew just how much railways charged. They could undercut them for goods they found it convenient to carry, but overcharge for others. In this way, they selected just what they wanted, while the railways were left with articles like coal. In fact, though, they held their own with freight traffic until the Second World War. In 1939, road transport carried 100 million tonnes of goods, and the railways 265 million tonnes.

During the Second World War, petrol was rationed and all but essential travel by road came to an end. Almost the whole burden of inland transport was thrown onto the railways, which were once again busy and making good profits. In the long run, though, this worked to their disadvantage, because there was a minimum of repair and maintenance. When the war ended, track and rolling stock were virtually worn out.

After 1945, traffic soon went back to the roads. More and more people were able to afford cars, while heavy lorries, helped by motorways, took a lot of freight. From 1952 to 1962, for example, freight traffic on the railways fell by a quarter, while on the roads it almost doubled.

The battle is not over, though. In the 1970's petrol became expensive, roads congested, and the railways more efficient. If a channel tunnel is ever built, the railways could do well on several important routes.

Technical Improvements. The railways tried to meet the challenge from the roads by making improvements. Before 1939 they gave some of their services a little glamour with engines like the "Silver Jubilee" and the "Coronation Scot". They increased the speed of their trains. In 1914 only four services ran at an average speed of over 100 km.p.h., while in 1938, there were 107. That same year the "Mallard" travelled at just over 200 km.p.h., a record that was unbroken until the 1970's.

The London and Suburban lines were electrified, making them more efficient, and giving passengers a faster, cleaner and more comfortable run.

238 *An early electrified line; Manchester to Altrincham*

For freight they introduced containers, which made it easier to transport delicate goods. They also had vans and lorries so that they could give their customers a door to door service.

Since 1945, improvements have continued. Main lines have been electrified as, for example, London to Birmingham and Manchester. Elsewhere, diesels have replaced steam locomotives. For passengers, there are fast inter-city services, and for goods there are freightliner trains.

It must be remembered, too, that all these improvements have been carried out in spite of falling profits down to 1956, and considerable losses since then.

Organisation. In the nineteenth century the government tried to encourage competition. They felt it would make railways more efficient, and keep down fares. They changed their minds during the first world war when they took them over and ran them as one organisation. It became clear how much time and money could be saved in such ways as cutting out duplicate services and pooling rolling stock, so that it could travel on any line, not just that of its owners.

When the First World War ended, many people wanted the railways nationalised, but the government returned them to their owners. It did, however, pass the Railways Act of 1921 which compelled the 125 separate companies to amalgamate into just four. They were the London, Midland and Scottish (L.M.S.), the London and North-Eastern Railway (L.N.E.R.), the Great Western Railway (G.W.R.) and the Southern Railway (S.R.). Each company had complete control in its own area so that if, for example, there were two competing services anywhere, then it could stop one of them. From trying to prevent monopolies, the government was now encouraging them. To protect the public from overcharging they fixed the combined profits from all four companies at £51 million a year. They need not have worried, because the best the railways ever did was in 1928 when they made £41 million.

During the Second World War the government again took over the railways, and when it ended, decided to nationalise them. Parliament did so by the Transport Act of 1947. There was little choice. The railways needed so much spent on them, and were likely to make so little profit in peace time, that if they had gone back to private ownership, they would have fallen into ruin. Railwaymen knew this quite well, so nationalisation was also needed to show them their jobs were safe, and keep up their morale.

What nationalisation could not do, though, was to stop competition from the roads. Modernisation plans achieved too little and by 1956 the railways were losing money. Dr. Beeching, the Chairman of British Rail, was asked what should be done and his answer, given in the Beeching 239

Report of 1963, was to close unprofitable lines and stations. His idea was carried out, so that by 1970 20 000 miles of track were reduced to 13 000. The railways have gone on losing money, but not as quickly as they would have done without the "Beeching Axe".

Like other Victorian industries the railways faced competition in the twentieth century. They fought it by trying to become more efficient and by reducing their size. Neither method brought much success, but they have refused to die, and are still essential for the economy of the country.

Part 2　Shipping

In shipping, as in railways, there was a good deal of technical progress in the twentieth century, but at the same time there were problems because of competition of various kinds.

Technical Changes. In the first place there have been new aids to navigation. The gyro compass was invented in 1908, while during the Second World War there was the development of the Decca navigation device and, even more important, radar.

Engines were improved. First of all, oil fuel was used instead of coal to drive steam turbines, then diesel engines replaced steam. They take up less room for the same power, setting space free for cargo.

Some remarkable ships were built. Before the Second World War the transatlantic liners were the pride of the merchant navy. There was the *Queen Mary* of 82 000 tonnes, launched in 1934, and the *Queen Elizabeth* of 85 000 tonnes, launched in 1938. With their cinemas, swimming pools, bars and restaurants, they were the last word in floating luxury hotels.

Since the war it is the cargo ship that has developed. There are container vessels which are easy to load and unload, and there are ships designed especially for particular cargoes. The most important are, of course, oil tankers. The giants among them are probably the most impressive merchant vessels now afloat.

Problems in the Shipping Industry. Before the Second World War it was the cargo vessels that faced the most serious problems. There was a decline in world trade, while the number of ships was increasing; other governments paid their shipping companies subsidies while, up until 1935, our own did not; some foreigners, like the Greeks, cut their costs and their charges by paying their sailors low wages; Great Britain no longer exported as much coal, so many ships had to make their outward voyages in ballast.

Liners, on the other hand, fared rather better. They belonged to large, well organised companies, and they had a regular income from mail. None the less, one firm, the Royal Mail Company, collapsed during the depression, in 1931.

After the war, cargo vessels, especially oil tankers, did relatively well because world trade was booming. Liners, on the other hand, met competition from passenger aircraft, and found it increasingly difficult to make a profit. The *Q.E. 1* ended her life as the University of Hongkong, while building the *Q.E. 2* might yet prove an expensive mistake.

"It was possible for a single solitary passenger to turn up for tea in the dim depths of the grand saloon and sit, magnificently alone, while a dozen white-jacketed stewards stood about, alert to his command. Then, as he chose his sandwiches and cakes a shadowy figure at the piano would shiver the air with selections from "Rose Marie" and "Desert Song". Not even the dining room in "Citizen Kane" was emptier."
(Brinnin—*The Sway of the Grand Saloon*.)

Questions

The picture shows the restaurant of the Queen Mary in 1939

1. Can you tell this picture was taken on a ship?
2. What has been done to make the room luxurious?
3. What does the number of waiters tell you about the service?
4. Why did the Cunard Company take so much trouble?
5. The extract describes the same room in 1965.

Say what change has taken place and explain why.

STOPPING-TRAIN SERVICES

Stopping services developed as the predominant form of rural public transport in the last century, when the only alternative was the horse-drawn vehicle and when the availability of private transport of any kind was very limited. Even in those days, when there was no satisfactory alternative, many of them failed to pay. Today, rail stopping services and bus services serve the same purpose. Buses carry the greater part of the passengers moving by public transport in rural areas, and, as well as competing with each other, both forms of public transport are fighting a losing battle against private transport. In 1938 the number of private cars was 1 944 000 and in 1961 there were 6 000 000. In addition, in 1961 there were 1 900 000 power driven cycles.

It is questionable whether British Railways meet as much as 10% of the total and declining demand for public rural transport. To do so, they provide services accounting for about 40% of the total passenger train mileage of the railways as a whole, and most of the trains carry an average of less than a bus-load and lose nearly twice as much as they collect in fares.

It is obvious that a high proportion of stopping train services ought to be discontinued as soon as possible, and that many of the lightly loaded lines over which they operate ought to close as well unless they carry exceptional freight traffic. (*Beeching Report*—1963.)

Questions

1. When were stopping trains once important?
2. What disadvantage have they always had?
3. What alternatives do people have now?
4. What share of public transport in the rural areas does British Rail have?
5. What proportion of its total passenger services goes to meet this small need?
6. How much of the cost of stopping train services is met by the fares they collect?
7. What is the solution to the problem?

QUEEN ELIZABETH 1 IN A STORM

With each swell her beautifully raked prow rose majestically; then she settled, again slowly, down into the sea. As she descended, the enormous force of the ocean was absorbed along the plates all down her hull, a fifth of a mile to her stern. Furniture shuddered and the wood panelling groaned. In this sea, long passageways paralleling the hull were uphill then downhill walks, and one had the feeling that the tubelike hallways gave a twist as the liner drove against the sea. Meanwhile thirty-seven large public rooms rose, fell and shook.

Pitch and roll are old enemies to Commodore Marr. Pitch he blames as the primary cause of seasickness. Roll has its hazards as well. The trouble arises as a passenger walks parallel to the ship's course, and a roll suddenly forces him in an opposite direction. Then he may find himself sprawling on the deck or bouncing his head off a bulkhead.

The people who operate ships like the *Queen Elizabeth* never use expensive advertising space to illustrate their liners sailing through rough weather. The advertisements feature open-deck scenes with people relaxing, playing games, or swimming in a sunlit pool against a brilliant blue sea in the background.

COMMODORE MARR EXPLAINS CUNARD'S POLICY

We're as much in the hotel business these days as in the shipping business. Cunard wants us to make each crossing more and more like a cruise. You know our slogan, "Getting there is half the fun." (Leonard Stevens—*The Elizabeth*.)

Questions

1. In what ways does the storm make life unpleasant and dangerous?
2. What is the difference between "pitch" and "roll"?
3. How do ship owners advertise voyages?
4. What image is the Cunard Company trying to give of a voyage on one of its ships?
5. Why are most people more likely to travel by aeroplane?

Questions—Chapter Thirty-Seven

1. Why is motor transport usually more convenient for passengers than rail?
2. How did road transport companies compete with railways for freight?
3. How did the war affect the railways?
4. Why has competition from road transport increased since 1945?
5. How were steam locomotives improved?
6. How were the London and Suburban lines improved?
7. How was the carriage of freight made more efficient?
8. What improvements have been made since the war?
9. Why did nineteenth century governments encourage competition between railways?
10. When and why did they change their minds?
11. Describe the Railways Act of 1921.
12. When and why were the railways nationalised?
13. What was the "Beeching Axe? Why was it needed?
14. Name three new aids to navigation.
15. How were ships' engines improved?
16. Describe the transatlantic liners.
17. How have cargo ships developed since the war?
18. What problems did cargo ships face before the war?
19. Why did passenger liners do better?
20. Why has the position been reversed since the war?

Further Work

1. Collect pictures of steam locomotives built since 1918.
2. What railway lines near you have been closed? When was this done?
3. How have others been modernised?
4. What future do you see for railways in Britain?
5. Consider any journeys you have made by train recently. Why did you not make them by road?
6. Collect pictures and descriptions of merchant ships built since 1918. Which is the largest?
7. Read more about the history of the "Queens".
8. Find advertisements issued by airlines and shipping companies. How do they try to attract passengers?

CHAPTER 38

Road Transport

Following the growth of the railways, long-distance travel by road virtually ceased, and turnpike trusts were driven out of business. Most of them had vanished by the 1870's, and the last one went in 1895.

The first sign of a revival of the road came with the bicycle. The motor vehicle soon followed and by 1914 there were a quarter of a million of them. After the First World War, the motor industry began to produce vehicles of all kinds in even greater quantity, and prices fell. There were goods vehicles, public transport vehicles and, above all, cheap family cars. "Popular motoring" brought a revolution in transport and many other changes as well.

The Bicycle. There had been bicycles of a sort since the early nineteenth century, but they were little more than toys. The problem was to make the machine cover enough ground for each turn of the pedals. One answer was the penny-farthing of the 1870's, but with its front-wheel drive it was difficult to steer, and the rider was dangerously high off the ground. Then, after 1885, there were "safety bicycles", which were the same, in principle, as modern bicycles. They became a good deal more comfortable after Dunlop started making his pneumatic tyres in 1888.

The bicycle brought a small revolution in transport for ordinary people. They had much more freedom of movement, both for going to work and for pleasure. Furthermore, there had to be a new industry to manufacture bicycles. It included firms with such names as Humber, Rover, Sunbeam and Triumph.

The First Cars. The pioneer work was done in France and Germany.
244 The first step came in 1859 when Lenoir, a Frenchman, invented the gas

engine. It was stationary, being used to drive machinery, but it is important in the history of the motor car, because it was the first internal combustion engine. There were even attempts to use it to drive vehicles, but it was heavy for its power, and slow.

Then, in 1884, a German called Daimler made an engine that burnt petrol. It was a good deal lighter than any gas engine of the same power, and it ran much more quickly. At the same time another German, Benz, was experimenting with mechanically propelled vehicles. In 1888 he produced the first petrol driven cars for sale.

In the 1890's the Germans made good progress and the French, perhaps, even better. In 1895 they were able to organise a race from Paris to Bordeaux and back. One of their inventors, Emile Lavassor, drove the 1168 kilometres in 48 hours.

In Britain, there were legal problems. Back in 1865 Parliament had passed the Red Flag Act which said that any mechanical vehicle must have three men with it, one going ahead with a red flag. There was also a speed limit of 4 m.p.h. The Act was meant for the huge steam-driven traction engines of the 1860's and for them it was reasonable enough. However, it would have made motoring impossible. Because of this, Parliament passed the Locomotives on Highways Act of 1896. It abolished the rule that each vehicle must have three attendants and raised the speed limit to 14 m.p.h. Motorists celebrated with a run to Brighton.

The first important British car was built by Fred and George Lanchester in 1896. Others followed including, ten years later, the Rolls-Royce *Silver Ghost*. The name suggests the sort of thing customers wanted—something luxurious and silent. Motoring was a rich man's hobby, and the more expensive cars cost well over £1000, or as much as a working man could earn in seven years. However, by 1914, it was possible to buy a Morris-Oxford for £175.

Popular Motoring. Cheap cars were first made in America, where Henry Ford began mass producing his *Model T* in 1909. In 1914 they cost £115. After the war English manufacturers like William Morris and Herbert Austin began to copy Ford. The price of cars fell so that ordinary people could buy them. In 1939 one family in eight owned a car.

Heavy Goods Vehicles. Rudolph Diesel invented his engine in 1892. With a petrol engine, the fuel is ignited by an electric spark, but in a diesel it happens by compressing the gases. Diesels are heavier than petrol engines, and they do not have the same acceleration, but they burn a lower grade of fuel and are much less likely to go wrong. They proved their worth in the First World War, and were widely used after 1918. 245

A Rolls-Royce Silver Ghost

Public Transport. The first horse drawn buses appeared in the 1830's. In the 1860's they had horse drawn trams which were able to take heavier loads. From 1891 there were electric trams and, for a time, they were a success, being cheap and easy to run. As other traffic increased, though, they became a nuisance. Their lines had to run down the middle of the streets because of parked vehicles, so they were particularly troublesome when they stopped. The last London tram ran in 1952. Trolley buses were an improvement in that they could avoid other vehicles, but like trams they had to follow their overhead cables and could not vary their routes.

The motor bus has proved better than either of its rivals. The first were made in 1898 and by 1907 there were 900 in London alone. There, particularly, their numbers grew rapidly and in 1930 there were 500 companies, many of them running along the same routes. The drivers raced and tried to box each other in, often causing accidents. Parliament had to intervene and in 1933 set up the London Passenger Transport Board. It was not only given a monopoly of the bus services, but also took over the trams and the underground.

Bus services ran in provincial towns, and they also went into the countryside where, along with the car, they completely changed village life.

246

Roads. As long as the turnpike trusts lasted they maintained the main roads more or less efficiently, but when the railways drove them out of business the parishes once again took charge. This lasted, with few changes, until the Local Government Act of 1888 created County Councils and gave them responsibility for the roads. Then, in 1909, the Central Road Board was set up which put taxes on vehicles and on petrol in order to pay for the new roads that motor transport required. The road fund grew so well that the government could not resist raiding it in times of difficulty. Today the motorist pays for a good deal more than the roads he uses.

In road construction the most important change was the use of "tar macadam". The older roads had surfaces of loose chippings and the iron tyres of horse-drawn vehicles gradually compacted them, like a steam-roller. Pneumatic tyres, on the other hand, made the dust and gravel fly. Several organisations tackled the problem, like the National Physical Laboratory and the Road Improvement Society. They found they had their best results with tar, either from coal or the asphalt lakes in Trinidad. First it was sprayed on the surface, but they soon discovered it was better to mix it with the road metal. Fortunately they already had the steam-roller, which had come into use in the 1880's.

There were new roads as well as new surfaces. Between the wars the Great West Road was built, and a number of by-passes, like the one at Kingston. However, there was no major programme until well after the Second World War. In 1959 the M 1 motorway from London to Birmingham opened, and today a coherent motorway network is at last appearing. Like the canals, turnpike roads and railways before it, it serves London and the main industrial areas.

There have been attempts to make roads safer. The period between the wars saw driving tests, the speed limit in built-up areas, pedestrian crossings and traffic lights. Compulsory third party insurance has at least made sure that innocent victims—or their families—have compensation. A few more people are now killed or injured on the roads than in the 1930's, but we must remember there are millions more vehicles, so that all these measures have had some success.

Effects of Motor Transport. It is difficult to find any aspect of life that has not been influenced by motor transport. Everyone depends on it in one way or another. The easy movement of people and goods has brought a revolution in work and in leisure. An important new industry, with many allied industries, has grown up. Since the Second World War the export of cars has been important for the economy.

However, along with the benefits, there are problems. The railways, which are too useful to close altogether, are unable to make a profit; 247

noise and fumes pollute the air; motorways scar the countryside and use good farming land; traffic ruins the cities. The car has added to the pressures of living. Using the roads is a severe test for drivers, passengers and pedestrians alike. Above all, there is the misery caused by accidents, for a thousand people are injured every day, and twenty are killed.

Compare the road space needed by (a) a bus passenger (b) a car passenger.
6. What steps are being taken to avoid jams like this one?

THE INVENTION OF THE MOTOR CAR
The motor car was invented by everybody and nobody. The wheel is found on carved pictures of 4000 B.C. Early in the 14th century Ackermann developed a front-wheel layout for carriages on which today's car steering is based. In the seventeenth century Christian Huyghens suggested the internal combustion engine. Farish and Cecil built an engine worked by the explosion of hydrogen gas in 1820 and in 1838 Barnett was running one powered by coal gas. Around the same time, Faraday invented the generator which would provide the electricity for the lamps invented by Swan which would light the way for road vehicles. Mackenzie patented a clutch in 1865 and Levassor derived from it the car clutch for his Panhard-Levassor cars. Everyone knows, however, that in 1885 Karl Benz developed an automobile. Benz's car got its fuel mixture by drawing air over the surface of petrol in the tank; a more advanced carburettor was invented by Maybach. The Marquis de Dion developed a rear suspension that is still used in many cars, for example, the Rover 2000. One of the outstanding inventors of the car was Frederick Lanchester. It is suggested that of 36 major car components Lanchester invented 18, including the disc brake. Kettering's "self starter" of 1912 became popularised, therefore making it possible to start a car without risking life and limb. By the 1920's most major items had been invented; however, the process continues.
(Rhys—*The Motor Industry.* 1972.)

Questions
1. Which of the problems created by motor transport are illustrated here? How are some of the drivers adding to the problems?
2. How many of the vehicles are (a) goods vehicles (b) buses (c) private cars and taxis.
3. Estimate how much road space is taken by each group.
4. Which group would you exclude from the street to ease the congestion?
5. Estimate how many people there are in (a) the buses (b) the cars. Assume the buses are full (this is the rush hour) and that there are two people in each car.

Questions

1. Explain the first sentence in this document.
2. Who is said to have made the first car?
3. What inventions came before it?
4. What improvements followed?
5. How were cars started before self starters?
In what way might this be dangerous?
6. Name some of the improvements that have been made since the 1920's.

THE ROAD PROBLEM OF 1909

I propose dealing with the new but increasingly troublesome problem of motor traffic. Any man who considers the damage which is done to the roads, the rapid increase in the expense of road maintenance, the harm done to rural life by the dust clouds which follow in the wake of these vehicles, above all, the appalling list of casualties to innocent pedestrians, especially to children, must come to the conclusion that this is a question which demands immediate notice of the Central Government. The question of road construction seemed to have been disposed of by the railways, but the advent of the motor has once more brought it to the front. It is quite clear that our present system of roads and of road-making is inadequate. Roads are too narrow, corners are too frequent and too sharp, high hedges have their dangers, and the old metalling, suited as it was to the vehicles we were accustomed to, is utterly unfitted for the motor-car.

The State has for a very long period done nothing at all for our roads. I believe that no main road has been made out of London for eighty years. The general public and the motorists are crying out for something to be done and we propose to make a real start. The brunt of the expense must be borne by the motorists, and to do them justice they are willing to subscribe handsomely so long as a guarantee is given that the funds will be devoted exclusively to the improvement of the roads.
(David Lloyd George—Budget Speech. 1909.)

Questions

1. What problems has the motor car caused?
2. Why had road making become unimportant?
3. In what ways are roads inadequate for cars?
4. What was the old type of metalling? What did cart wheels do to it? Why did cars damage it?
5. What shows that the state neglected the roads?
6. Who is to pay for the new roads?
7. What guarantee will they have?
8. Was this promise kept?

Questions—Chapter Thirty-Eight

1. What was the main problem in bicycle design? How was it first solved?
2. What kind of bicycle was developed in the 1880's?
3. Who invented the gas engine? What kind of engine is it?
4. Where was the car first developed?
5. What work was done by (a) Daimler (b) Benz?
6. What motoring event was there in France in 1895?
7. What legal problems were there for British motorists?
8. Describe the Locomotives on Highways Act of 1896.
9. Name some of the first car makers in Britain.
10. Who made it possible for ordinary people to own cars? How?
11. Who invented the diesel engine? What are its advantages? What vehicles use it in the main?
12. What public transport was there before motor buses?
13. When were motor buses first made?
14. When was the London Transport Board set up? Why?
15. What Board was set up in 1909?
16. How did it raise money? How was the money spent?
17. How were road surfaces improved?
18. What new roads were built before the war and since?
19. What benefits has motor transport brought?
20. What problems has it created?

249

Further Work

1. Collect pictures of early motor vehicles.
2. Read more about Lanchester, Rolls and Royce.
3. Ask older people to tell you about their experiences of the early days of motoring.
4. What public authorities are responsible for roads today?
5. What road improvements have taken place in your area since the war? What others are planned?
6. Study a map of the motorway network. How do you think it will compare in importance in the history of transport, with turnpikes, canals and railways?
7. How do you imagine road transport is going to develop during your lifetime?

CHAPTER 39

Air Transport

In Paris in 1783, two men went up in a hot air balloon, and became the first ever to fly. In the same year another Frenchman flew in a balloon filled with hydrogen which proved to be more reliable than hot air. During the nineteenth century flying in hydrogen balloons became quite common. People did it for pleasure, while in time of war, balloons were useful for spotting. There were also attempts to make airships by having cigar-shaped gas-bags with propellers fitted. However, turning the propellers by hand needed too much strength, while steam engines were too heavy.

At the same time that the balloonists were making their experiments, they and others were studying heavier than air machines. For a long time men had been trying to fly by imitating the wing-flapping of birds, but in the early nineteenth century, Sir George Cayley decided that the only way would be to have a fixed-wing aircraft, with a separate source of power. There were numerous experiments and some successful flying models were made, worked by clockwork or elastic. Men actually flew as well, but this was in gliders. All attempts to power aircraft with steam engines failed.

Then came the internal combustion engine. Lenoir invented the first, worked by gas, and later on Daimler found how to fuel it with petrol. Within twenty years, men were flying both in airships and in aeroplanes.

Airships. The earliest airships were French, but the best known were those that Count von Zeppelin built in Germany. The first, experimental, Zeppelin, was made in 1900, and by 1910 there were five in regular service. In the next four years they carried, between them, some 35 000 passengers, and without any loss of life.

251

A Handley-Page Hannibal of Imperial Airways

During the war airships were of little value, but afterwards they travelled the world—at a sedate 100 km.p.h. The Graf Zeppelin, especially, was a success, and covered over one and a half million kilometres during her working life from 1928 to 1937. Unfortunately there were a good many accidents, as when the British R 101 crashed on its maiden flight, and when the German Hindenburg burst into flames at its mooring tower. By the 1930's it was clear that the future lay with the aeroplane.

Aeroplanes before 1918. The first men to fly in a heavier than air machine were two young Americans, Wilbur and Orville Wright. They had the advantage of the internal combustion engine, and of the research that scientists had been making on aerodynamics for a hundred years previously. None the less, theirs was a great achievement. They were prepared to be methodical and started by building gliders. Only when they had made one that could be fully controlled did they try powered flight. This was at Kittyhawk in North Carolina, in 1903. Their Flyer I stayed in the air for twelve seconds at the first attempt, and, finally, for nearly a minute. In 1905 they made their Flyer III which they could manoeuvre as they wished, and would fly for half an hour.

Other experiments followed in America and in Europe. There was a famous air meeting at Reims in 1909, and the same year, Louis Blériot flew the English Channel. Progress was now rapid, so that by 1914 most of the technical problems had been solved.

In the war aircraft were first used for spotting, and later there were fighters and bombers as well. They increased in power, size, speed, and numbers. By 1918 there were thousands of planes in service.

Aeroplanes. 1918-1939. The period between the wars saw the development of civil aviation.

In the first place, a number of pioneer flights showed that long distance air travel was possible. In 1919 Alcock and Brown made the first Atlantic crossing. Their Vickers "Vimy" bomber took them from Newfoundland to Ireland in 16 hours, an average speed of 188 km.p.h. The same year Keith and Ross Smith flew from England to Australia, a journey that took 28 days. However, it was Charles Lindbergh's solo flight from New York to Paris in 1927 that caused the biggest sensation. His aeroplane was called *The Spirit of St. Louis*. The young American was 33 hours in the air without proper navigation aids and without any wireless to keep in contact with the ground. Such men, and others like them, prepared the way for commercial flights.

In Britain, civil aviation began in 1919, with two aircraft going between London and Paris. Other companies followed, but none of them could make a profit and by 1921 they were all out of business. For the safety of the country, no government could allow such a thing to happen, so Winston Churchill, who was Secretary of State for War, found the companies a subsidy, and their aircraft flew again.

In 1924, four of them combined as Imperial Airways and started services all over the world, for example to India, Australia and South Africa. By 1939 they had nearly 80 aircraft and in the fifteen years had not lost a single passenger. Financially, though, the company was a failure. It had a heavy subsidy from the government and, like the coaches and steamships before it, was thankful to carry mail. Only about 30% of its revenue came from passengers.

In 1935 another company was formed, and also given a large subsidy. This was British Airways, which operated in Europe.

There was some discontent because so much public money was going to private companies, so in 1939 the government nationalised them both, and amalgamated them to form the British Overseas Airways Corporation.

The Second World War. In the First World War, aircraft were important; in the second, they were vital. A Ministry of Aircraft Production was set up under Lord Beaverbrook, and the construction of 253 aircraft became the largest industry in Britain. It produced fighters, like the Hurricane and Spitfire, bombers, like the Wellington and Lancaster, and fighter bombers, like the Mosquito. The war was decided by command of the air although, of course, the British contribution did not match the American.

From 1944 to the Present. Following the war, Britain found herself with an aircraft industry far larger than she needed. The answer was to expand our own civilian airlines and to make aircraft for export. The industry was greatly helped by the jet engine. This had been invented by Sir Frank Whittle and was being used for military aircraft as the war was ending. It proved ideal for passenger traffic. A jet engine gives more speed than one driven by pistons and allows aircraft to fly much higher, above atmospheric disturbances. The importance of the jet is shown by the number of passenger miles flown in British aircraft alone. It was 300 million in 1945 and 10 000 million in 1969.

The British first produced Comets and later, Viscounts, Britannias and VC 10's. Their success gave our manufacturers and our government the impression that there were passengers who were willing to pay ever increasing fares, provided they could travel at ever increasing speeds. Accordingly, in co-operation with the French, they started the Concorde project. This machine made its maiden flight in 1969 and showed its paces in 1973 by flying from Washington to Paris in 3½ hours. Technically it is a success, but not economically. Oddly enough it has the same fault as the early steamships in that it can carry little more than its own fuel.

Effects of Air Transport. The aeroplane has had nothing like the same direct influence as the motor car on the daily life of the ordinary person. However, there have been important effects on the economy of the country. Aircraft allow business people, mail and light freight to travel much quicker than they did before. An important new industry has grown up, and many allied industries along with it. Aircraft have accounted for a good portion of our exports, since the war.

However, there has been a similar price to pay as for the motor car. Noise pollution is a nuisance everywhere, and near airports it is unbearable. There have been deaths, too. Modern aircraft carry so many passengers that any crash is a major disaster.

Questions

1. What is the name written on the aircraft?
2. What is the name of the pilot?
3. What flight did the pilot make in this aircraft? When?
4. How long did the flight last? Why was it difficult and dangerous?
5. Why was it a landmark in the history of flying?
6. Why were pioneer flights of this kind important?

FLIGHT FROM NEWCASTLE TO EDINBURGH, 1911

From the very moment I left Newcastle I was not sure of my course. It would have been very much easier for me to have taken the sea route, though longer. However, I elected to follow the railway. A few miles from Newcastle strong air currents threatened me with a gale. I rose to a great height to escape them, but it was of course difficult to see the way clearly. Then the wind ahead hindered my speed, though I was flying at 5000 ft. The lakes and ponds that I could see, and which could have been used as guiding marks, were not marked on my War Office map. All of a sudden I was caught in a frightful gale. Large drops of rain began to lash my face. Strong currents hindered my progress and my machine was tossed and pitched in the most terrifying way. I was drawn upwards and pushed downwards and the rain prevented me from seeing anything around me. It was wiser to come down lower so as to find my way. Just then a column of air literally pulled me down to about 400 ft., much nearer the surface of the globe the I liked to be. I saw too well the moss-grown crags and mountain valleys. And thus in the gale I crossed mountains, passes, rivers, taking note of the smallest landmarks, flying at a low altitude rather than lose my way. Fortunately my struggle was coming to an end, for Edinburgh Castle was in sight. I soon saw a huge petrol fire which had been lit. I alighted in pouring rain and in a strong gale.

(Beaumont—*My Three Big Flights.*)

Questions
1. *Locate Newcastle and Edinburgh on a map. How far apart are they? (Beaumont took two hours).*
2. *How did Beaumont find his way?*
3. *Why would the sea route have been easier?*
4. *Why did he fly at a low altitude? Why was this dangerous?*
5. *How did he know where to land?*
6. *Why do modern pilots find navigation easier?*

Questions
1. *What advantage does the aeroplane have?*
2. *What type of transatlantic aeroplane does the writer forsee? How fast will it travel?*
3. *Why is the airship safer?*
4. *What other advantages do airships have?*
5. *How fast will airships travel? How will their greater speed help them?*
6. *When and why were airships abandoned?*

AIRSHIPS OR AEROPLANES?
There must be no exclusion of either airships or aeroplanes. When it is necessary to travel very rapidly one will have recourse to the aeroplane, and without doubt we shall see "aeroplane liners" of huge dimensions, carrying numerous passengers. Perhaps they will be built even for transatlantic passages, as the "hull" with which they must necessarily be equipped will render landing less dangerous upon the water. Transatlantic journeys would be made at speeds exceeding 200 kilometres per hour; that is to say, one would travel from Europe to the United States in a single day! But when this speed is unnecessary, it appears scarcely possible to disclaim the envelope charged with gas. Even if it travels at less speed, it has the advantage of sustaining the aerial navigator without the help of a motor. Consequently, here is safety, and should the motor of an airship break down, one is always master, and able to continue the journey "before the wind" or to land. Moreover, an airship can carry many more passengers; it can carry them in greater comfort; when it will have attained a speed of 60 or 70 kilometres per hour instead of 40 or 45, it will be able to set out at any time; lastly, it can stop at any point in the aerial ocean, which an aeroplane cannot do. Its career is far from ended; it has no more than begun, and it will develop side by side with the aeroplane.

256 (Berget—*Conquest of the Air.* 1909.)

Questions—Chapter Thirty-Nine
1. *When was the first balloon flight?*
2. *How were balloons used in the 19th century?*
3. *What did Sir George Cayley discover?*
4. *What engine, suitable for aircraft, was invented?*
5. *Who built airships in Germany?*
6. *Why were airships abandoned?*
7. *Who built the first heavier than air machine? When and where did they make their first flight?*
8. *Who first flew the English Channel? When?*
9. *How did aircraft develop during World War One?*
10. *Describe the flights of: Alcock and Brown; Keith and Ross Smith; Charles Lindbergh.*
11. *Why did the government subsidise airlines?*
12. *Which company operated all over the world? Which operated in Europe?*
13. *What happened to them in 1939?*
14. *Who took charge of aircraft production during the Second World War?*
15. *Name some of the aircraft that were made.*
16. *Why did Britain develop her civil airlines after the war?*
17. *Who invented the jet engine? What is its value?*
18. *Name some of the civilian aircraft that were developed. What project was started with the French?*
19. *How has the aeroplane affected the economy?*
20. *What problems has it created?*

Further Work

1. Read more about the early balloon flights.
2. Read about the history of the airship.
3. Find out more about the Wright brothers' work.
4. Read the stories of Alcock and Brown, Keith and Ross Smith, Charles Lindbergh and other pioneers.
5. Read about the war in the air during both World Wars. What were the main differences?
6. Discover what you can about the Concorde project. Why has it led to such a lot of argument?
7. Ask older people about the changes they have seen in air transport.
8. What do you think is the future of air transport?

SECTION ELEVEN
Industry Since 1914

CHAPTER 40

The Old Staple Industries

In the nineteenth century British prosperity depended on certain well-established industries like coal, cotton, shipbuilding, iron and steel and engineering. They reached their peak just before the First World War and remained important while it lasted, as also during the short boom that followed. After 1921, though, they ran into difficulty. With their antiquated equipment and methods they faced competition from newer, more efficient industrial countries like the U.S.A., Germany and Japan. At the same time trade was slack all over the world, especially during the slumps of the early 1920's and 1930's. British production fell, which meant unemployment, lower wages and bad industrial relations.

The Second World War brought the old industries back to life again, and when it was over the widespread destruction in Europe and Japan gave them an excellent opportunity. They failed to take it and soon other countries had left Britain far behind.

Coal. Coal has been, perhaps, the most unhappy of British industries. During the First World War there was a demand for coal, but after 1920 it fell away. Oil was now a serious competitor, especially for ships. Furthermore we lost our exports because other countries, notably Germany and the U.S.A., were producing it more cheaply. Production fell, so there was unemployment, and mine owners tried to cut costs by cutting wages. After a bitter strike in 1921 they forced the men to accept longer hours and less money. There was another strike in 1926, which provoked the general strike, but once again the employers won.

During the Second World War demand shot up, so much so that the government had to send a good number of conscripts to the mines instead of to the army. They were known as "Bevin boys". The shortage of fuel continued when the war was over while in 1947 the industry was 259 nationalised, which was something the miners had wanted for a long time. There should have been prosperity and better labour relations, but there was neither.

By the 1940's a lot of the best seams had been worked out, so that too many pits were inefficient; the government insisted that the price of coal should be kept low, so the National Coal Board made heavy losses; few young men became miners, which meant the labour force was ageing; hourly wages increased but the men used this, not to earn more, but to work less and absenteeism was rife; there were strikes, too, and though they were usually unofficial, and short, there were many of them. Output did not rise above two hundred million tonnes in the best of years so that Britain actually had to import coal from abroad, which in 1913 would have seemed unbelievable.

There were changes when Lord Robens became Chairman of the National Coal Board in 1952. He closed many of the unprofitable pits and mechanised the others. The industry was more efficient, but it came nowhere near meeting the country's needs. Indeed it was planned that by 1980 coal would produce only one third of our energy. There was nuclear power to take its place in part, but most of all we came to depend on imported oil.

260 *Modern coal-cutting machinery*

Cotton. The story of cotton is similar to that of coal.

During the First World War imports of raw cotton were cut because shipping space was needed for more important raw materials. Foreign competition had been growing before the war and now our rivals took advantage of the shortage of British goods to develop their own industries even more quickly. The most important were India and Japan. This continued after the war, and in India many of the new mills were equipped with machinery made in Lancashire. The foreign factories were efficient and their labour was cheap, so the British industry could not compete and vital export markets were lost. In 1913 we controlled 60% of world's export trade in cotton goods, but by 1939, only 30%. Some factories closed, and in the remainder, many machines stood idle.

Like the coal industry, cotton revived during the second world war, and afterwards the destruction in Germany and Japan gave Britain the chance to capture their markets. The industry could not meet the challenge though, because its equipment and methods were out of date and soon our former enemies had rebuilt their factories. Moreover, on top of the foreign competition, man-made fibres were becoming popular. The cotton industry again sank into decline and by 1959 it was working at only half its capacity.

The cure was much the same as for coal. There was no nationalisation, but many mills were closed and the rest had new equipment, so that they were more efficient. Between 1956 and 1961, productivity rose 10%. None the less this is pathetic compared with an increase of over 50% in Italy, during the same time. By the late 1960's our output was one eighth of what it had been in 1913, and we were even importing from India and Hong Kong.

Shipbuilding. Shipbuilding prospered during the First World War because of orders from the Royal Navy, and because U-boats sank so many merchant vessels. However, we needed all the ships we could build, and no longer sold them to foreigners. They developed their own yards, especially Holland, Norway, Sweden and above all, Japan.

After the war there were many losses to be made good, but the boom soon collapsed. British shipyards were old, their costs were high and they were slow to change from steamships to the more popular motor ships. The main problem, though, was that few new vessels were wanted at the best of times, while during the depression of the early 1930's building stopped almost completely.

The Second World War revived the industry, and when it was over, the destruction of yards in Germany and Japan gave Britain an excellent opportunity. She failed to take it. Our industry was out of date while the craft unions held endless strikes over who-does-what disputes.   261

Between the wars we had still produced half the world's tonnage, but by 1956 our share had fallen to 14%. Germany was comfortably ahead of us and Japan even more so. She now builds twice as many ships as her three closest rivals. Our own industry stays alive only with the aid of massive grants from the government.

Steel and Engineering. Steel and engineering were important during the First World War, for the making of armaments and building ships. Soon after the war ended, though, they found themselves in the same position as the other industries.

Happily for them, the bad times did not last. Steel output, for example, which had only been 5 million tonnes in 1931, increased to 13 million tonnes by 1939. The Second World War, of course, meant an enormous increase in output and at the end a leading competitor, Germany, was in ruins. British manufacturers had a golden opportunity, but once again they failed to take it. In 1950 we made 10% of the world's steel and in 1966 only 5%. However, this only meant that other countries had done better than us. Our own output had grown considerably. We made 12.7 million tonnes in 1946, 16.3 million tonnes in 1950, and 33 million tonnes in 1966.

Unlike the other old industries, steel and engineering prospered, which was because they had found new customers. In the nineteenth century they supplied firms making railways, steamships and textiles, but when they were no longer as important there were others to take their place, producing, for example, motor cars, aircraft, plastics and a wide range of electrical goods.

Questions
1. Which part of the mine is this?
2. The picture was intended to show a new type of safety helmet introduced in 1935. That, and the pit prop and light, represent 200 years of progress in this particular job. How would a miner of 1735 have found them different? In what ways would his work have been similar to that of the miner of 1935?
3. Why were coal owners slow to introduce new methods and machinery in the 1930's?
4. When were steps taken to modernise the mines? Who was largely responsible?

INDUSTRIAL DISCONTENT IN AN OLD INDUSTRY—COAL
Industrial relations are an even more important factor in efficiency than technical achievement, and the record of the industry is bad. Over one third of the losses from disputes over the past twenty years were suffered by the coal industry which accounts for less than 4% of the working population. Why should worker-management relations in the coal industry be so difficult? A great deal is made of the physical strain, dirt and danger, but custom and tradition count for a great deal. Memories are long in an industry where father is often followed by son and where mining communities are often set apart and self-contained. The tradition in such areas is one of extreme militancy. A man with a grievance will leave the pit and, without hesitation or knowledge of the case, the rest of the men will follow. Customary practices and wage differentials which have been fought for at great cost in the past will now be vigorously defended however irrelevant to present working methods and however much a hinderance to efficient management they become. There have been many bitter episodes in their past relations with the owners and it takes very little to reopen old sores. The greatest

263

obstacle the National Coal Board has to face is the cloud of suspicion and hostility that still hangs over the industry. For the moment the miners keep their traditional weapons, the lightning strike, the "go-slow" and the "stay down". What is most difficult to explain is why the position has not been improved by nationalisation. The miners have achieved their most cherished objective. The "wicked coal-owners" have gone.
(Beacham—The Coal Industry. 1961.)

Questions
1. Coal is an old industry. How does this help explain its bad record for strikes?
2. Describe the methods and attitudes of the miners.
3. When was nationalisation? Why should it have improved matters? Has it done so?

OUTDATED EQUIPMENT IN AN OLD INDUSTRY—COTTON
A. Oldham boss's view of foreign competition, 1911:
"In the first place we've got the only climate in the world where cotton goods in any quantity can ever be produced. In the second, no foreign Johnnies can ever be bred that can spin and weave like Lancashire lads and lasses. In the third place there are more spindles in Oldham than all of the rest of the world put together. And last of all, if they had the climate, the men and the spindles, which they never can have, foreigners could never find the brains Lancashire men have for the job."
B. Lancashire 1976:
In the once great spinning towns of Bolton and Oldham there are no mules left; the only demand for them is from scrap merchants. "The mule was, and is, the best machine in the world able to spin from the finest to the coarsest thread," says Dr. Hills. If Spodden Manufacturing with its six pairs of mules goes down, it will do so fighting. On some of the most venerable plant in the world it is producing textiles and making profits. "If mules are treated properly," says Ronnie

Wood, "they will spin for ever." But this philosophy is dying like the mule itself. A modern ring frame produces half as much again as a mule. But an advanced break spinner will turn out two-thirds more yarn than the ring. The big groups know the way they have to go to stay in business. Yet, as if Lancashire has not suffered enough with textile manpower down to 80 000 from 600 000 at the turn of the century, more mill closures are expected in the next few days.
(*Sunday Times, June 13th 1976.*)

Questions
1. Who invented the mule? When?
2. Describe the Oldham boss's attitude. How would it lead to keeping old equipment?
3. What do Dr. Hills and Mr. Wood think of mules?
4. What action are the big firms taking?
5. How have workers been affected by the slow modernisation of the industry?

Questions—Chapter Forty
1. What were the old staple industries?
2. When and why did coal production fall?
3. What happened to the coal industry during the Second World War?
4. What happened to it in 1947?
5. What problems did it have after the war?
6. Who was Lord Robens? What was his policy?
7. How did World War I affect the cotton industry?
8. What foreigners competed successfully with the British cotton industry? Why did they succeed?
9. What opportunity was there after World War II?
10. Why did the industry not take it?
11. What changes have been made since the 1950's?
12. Why did shipbuilding prosper during World War I?
13. Why did it decline afterwards?
14. What opportunity was there after World War II?

15. Why did the shipping industry not take it?
16. How has it managed to survive?
17. Why were steel and engineering prosperous during the two World Wars?
18. What opportunity did they have after World War II?
19. How far did they take advantage of it?
20. Why have engineering and steel remained more prosperous than the other old industries?

Further Work

1. Collect news items about the old industries.
2. Ask older people to tell you about the economic problems during and between the wars. Compare what they tell you with what you read in books.
3. Compare the problems and achievements of Lord Robens and Dr. Beeching.
4. What events in the 1970's stopped the declining importance of coal mining?
5. List items of clothing and soft furnishing you have in your home. How many are pure cotton?
6. Find out more about the recovery of Germany and Japan since the war. What other countries have made good progress? Why have they succeeded?
7. If you had to make plans for the old industries what would you do and why?

CHAPTER 41

The New Industries— Power

The new industries of the nineteenth century depended on steam engines; those of the twentieth century rely on electric motors. Oil is another important source of power.

As we have seen, the old staple industries that had brought prosperity in Victorian times declined in the twentieth century, but at the same time new ones were growing. Between the wars the traditional industrial areas on the coal fields of South Wales, the North and Scotland sank into a decay that brought poverty and mass unemployment. On the other hand, the Midlands and South-East England prospered. New factories were built that used electric power, and along with them were housing estates, shopping centres and schools.

Before 1939, though, the new industries were not strong enough to rid the country of its dead weight of one million unemployed, and after 1950 they were unable to compete with foreigners. They did not have the success story they might have done.

Electricity Supply. Electricity supply is an industry that has prospered, but it did not begin well. In the years just after the First World War it was backward and chaotic. There were over 450 separate organisations supplying electricity, some of which were private companies, and some local authorities. A few were large, but most of them were small and inefficient. Some supplied a.c. and some d.c., and there were many different voltages.

The organisation improved after 1926 when Parliament passed the Electricity Supply Act. This Act set up a Central Electricity Board which was responsible for creating a national grid. The grid is a network of cables which covers the country. The Central Electricity Board bought current from the companies that were generating it, fed it into the grid,

Early generating equipment

and then distributed it to customers. The Board could ensure the supply of electricity at all times and to all places, while at off-peak periods the less efficient power stations could be shut off, while the best ones kept on working. The Board encouraged suppliers to standardise their voltages, and to close the smaller, inefficient power stations.

By 1934, the grid was complete, and the number of stations reduced to 144, many of them being new super-stations.

In 1947 the industry was nationalised and put under the control of the Central Electricity Generating Board. The country was divided into twelve areas, each one with its own Area Board.

Nationalisation brought an important advantage, in that the industry has enough money to keep up to date. It is needed for scientific research and to provide new power stations and equipment. For one thing, the supply of electricity no longer depends entirely on coal. We have oil as well and, increasingly, atomic power.

Electricity has brought important changes.

In the first place it has greatly increased the standard of living. Power failures from time to time show only too well what life would be without it.

Secondly, it has transformed industry. The steam engine was valuable in its day, but is bulky, difficult to start and stop, and inefficient. It tied British industry to the coal fields, because away from them it was too expensive to use. On the other hand, the electric motor is compact, easy to start and stop, and well over ninety per cent efficient. Moreover, as the national grid goes everywhere, the electric motor can be used everywhere. Electricity has freed industry from the coal fields so that in the twentieth century factories have been built in the Midlands, the South and the South-East.

Electricity supply is an important industry in itself, giving employment to thousands. It was particularly lucky that the grid was being set up in the early 1930's because the task gave employment to 100 000 men, right through the depression. There is also a completely new industry, electrical engineering.

Oil. Before the Second World War, oil refining was not important in Britain. We bought most of our petrol from the United States and only processed about two million metric tonnes of oil in our own country. After the war, though, we had no dollars to buy American petrol, so the government decided that instead we should import crude oil from the Middle East and refine it ourselves. In 1950 we processed 11½ million metric tonnes, and in 1970, 112 million.

To bring in the oil was a growing fleet of tankers, some of them giants. Refineries have been built around the coast, and these, too, are large. The bigger they are, the cheaper they are to run. The Esso refinery at Fawley, for example, has a capacity of more than double the output of the entire country in 1938. The oil companies are large, too, being international giants like Esso, Shell and B.P.

However, the industry is impressive for more than its size. It has grown remarkably quickly, it has a high level of productivity, and it has saved us a considerable amount of money on our bill for imports. Furthermore, oil refining has given rise to the petro-chemical industries which are important in their own right.

However, when we compare the rate of growth in Britain with that in other countries, it does not look so spectacular:

Oil Refining		
Thousands of Tonnes		
	1950	1960	1970
Japan	2600	32 130	165 000
West Germany	4700	39 700	117 800
Italy	5900	41 400	157 200
U.K.	11 500	49 200	112 000

The lead that Great Britain had in 1950 was lost. However, since the discoveries around our coasts it does seem that the oil industry has a bright future.

"Aerial view of Fawley Refinery from the west. The refinery occupies a 1250 acre site and has a throughput capacity of 19 million tons a year. To date, the capital expenditure on plant and equipment amounts to £140 million."—Esso Company.

Questions
1. Find Fawley on a map. Why is it a good place to build a refinery?
2. When did Britain begin to build her own refineries, and why?
3. What vessels call here? Locate where they dock.
4. What are the products that leave an oil refinery?
5. Locate the power station at the top right-hand corner. Why is it so close to the refinery?
6. Oil is known as a "primary fuel" and electricity as a "secondary fuel". Why is this?

269

CHANGES IN BRITAIN'S FUEL SUPPLIES

The discovery of natural gas in the North Sea is a major event in the evolution of Britain's energy supplies. It follows closely upon the coming of age of nuclear power as a potential major source of energy. Together, these two developments will lead to fundamental changes in the pattern of energy supply in the coming years. A decade ago coal supplied 85% of our primary fuel, and oil most of the remainder. We are still basically a two-fuel economy but oil's share had grown to 37% of the total in 1966 and coal's share had dropped to under 60%. There is no shortage of either coal or oil in the ground, but whereas for coal we need not look beyond our own borders, for oil we are at present wholly dependent on foreign sources. This presents problems. The pattern of availability and supply is changing. The quantity of natural gas already found in the North Sea is sufficient to replace town gas completely in the course of a few years and, at the right price, to bring about a major expansion of the market for gas. Nuclear power has emerged from its experimental stage into a proven source of energy, with supplies of uranium and plutonium sufficiently assured to place no limitation on its further growth within the foreseeable future. Though the dominance of coal and oil as primary fuel sources will continue for many years to come, they will be competing with nuclear power and natural gas. We are moving from a two-fuel to a four-fuel economy.

(Ministry of Power—Fuel Policy 1967.)

Questions

1. How have oil and coal changed in importance?
2. What two new primary fuels are being developed?
3. How has this changed the nature of the economy?
4. How has relying on foreign oil caused problems?
5. What secondary fuel is going out of use?
6. What important development in Britain's fuel supplies would be mentioned in any report today?

SHELL'S HELICOPTER VIEW

Shell's top executives in London hardly regard themselves as part of life in Britain at all, and try to cultivate what they call the "helicopter view". "England," said one, "is just as much abroad to us as Venezuela." Like Government officials they use millions and billions as normal units of discussion."Six nothings don't overawe me," said the managing director in charge of planning, "it all comes down to simple principles in the end." Shell has taken out catastrophe insurance to protect it against major disaster, "But," said one of its senior finance men, "we wouldn't worry about £2m. After all, you don't insure your fountain pen."

Shell's complex of offices on the south bank of the Thames has 3000 rooms, the largest private telephone exchange in Britain, a swimming pool of international standard, a rifle range, a cinema and four squash courts; and about 4600 people work there. Yet Shell Centre is only half—though the larger half—of the Royal Dutch Shell Group's central offices. The other is in The Hague. Between them they control the second largest oil group in the world, with over £3500m. of assets. Shell supplies fourteen per cent of all the oil sold in the non-Communist world: has interests in oil-fields in twenty-six countries; owns or has an interest in seventy-nine refineries and 41 000 miles of pipeline; and either owns or has on charter well over twenty-two million tons of shipping, a sixth of the world's tanker tonnage. On an average day, Shell has four hundred ships at sea.

(Graham Turner—Business in Britain. 1971.)

Questions

1. What is meant by a "helicopter view"?
2. Explain the remarks, "six nothings don't overawe me" and "You don't insure your fountain pen."
3. What is the full title of Shell?

4. Describe its head offices in London.
5. Where else does it have a head office?
6. List the assets owned by Shell.

Questions—Chapter Forty-One
1. In what ways was the electricity supply industry backward in the 1920's?
2. What Act did Parliament pass in 1926?
3. What Board was set up?
4. How did the National Grid work?
5. Name two things the Board encouraged.
6. When was the industry nationalised?
7. How was it organised under nationalisation?
8. What advantages have nationalisation brought?
9. Think of some ways electricity has improved the standard of living.
10. How has electricity affected the location of industry?
11. How has it helped employment?
12. What new industry has been created?
13. How did we obtain our petrol before 1939?
14. When and why did oil refining become important in Britain?
15. How much did the industry grow between 1950 and 1970?

16. Name three things that show the industry is organised on a large scale.
17. In what other ways is it impressive?
18. What new industry has been created?
19. How did the rate of growth of Britain's oil industry compare with other countries?
20. What prospects does the industry have?

Further Work
1. Find out about the early days of the electricity industry, during the 19th century.
2. Find what you can about your nearest power station.
3. Ask old people to tell you what life was like without electricity.
4. Find pictures of equipment used by the oil industry for prospecting, drilling and transport.
5. Find out how an oil refinery works.
6. What goods does the petro-chemical industry make?
7. What were the main sources of power in the past?
8. Imagine it is the 21st century. Describe the ways Britain is obtaining power.

CHAPTER 42

The New Industries— Motor Vehicles and Aircraft

The Motor Vehicle Industry. The motor vehicle industry grew rapidly. Just before the First World War it produced 34 000 cars a year, in 1939, over half a million and by the 1960's, comfortably over two millions. This was due to an ever increasing demand, and also because the industry became more efficient.

In the early days there were many firms in the business, employing craftsmen to make cars in small batches, or even individually. There were few cars that looked alike, or were even much alike mechanically. An owner had to pay a lot for his vehicle, and he had serious problems when he needed spare parts. In 1920 there were still 96 manufacturers, but by 1939 there were only twenty, and six of these made 90% of all cars produced. They were Morris, Austin, Ford, Vauxhall, Rootes and Standard. After the war, Morris and Austin combined to form the British Motor Corporation, while Standard linked up with two smaller firms, Leyland and Triumph. B.M.C. and Standard-Triumph are now part of British Leyland.

At the same time the firms that supply components have grown in size. For example, Lucas produce most of the electrical parts, Girling, brakes and clutches, Champion, spark plugs, and Dunlop, tyres.

Amalgamation is important, because with a few big firms it is easier to have standardised parts. The value of this came out clearly in the First World War, but it is just as essential for civilian motoring in time of peace. Firms making components can keep their prices lower, while a garage can carry out repairs more easily.

Furthermore, only large firms can use mass production. The complicated process of assembling a car is broken down into many small, easy steps that need only semi-skilled labour. The vehicles move slowly along a production line at just the right speed to allow each man to do his job

Production line at the Austin factory

without having to hurry or, theoretically, without being able to stand idle. This was the method Henry Ford developed in America and Morris and Austin introduced to Britain in the 1920's. Without it, the motor car would still be a rare form of transport.

There have been new techniques that save time and money. Bodies were once built from separate pieces, like coaches. They were painted by hand, coat after coat being put on and rubbed down until, finally, the whole thing was varnished. Now a complete body is stamped in one piece in a press and is sprayed with, or dipped in, cellulose paint.

At first mass production brought down the price of cars. The average was £308 in 1912, and £130 in 1936 which, of course, encouraged people to buy. Since 1945 prices have gone up rapidly, but this is because of the cost of labour and materials. Techniques have gone on improving. For example, in 1950 the industry produced 3.3 cars a year for every man employed, while in 1959 this figure was 5.2.

The motor vehicle industry could not grow alone. It encouraged glass, steel, rubber, electrical and mechanical engineering and oil refining. 273

The work of garages is also important, employing thousands of people. Car manufacturers do not normally use raw materials. They assemble parts made in a variety of places, so in setting up a plant, one town is as likely to be convenient for them as another. In fact they have chosen the Midlands and the South-East where they have helped to bring a good deal of prosperity. The government, on the other hand, has encouraged them to go into the depressed areas of the old staple industries—South Wales, the North of England and Scotland. They have had some success. Ford, for example, has opened a works at Halewood, on Merseyside.

It remains to see how car manufacturing in this country compares with others.

At first, the government taxed cars according to the size of their engines, so manufacturers made small, low powered vehicles which had little sale abroad. Before 1939 only about one eighth were exported. This did not matter, because between the wars, Britain had no cause to worry about exports. After the war, though, we had to find them, and quickly. The old staple industries could not meet the need, so others had to. The motor vehicle industry seemed well placed. During the war it had expanded greatly to make military vehicles and it was easy enough for it to change to civilian uses. German industry was in ruins and few countries had enough dollars to buy from America. The markets of the world lay open and British manufacturers had an excellent opportunity. They soon increased their production to well above the pre-war level, and they exported 80% of all that they made.

However, the number of dissatisfied customers grew with the number of sales. The British neglected quality, and they neglected spare parts and servicing, so that they only did well as long as they had no competition. Soon the industries of Europe and Japan revived and they offered a quality and a reliability not matched by Britain. Moreover, though our own manufacturers increased their efficiency, as we have seen, this was nothing to what happened abroad. Between 1955 and 1964 our output went up 90%, while in the same period other countries increased theirs by 200%. Japan did particularly well, and is now second only to the U.S.A. We are losing our share of markets abroad, while even in our own country the number of foreign cars is growing rapidly—this in spite of heavy import duties.

The Aircraft Industry. The aircraft industry hardly existed before 1914, but it did become quite important during the First World War. Afterwards, though, it declined for a time. The commercial airlines were finding it hard to make money, so that building for them was risky.

Things changed in the 1930's when the Royal Air Force began to place regular orders. Firms grew in size and there was a good deal of research which resulted in aircraft like the Hurricane and the Spitfire—fortunately for Great Britain.

The fall of France and the threat of invasion in 1940 meant that the building of aircraft was a top priority. There was a Ministry of Aircraft Production under Lord Beaverbrook, and through his guidance the industry grew rapidly. In 1938, 2800 aircraft had been built, while in 1944 there were nearly ten times as many. Moreover the average size was about double.

When the war ended, the industry was well-organised and up-to-date. It was able to adapt itself easily to civilian work, and to take advantage of the new jet and turbo-jet engines that were ideal for large passenger aircraft. Thanks to help from the government there was plenty of scientific research and the industry kept its technical lead for some years. It could not last, though. This time it was the Americans who overtook us. They not only had the advantage of their great wealth, but also had a good domestic market, since they can use large numbers of aircraft in their own country.

Faced with this problem, the British government decided to increase efficiency by cutting down the number of firms even more. Four of them making airframes amalgamated to form B.A.C. and three others made up Hawker Siddeley. Similarly there were just two firms for engines, Rolls-Royce and Bristol Siddeley.

To overcome the problem of America's superior wealth, the British and French decided to combine their resources and build the Concorde. The result was that hundreds of millions of pounds of the taxpayers' money have been spent on an aircraft which is a commercial failure. Moreover, by developing our industry in the wrong direction we have increased the Americans' lead instead of reducing it. Their slower, but much larger aircraft, make profits and on long flights they can even take their passengers more quickly to their destinations because they do not have to stop repeatedly to refuel.

A man is fitting his second gear box into the engine. Select the gear box, lift it with the hoist and stick it into the holds in the middle of the engine. It's quicker if you do it without the hoist, but watch your back. Screw down the top bolts and secure the gear box to the engine. In the next six hours he will have a coffee break and a dinner break, and he will have installed another 200 gear boxes. Forty an hour, 320 a shift.

(Beynon—*Working for Ford.*)

Questions

1. What are the men in the picture assembling?
2. What production technique is being used?
3. Who first developed it for motor cars?
4. Who introduced it to Britain? When?
5. What advantage does it have for the manufacturer?
6. What is it like to work in this way?

LOCATION OF THE MOTOR VEHICLE INDUSTRY, 1935-1965

Historically the industry developed out of the cycle manufacturers of Coventry. By 1935 the industry was mainly in the West Midlands and London/Southeast area where over 85% of its factories were. But during the 1930's Britain faced a critical problem of unemployment. The areas most affected were those that had produced the "old" staples of the export trade: cotton, coal, steel and ships. The government developed a policy with the primary aim of directing the flow of industries into the depressed areas. The fact that these areas were unattractive to the new industries made it necessary for the government to find emphatic means to persuade them. The Treasury was empowered to assist firms financially. Further, anyone wishing to construct a new factory had to have an Industrial Development Certificate from the Board of Trade. In 1960 the prospects for the motor industry were good and all the major companies planned to expand. The plans came under the scrutiny of the Board of Trade, and that body required that the companies seek locations outside the London and Birmingham areas. Naturally, most firms wanted to expand where they were already established and their linkages with suppliers and outlets known. However, Ford, Vauxhall and B.M.C. agreed to build at Merseyside; B.M.C., Rootes and Pressed Steel selected locations in Central Scotland and B.M.C. and Rover agreed to expansion in South Wales. The development of the industry in these regions has had the effect of increasing the dispersion of the industry. (Goodwin—*Structure of the Motor Vehicle Industry*.)

Questions
1. *Where did the motor industry grow up?*
2. *How did the government encourage new industries to go into areas of high unemployment?*
3. *Where did the motor industry expand in the 1960's? Why were companies unwilling to go there?*
4. *How did expanding there affect the industry?*
5. *What disadvantages do you think this caused?*

CONCORDE
In November 1962 there was an agreement between France and the United Kingdom to share, on the basis of equal responsibility, the costs, development and production work and the proceeds of sales of a supersonic air transport to be known as Concorde. Concorde will carry 128 passengers and will have a cruising speed of Mach 2 (1320 mph). Its range is 3250 miles, enabling a non-stop service across the Atlantic taking only 3½ hours, compared with some 7 hours by subsonic jet airliner.
To minimise supersonic drag, the fuselage is long and slender and the wing ogee-shaped. Much of the structure consists of a tough heat and creep resistant aluminium alloy known as Hiduminium RR58. The cost of Concorde was estimated

in May 1972 at £970m. divided equally between Britain and France.
Following the decision by the U.S. Government to withdraw financial support from the development of a supersonic transport, the only aircraft similar to Concorde is the Russian Tupolev TU-144 which made its first flight in 1968.
The problems of sonic boom have yet to be fully solved. Even if supersonic flights are banned over populated land area, the manufacturers claim that a big market would remain, as three-quarters of the world's air traffic is carried on ocean routes. Concorde's design aim is that its engines should be no noisier than those of existing subsonic jets, and silencers of a new design are being developed.
(Central Office of Information—*Aerospace*. 1972.)

Questions
1. *Why did Britain and France make Concorde together?*
2. *Describe Concorde's performance.*
3. *What technical problems are mentioned here?*
4. *How were they overcome?*
5. *What will Concorde cost per head of population?*
6. *What is Concorde's only rival?*
7. *What disadvantage will make Concorde unpopular?*
8. *What does this writer say about them?*

Questions—Chapter Forty-Two
1. *How was the car industry organised in the early days?*
2. *What disadvantages did this cause?*
3. *How many car manufacturers were there in 1920 and in 1939?*
4. *Why was amalgamation important?*
5. *How is mass production organised?*
6. *How has the making of car bodies changed?*
7. *How did mass production affect prices?*
8. *What other industries has the car industry encouraged?*
9. *Where did the car industry grow up?*
10. *Where has it been made to expand?*
11. *Why were few cars exported before 1939?*

277

12. Why were many exported after the war?

13. Why did British manufacturers lose markets?

14. When was the aircraft industry first important?

15. Why did it decline, then recover, between the wars?

16. Who organised aircraft production during the war?

17. Why was the industry well placed after the war?

18. Which country overtook Britain and why?

19. How did the government try to increase efficiency?

20. What project was started with the French?

Further Work

1. What existing industries first attracted the motor car industry to the Midlands?

2. Count the number of cars in a car park. What proportion are British and what are foreign?

3. Find out how many cars are produced per man each year in Britain, France, West Germany and Japan.

4. Find out about some of the aircraft built in Britain during and since the war.

5. This book was written in 1976. What has happened about Concorde since then?

6. The documents give two examples of government direction of industry. Give more examples in the motor vehicle, aircraft and other industries. What advantages and what problems have resulted?

CHAPTER 43

The New Industries— Electrical Engineering, Chemicals and Man-Made Fibres

Electrical Engineering. Electrical engineering has grown along with electricity supply.

In the first place it has provided equipment for the people who make electricity—such things as generators, motors and cables. Secondly it has made equipment for those who use electricity. There are heavy electrical goods like motors for factories and railway locomotives. There are complicated electronic devices like radar and computers. There are light electrical goods, too. Many are used in cars or aeroplanes, and many others are used in the home. When we talk of a rising standard of living we mean, as much as anything, owning an increasing number of electrical gadgets. A normal house can have up to twenty of these, ranging from the colour T.V. set to a hair drier and perhaps worth, all together, £1000.

The industry is well organised, and many of the firms are large. There was, for example, Electrical and Musical Industries (E.M.I.) a big combine, formed in 1931. This in turn was taken over by G.E.C. in 1967. Factories tend to be large, too. As early as 1935 half the people in electrical engineering were in factories with over 1000 employees. There has been little unemployment in the industry. In 1937 it had only three per cent out of work, while in shipbuilding, for example, the figure was 24%. There has also been a high level of exports, both before and after the war.

As in all well-conducted industries, much money is spent on research and there is progress the whole time. Radar was particularly important. Its development before the war probably saved the country from invasion because without it the R.A.F. could hardly have won the Battle of Britain.

Since the war there has been the computer. The pioneer work was done in the nineteenth century, particularly by Charles Babbage who 279 adopted the idea of using punched cards from the Jacquard loom. Automatic calculating machines, like the comptometer, were common enough in the early part of the twentieth century, but there were no electronic computers until the second world war. The first were made in America, but invaluable research was done by British scientists like Dr. M. V. Wilkes of Cambridge University. The large sums of money needed to manufacture computers commercially came from the government, and large electronics firms like Ferranti.

The first British firm to have a computer were the restaurant owners, J. Lyons & Co., who installed one in 1951. Since then most big organisations have been using them. They are valuable in helping organise industry, and in commerce and banking. Moreover, a computer can replace a man in controlling machinery. This is what is meant by "automation".

Technically, the British were ahead of the Americans in the 1950's, but they could not find the money to keep their lead, and have since fallen behind.

Indeed, this is true of the British electronics industry as a whole. It has continued to grow, but not as rapidly as in other countries.

280 *The ICL 2903 computer system*

The Chemical Industry. The chemical industry is not one industry, but many. The following list shows how varied they are. First the chemical is given and then some of the goods that it helps to make:

Caustic Soda — soap, rayon, glass, paper.
Sulphuric Acid — fertilisers, rayon, steel.
Coal Tar — dyes.
Nitrogen — explosives and fertilisers.
Petro-chemicals — detergents, man-made fibres, fertilisers, sprays and plastics.

There are also what are known as "fine chemicals" which include pharmaceuticals.

Before 1914 the chemical industry was in poor shape, largely because it did not employ enough trained scientists. The First World War brought changes, however. We badly needed explosives and fertilisers, so there were frantic efforts to bring the industry up to date, with the government giving a good deal of money. Research slackened a little when government help dried up in 1920, but during the Second World War it more than made up the lost ground. For example there was the development of antibiotics and of pesticides like D.D.T. while even the humble sea-sickness pills helped to make the D-Day landings a success.

Technical progress continued after the war. The manufacture of petro-chemicals began because of the growth of oil refining. Pharmaceuticals became important, too—the National Health Service found plenty of good customers for this branch of the industry.

Moreover, during the Second World War, German industry was destroyed and British manufacturers took full advantage of the fact. Between 1946 and 1950 they increased output by 40% while, for the first time, there were considerable exports.

The organisation of the industry helped it to succeed. It is made up of large firms, and even they are dominated by one giant. This is Imperial Chemical Industries, created in 1926 by the merger of four big companies. I.C.I. went on to absorb many others, and in 1961 even tried to take over Courtaulds, one of its few serious rivals.

When industrialists build up a big empire, they are trying to create a monopoly which enables them to charge whatever prices they like. Here they succeeded only in part. What the big firms did manage to do, though, was to find the money needed for scientific research, which small organisations could never have done.

All went well until 1950, by which time Germany had recovered. Her rate of growth was much higher than Britain's and she invaded many of our export markets. From time to time there were world-wide shortages of chemicals which German industry surged ahead to satisfy. Britain on the other hand, met the need by increasing her imports, instead of 281 increasing her production. We can see what happened by looking at one key product, sulphuric acid:

Sulphuric Acid			
Thousands of Tonnes			
	1948	1960	1969
U.K.	1580	2745	3287
West Germany	810	3170	4481

Man-Made Fibres. The first man-made fibre was rayon. It was manufactured in France from about 1890 onwards, and soon afterwards in Great Britain, where it was taken up by the old established silk firm of Courtaulds. Rayon is made from the cellulose in wood pulp. Because of its lightness and shiny appearance it is used as a substitute for silk and indeed it is often known as artificial silk.

In 1927, the Americans found how to make nylon, and in 1940, the British found how to make terylene. Both became important after the war and have been joined by many other similar products like Orlon and Ardil. They can act as substitutes for all the traditional fibres, silk, cotton, linen and wool. They can also be mixed with them to make a cloth cheaper and more hard-wearing than one of natural fibres alone.

As artificial silk was hardly needed in war time, the rayon industry did not do well during the First World War. Afterwards, though, it grew at the astonishing rate of nearly 16% a year. Cars and electrical goods came next at 10%, while the figure for British industry as a whole was 2%.

If anything, the Second World War helped the industry because artificial fibres were found to have military uses, for example to make parachute cords, or to take the place of cotton in tyres. At the end of the war rayon was, as we have seen, joined by a whole range of other artificial fibres, while the natural ones, especially wool, became for a time extremely expensive. As a result the industry kept up its good rate of growth.

Man-made fibres have improved our standard of living. Everyone has far more clothes than before, and in a much greater variety of fabric and colour. Along with the washing machine the new materials ended a traditional piece of household drudgery, the 'Monday wash'. This has 282 done a lot towards freeing women for full-time employment.

As with so many successful industries, firms are large. Two of the most important were Courtaulds and British Celanese and they merged in 1957. Thanks to their size such organisations have been able to spend a lot of money on research and, down to 1950, introduce new equipment and methods rapidly enough.

Unhappily, this new industry which had begun so well, lost ground to foreign competitors after 1950. It has indeed gone on growing, but technical changes have not come nearly fast enough in the British industry to allow it to keep pace. We have only to compare the British output of rayon with that of Japan:

Rayon Filament—Staple			
Thousands of Tonnes			
	1948	1960	1969
U.K.	106	208	266
Japan	32	434	515

I.C.L. COMPUTER—MANUFACTURER'S DESCRIPTION

Immediate answers to enquiries can be given on a display screen. You can assess the urgent order situation, check the critical stocks position, investigate credit risks etc. in seconds.

Any computer can only be as good as the information it is given. With the ICL 2903 you can put information into it much quicker simply by typing it straight in on a keyboard without the necessity of first putting it onto punched cards.

The screen shows exactly what information is being fed into the computer at any time.

Questions

1. What work will this computer do?
2. What decides how well it will perform?
3. What is the purpose of the keyboard?
4. What older method does it replace?
5. Name two uses for the screen.

283

ELECTRONICS IN INDUSTRY

Electronic methods, including industrial television, make possible the continuous control of a number of processes where human control would be dangerous or impossible, as in parts of the chemical and oil industries, and nuclear power. Such methods also give more accurate control, as in the operation of a paper mill or a newspaper press. Photo-electric devices are now used as batch counters: thus the little eye will observe the rapid passage of objects down a chute and when a gross has gone will divert the second batch into a different channel. Similar devices spot the bottle that is not quite full, and their mechanical adjuncts will toss it coldly aside. Photo-cells will report when there are pin-holes in sheet steel or, as bright-hot steel bars roll past them, their excitement will grow till, at the appropriate point, they bring down the crashing guillotine. But it is the computer that has attracted most attention. There are three main types: first the mathematical machine, whether analogue or digital, for use in scientific establishments; secondly the digital computer for handling business accounts; then the computer that can control machinery. Suppose a piece of metal of a complicated shape is required: the specifications are fed on punched cards into a small computer which then regulates a machine tool in such a way that the object will be cut from a solid block of metal.

(Wilson—*The Electronics Industry.* 1958.)

SCOTLAND'S NEWEST INDUSTRY

In Aberdeen and District there are now over 200 companies directly involved in the offshore oil industry and well over 300 supplying it.

It is difficult to measure the number of jobs that have been created as a spin-off from the growing oil industry. It is certainly considerable. Aberdeen Airport has passenger traffic increasing at an annual rate of over 35 per cent.

The oil companies have moved into a variety of premises and there are many new offices, warehouses and factories. The cost runs into many millions of pounds. In addition new hotels are being built. At Peterhead major developments are in hand for the Harbour of Refuge, a square mile of deep water enclosed by two massive granite breakwaters. A particularly significant development is the decision by two major manufacturers of oilfield equipment to set up factories near Aberdeen. B.P. have ordered four production platforms. The biggest, being built at Nigg Bay will be the largest ever, costing £40m. and weighing 57 000 tons. It will be pile-driven into the sea bed in 400 feet of water. The full height when complete is about 700 feet. North East Scotland's indigenous industries are expanding with considerable investment in food and fish processing plant, cold storage and distilleries. Several oil industry training centres are proposed. Aberdeen University has established a Master of Science course in Petroleum Technology.

An active Petroleum Wives' Club has also been formed.

(North East Scotland Development Authority. 1973.)

Questions
1. Name the electronic devices mentioned in the first half of this extract.
2. What work will they do?
3. Why is it better the work should be done by them rather than by people?
4. Name three different places where computers are used. Where does the one on the front of this card belong?
5. Find out the difference between digital and analogue computers.

Questions
1. Find the places mentioned on a map.
2. How many firms are involved in the oil business in the Aberdeen area?
3. List the industries and activities stimulated by the oil industry. Explain why this has happened. Think of others likely to be affected.
4. Find out how the people in the Aberdeen area made a living before the discovery of oil.

Questions—Chapter Forty-Three

1. List the main products of the electrical engineering industry and say who buys them.
2. Name a large electronics firm. How large were factories, before the war?
3. How has the industry helped the economy?
4. What discovery helped to win the war?
5. Describe the development of the computer. Which was the first British firm to have one?
6. What work can computers do?
7. Why did the British lose their lead in computers?
8. Name five important chemicals and some of the goods made from them.
9. What happened to the chemical industry during the two World Wars?
10. Name two branches of the industry that have prospered since the war.
11. What advantage did the British industry have after the war?
12. Name a large chemical firm. What is the advantage of having large firms?
13. How has the British chemical industry compared with the German since 1950?

14. What was the first man-made fibre? Which was the first British firm to make it?
15. What other man-made fibres have been developed?
16. How fast did the industry grow between the wars?
17. How did the Second World War help the industry?
18. How have man-made fibres improved the standard of living?
19. Name an important firm. What are the advantages large firms enjoy?
20. How has the British industry compared with the Japanese since 1950?

Further Work

1. How do computers affect our daily lives?
2. Ask your grandmother to describe an old fashioned wash day. Why is the work easier today?
3. Collect news items about the new industries.
4. What industries were new in the 18th and 19th centuries? Compare them with those we have today.

CHAPTER 44 Industry— Conclusion

In the twentieth century we have to distinguish between the old staple industries like coal mining, cotton and shipbuilding, and the new industries like motor vehicle manufacture, man-made fibres and electrical engineering.

The old staple industries depended on exports and when, after 1920, they lost many of their overseas markets, they went into decline. At the same time the new industries began to develop, bringing prosperity to their workers and to parts of England, notably the Midlands and the South-East. Unfortunately the country was too slow in switching its energies to the new industries and they did not grow fast enough to save the rest of Great Britain from nearly twenty years of depression with never less than one million unemployed.

During the Second World War, most industries boomed. When it was over a few factories had been bombed, and in many machinery and equipment needed replacing. However, British industry was more or less intact, while that of two of her chief rivals, Germany and Japan, lay in ruins. Here was a golden opportunity, but Britain failed to take it.

In the first place the old industries, notably cotton and coal, hardly responded at all. Their output sagged and it was as if the good luck had never come their way. They were like a footballer who sees an empty goal before him, but lacks the strength to kick the ball into the net.

The new industries were different. They rushed to fill the vacuum caused by the misfortune of Germany and Japan, increasing production and seizing many world markets. The good times did not last long. By 1950 Germany and Japan had rebuilt their factories and were winning back their customers. They proved that Great Britain could only do well in international trade as long as she had no competitors.

For a long time now, Britain's economy has been growing much more slowly than that of other industrial powers.

What are the reasons? All sorts of people have been blamed—trade unions for insisting on high wages and calling strikes, working people for being idle and careless, employers for being inefficient and showing too little enterprise. There may be a certain amount of truth in this, but it is too much of a coincidence that all industries have been stricken with the same disease. Something outside industry is responsible, more 286 than anything within it.

The reason why almost any British factory lags behind its counterpart in, say, Germany, is quite simple. If one visits them both it is obvious that the British workman has older and less efficient equipment. However hard he tries he has no hope of keeping up with his continental rival.

Again, it is fairly easy to explain why British factories are using out of date machines, and it is because their owners have not bought new ones. To use the jargon of the economist, the level of investment in British industry is too low. Why this should be is more complicated, but two reasons are outstanding. In the first place, many people in Britain with money to invest have had more confidence in foreign industries than in our own. A good deal of British capital has gone abroad, much of it to Europe, where it has helped build factories for our successful rivals. By itself this might not matter too much and, after all, money invested wisely abroad will earn the country a good income.

There is another, more important reason, and that is the policy followed by our governments, both Socialist and Conservative.

In the years just after the war we were disposing of our Empire. Probably it was no economic value to us at any time, but as it broke up it was an enormous liability. Each colony that became independent did so with a lavish grant of economic aid, and the promise of more to follow. Probably we did no more than we were morally obliged, but a good deal of money that could have built up our own economy went to help underdeveloped countries.

Another great expense was the armed forces. The Conservatives have been, perhaps, more interested in these than the Socialists, but it was Ernest Bevin who, as Foreign Secretary, pleaded that he should not be sent "naked into the conference room". He meant that this country should have the atomic bomb and be able to negotiate on equal terms with the U.S.A. and the U.S.S.R. Trying to keep up with the Americans and the Russians has cost us dearly. To pay for our armed forces Britain has been crippled with taxation, and money that could have gone on new factories and machinery has bought tanks, nuclear submarines and hydrogen bombs.

Finally there have been the attempts to check unemployment. People have dreaded a return to the bad days of the 1930's when there were nearly four million out of work, so that any government that allowed unemployment to grow would be sure to lose votes at an election, and be in trouble with the Trade Unions.

From time to time it has been difficult to sell goods abroad so manufacturers have made less of them and have had to dismiss workers. When governments have seen this happening, they have increased public spending. In other words, they have used tax-payers' money to create jobs. People have gone into the civil service, local 287 government, the national health service, the social services, education and so on. Here they may or may not be useful for the community, but one thing is certain—they do not produce goods for export.

When trade has revived, industry has wanted workers again, but in the meantime they have found cosy jobs in the public sector which they do not want to leave. Goods have not been produced and foreigners have taken Britain's markets. Then further periods of unemployment have come along, still more jobs have been created in the public sector and fewer and fewer people have been available to work in factories. As industry grows smaller, the number of people it has to support grows larger. It is like the man who is losing his strength for work while his children demand more and more food, clothes and pocket money.

In the nineteenth century, Great Britain was the richest country in Europe; she is now one of the poorest.

In July 1976 the Chancellor of the Exchequer, Mr. Healey, announced cuts of £1000m. in public spending.

Questions
1. What is the figure shown in the building?

2. Why is she described as "Sleeping Beauty"?

3. Whom does the handsome prince represent?

4. What services are being cut by him?

5. How, since 1945, had governments used these services to check unemployment?

6. Why, in 1976, did it seem necessary to cut them?

Average Annual Growth Rates 1950-1962
Germany 7.2%   Austria 6.0%
France 4.4%   Italy 6.3%
Netherlands 4.9%   Ireland 1.3%
United Kingdom 2.6%

SOME AMERICAN OPINIONS OF BRITAIN'S ECONOMY

A. In many ways, Britain's economic performance since World War II outstrips any earlier period. Her rate of growth, her attainment of full employment are fit objects of pride, the more impressive because they were achieved despite the immense problems of postwar reconstruction, dwindling overseas earnings, and increased competition in export markets. Yet Britain seems burnt-out by comparison with her neighbours. Since the 1950's several West European countries have completed their postwar recovery and attained rapid growth, while the U.K. economy has grown less rapidly and has been plagued with crises.

B. In 1966 the Nottinghamshire miners opposed the seven-day operation of the first completely automatic coal pit in Britain. Their council's president explained that the miners would be obliged to work frequently on weekends, and "This the men feel would result in a serious loss of social life." Moreover, the local union opposed the offer of extra pay for weekend work on the grounds that this would cause unrest in the mining villages in the region.

This opposition delayed the opening of the mine for two years; and then it was opened only for 18 hour shifts instead of an optimal 21. What price "social life"? What price efficient coal production?

C. "Your society isn't going to hell, but it isn't going any other place either."—American business man.

AN ENGLISHMAN'S VIEW

One obvious reason why many British companies perform poorly is that the men who run them lack the will to do better. They aim low, are satisfied with modest performances and put a quiet life high on their list of priorities. For many, money is apparently not even a prime objective. Lord Kearton says he is more concerned to be able to please himself than to amass money; Lord Stokes does not know what he takes home after tax; Sir Peter Allen once remarked that he would prefer more leisure to a higher salary.

Many industrialists do not like what happens to U.S. businessmen as a result of their singleminded dedication. They feel it produces narrow-minded bores who are washed out at sixty; and they do not yet feel able to weep over the excellence of sales figures, as is not unknown at celebratory gatherings in the United States. In other words they are afraid of becoming zombies.

Company songs are used by some corporations in both the United States and Japan as a method of nurturing dedication. This would be unthinkable in Britain. As one British businessman sagely remarked, "If we had a company song, people would only start putting their own words to it." (Graham Turner—Business in Britain. 1971.)

Questions

1. Draw a bar diagram to illustrate the growth rates shown in the table.

2. What does the American writer say about Britain's record since the war?

3. Does the table of growth rates bear him out?

4. What did the Nottingham miners oppose? Why?

5. What was the result of the dispute?

6. What is the writer's opinion of it?

7. Explain the remark in Document C.

8. What does the English writer say is wrong with the attitudes of British business men?

9. What do they think of money?

10. In what way are they like the Nottingham miners?

11. What is the attitude of American business men?

12. What do British business men feel about them?

13. What is the purpose of a company song?

14. Why do British firms not have them?

15. What does this show about the attitude of British employees to their firms?

Questions—Chapter Forty-Four

1. Name some of the old staple industries.

2. Name some of the new industries.

3. When and why did the old industries decline?

4. Why did the new industries not prevent depression between the wars?

5. What advantage did Britain have after the war?

6. How did the old industries react?

7. How did the new industries react?

8. Why did they not continue to do well?

9. In what ways are trade unions to blame?

10. How are employers to blame?

11. Why are British factories less efficient than German ones?

12. Where has much British capital been invested?

13. How did the British Empire cause a great deal of expense?

14. What did Britain try to do in foreign affairs?

15. How did this lead to expense?

16. Why have governments been anxious about unemployment?

17. What has caused unemployment from time to time?

18. How have governments checked its growth?

19. How have these measures affected industry?

20. How does Britain compare with the rest of Europe?

Further Work

1. Find statistics comparing Britain's economy with other European countries.

2. Collect newspaper articles discussing British economic problems.

3. Look for examples of lavish public spending in your area—new schools, hospitals, roads, public buildings etc.

4. List the occupations of the parents of the children in your class. How many help to produce goods that are, or could be, sold abroad?

5. Britain's economy has been greatly helped by her "invisible" exports. What are they?

6. In your view, how important is it that Britain should be as rich as her European neighbours?

SECTION TWELVE
Social Changes Since 1900

CHAPTER 45

The Origins of the Welfare State 1906-1939

We have already seen what happened to the poor in the nineteenth century. In the first place, they were the responsibility of their neighbours, the local ratepayers, and secondly they were treated as a kind of sub-species of the human race, with the special name of "pauper". Under the Welfare State, however, the care of those in misfortune is a national duty, and not a local one. Moreover, the help is available for people in all walks of life. Everyone pays his insurance contributions and everyone can draw benefits as a matter of right. In theory, at least, we have no separate class of "pauper".

This comprehensive state service began well enough under the Liberal governments that were in power just before the First World War, but from 1921 to 1939 the problem of unemployment was so great that there was little progress. State insurance did not protect everyone and so for the others the poor law lingered on, remaining much the same in spite of an attempt to reform it in 1929.

The Liberal Reforms 1906-1914. The man who founded the welfare state was the Welsh radical, David Lloyd George, who, at that time, was Chancellor of the Exchequer. There is no doubt that he wanted to help the poor, but he was also anxious to win working class votes for the Liberal Party.

In order to deal with poverty, he might have reformed the Poor Laws, and since a Royal Commission had reported on them as recently as 1905, he had plenty of up-to-date information and advice. However, he chose to ignore it all, setting up his own system which, he hoped, would help people stay out of the workhouse. The problems lay with children, the elderly, the sick and the unemployed. Something was done for all of them.

For the children there were school meals, school medical examinations and in 1908 an Act known as the Children's Charter. It protected them from some of the worst sorts of cruelty and made it illegal for them to do unsuitable work. All this together did not amount to much. It was well known that children bore the brunt of the poverty among the working classes, but they have no votes, so little public money came their way.

For the elderly there was the Old Age Pensions Act of 1908. The pension was 5/- (25p) a week and to qualify one had to be over 70, of good character and have an income of less than £26 a year. On the other hand, all the money came from the government, so no-one had to pay contributions during his working life. Small though it was, the pension saved many an old person from the workhouse. If his family would give him a home, it would just pay for his keep.

Collecting the Old Age Pension—1909

For the unemployed there were first of all labour exchanges, set up by an Act of 1909. They were meant to help people find work.

However, Lloyd George's most important measure was the National Insurance Act of 1911. Part I of the Act was to help the sick. Any employee who fell ill was to have 10/- (50p) a week, and free medical attention. As it was an insurance scheme, there were regular contributions to make, which were compulsory. The employee himself paid 4d a week, and his employer 3d. The government added another 2d of the taxpayers' money, making a total of 9d (4p).

Lloyd George wanted everyone to have unemployment benefits as well, but it was felt that enough had already been done to upset the insurance companies. As a result Part II of the Act only gave protection to men in industries that were important, and where unemployment was common, mainly engineering and building. This involved about 2¼ million men. They paid an extra 2½d (1p) a week and if anyone lost his job he could have a dole of 6/- (30p) a week for up to 15 weeks in any one year.

Compulsory insurance was not popular. People were glad enough to draw their benefits when they needed them, but they disliked the deductions from their pay. Lloyd George told them they were having "ninepence for fourpence", but they were not impressed. A crowd of female servants spoke for all the working classes when they shouted at him, "Taffy was a Welshman, Taffy was a Thief".

1918-1939. In the years between the wars the pension scheme was expanded. People now had to make contributions during their working lives, but they had better pensions and they qualified earlier, men at 65 and women at 60.

However, the most important problem by far was to be unemployment. During the short boom that followed the war, they were not to know this, and in 1920 Parliament passed an optimistic Unemployment Insurance Act. It gave protection to almost all industrial workers—though not to farm labourers and domestic servants. In theory 12 million were now insured against unemployment, but the men who drafted the Act were still thinking of pre-war days, when only 4% of workers, or about half a million, were out of work at any one time. With this in mind they fixed contributions that proved to be much too low. Until 1939 there were never less than a million unemployed, and usually there were a lot more. Following the depression of 1921 the insurance fund was empty and the government was wondering what to do.

Many people, including the T.U.C., thought they should create jobs by starting public works, such as road building, but the government held the view that as the country was short of money, they should cut expenses, not increase them. Out of kindness to the unemployed they

294

would give an insured man money after the 26 weeks which the Act allowed. They called these payments "transitional benefits". So as to meet the drain on the fund, they borrowed, and in this way they muddled through until 1931. By then the country was in the throes of the worst trade depression it has ever known, with 2¾ million insured workers out of work and possibly a million others. Snowden, the Chancellor of the Exchequer, decided that everyone would have to make sacrifices, even the unemployed. He cut benefits by 10%, he increased contributions and, what caused most upset of all, he introduced a means test for transitional benefits. This meant that if the wife or child of an unemployed man had any earnings, then his dole was cut accordingly. The average British worker has something of the Andy Capp about him, and the indignity of having to go to his wife for his beer money was more than he could stand.

With the revival of trade in 1934 there was a new Unemployment Act which changed the insurance scheme so that the fund could cope with an unemployment figure of 17%. In fact it was never again as bad as that and in 1939 the Second World War brought its own drastic cure for unemployment.

The Poor Law. All the schemes, from Lloyd George's onwards, did not affect the Poor Law. It was still lurking in the background and indeed it was essential it should remain as long as so many people were not protected by the National Insurance Acts.

By the 1920's many Boards of Guardians were in trouble. With most of them, it was shortage of money. For example, during the depression of 1921 the number of people drawing relief jumped from 600 000 to 1½ million. Other Guardians deliberately went against official policies. They were the ones that had a majority of socialist members, as at Poplar in S.E. London. Here they took the view that they were Guardians of the poor, not of the ratepayers' money, and they gave so much help so readily that the Minister of Health had to intervene.

In the end, the Government decided to do what the Royal Commission of 1905 had recommended, and abolish Boards of Guardians. This was done by the Local Government Act of 1929, which also transferred their duties to Public Assistance Committees of the County Councils.

The Public Assistance Committees took over at the beginning of a trade depression so they were faced with cuts in spending and ever increasing demands from the poor. In most areas, people going for relief found the new authorities as niggardly as the old; elsewhere Socialist controlled councils gave the government the same headaches as the Poplar Guardians. Little had been achieved by changing the people who had administered the Poor Laws and it became clear that the only answer was to abolish them altogether.

family; there is the inability to obtain employment for economic reasons; and there is the inability of men to work owing to sickness, old age, or lack of physical stamina. Then there is the most fertile cause of all—a man's own improvident habits, such as drinking and gambling. Shame upon rich Britain that she should tolerate so much poverty among her people. The country that spent 250 millions to avenge an insult by an old Dutch farmer is not ashamed to see her children hungry and in rags. There is plenty of wealth in this country. What is wanted is a fairer distribution.
(David Lloyd George—*Slings and Arrows*.)

Questions
1. *What are the traditional ways of helping the poor?*
2. *Why are they not good enough?*
3. *Describe the work of Booth and Rowntree. (See Chapter 26).*
4. *What are the main causes of poverty?*
5. *Which of them were tackled by the Liberals between 1906 and 1914?*
6. *Explain the reference to the "old Dutch farmer."*
7. *Why must it be possible to relieve poverty?*
8. *According to Lloyd George, how can it be done?*

Questions
This is a picture of the Labour Exchange at Snow Hill, London, in 1930.
1. *What government established labour exchanges? When?*
2. *Why did so many people need to attend them in 1930 and 1931?*
3. *Where would these men have gone for help if the National Insurance Acts had not been passed?*
4. *What do you notice about the dress of the men wearing hats (not caps)?*
5. *What conclusion would you draw from this?*

LLOYD GEORGE DESCRIBES THE PROBLEM OF POVERTY. 1906.
Christians think that their main duty towards their unfortunate fellow-beings is discharged for the current half-year when they pay their poor-rate, and they certainly think that the charity which they dispense from time to time deals with the few odd cases that escape the meshes of the Poor Law. But the careful investigation of men like Mr. Booth and Mr. Rowntree has revealed a state of things which it would be difficult even for the orators of discontent to exaggerate. There are ten millions in this country enduring year after year the torture of living while lacking a sufficiency of the bare necessaries of life. What are some of the causes of poverty? There is the fact that a man's earnings are not adequate to maintain himself and his

WINSTON CHURCHILL DESCRIBES TO PARLIAMENT THE GOVERNMENT'S PLANS FOR COMPULSORY UNEMPLOYMENT INSURANCE
The trades marked out are those in which unemployment is not only high and chronic, but marked by seasonal and cyclical fluctuations. They are building, shipbuilding and engineering. That is a very considerable group of industries. They comprise 2¼ millions of adult males, or one third of the population in purely industrial work; that is to say excluding commercial, professional, agricultural and domestic occupations. Of the remaining two-thirds of the industrial population, nearly one half are in trades which, by the adoption of short-time or other arrangements, avoid the total discharge of a proportion of workmen from time to time.

So that this group of trades to which we propose to apply compulsory unemployment insurance covers nearly half of the whole field of unemployment. We will have to raise between 5d and 6d per week per head, and this sum will be met by contributions from the State, the workman and the employer. The House will see the connection of this to the Labour Exchanges. We propose to follow the example of Germany in respect of Insurance Cards to which stamps will be affixed week by week. When a worker loses his employment, all he will have to do is to take his card to the Labour Exchange which will find him a job or pay him his benefit.

(Churchill—*Liberalism and the Social Problem.* 1909.)

Questions

1. Which trades are to have compulsory insurance?
2. Why have they been chosen?
3. What occupations are excluded?
4. What proportion of unemployed will be insured?
5. How will the money be found?
6. What part will Labour Exchanges play?
7. Who first thought of Insurance Cards?
8. When did these proposals become law?
9. What other form of insurance was introduced at the same time?

Questions—Chapter Forty-Five

1. Which political party laid the foundations of the Welfare State? When?
2. Which of their politicians played a leading part?
3. What was done for children?
4. What was done for the elderly?
5. What was the purpose of labour exchanges?

6. What was the purpose of Part One of the National Insurance Act of 1911?
7. What benefits did it give? What were the contributions?
8. Describe Part Two of the Act.
9. How did the public feel about the Act?
10. What was the most serious social problem between the wars?
11. Describe the Unemployment Insurance Act of 1920. What mistake was made?
12. What were "transitional benefits"?
13. How many were unemployed in 1931? Why?
14. Who was Chancellor of the Exchequer? Describe three measures he took to deal with the crisis.
15. When and why did the situation improve?
16. Why was the Poor Law still necessary?
17. What problem did many Boards of Guardians face?
18. How did some of them defy official policies?
19. Who took over from Boards of Guardians? When?
20. Why was the change a failure?

Further Work

1. Find pictures that illustrate the problem of poverty between 1900 and 1939.
2. Read about the national insurance schemes Bismarck introduced in Germany.
3. Read about Lloyd George's budget of 1909, and the dispute it caused between the House of Commons and the House of Lords.
4. Ask people who were alive in the depression of 1931 to describe their experiences, and read about it in other books. Put together all the information you have found, and write your own account.
5. How did the depression of 1931 affect Germany?

CHAPTER 46

The Creation of the Welfare State 1939-1950

During the war years little could be done to improve the welfare services, but this did not stop people from thinking and planning. There was the evacuation of children from the slums which showed more clearly than ever before how much there was to do. Moreover there was a report on Social Insurance by Sir William Beveridge giving definite ideas on what should happen when peace finally came. In 1945, at the end of the war in Europe, the Labour Party won its first general election with a decisive majority. In what Hugh Dalton, their Chancellor of the Exchequer, later called "those five shining years from 1945 to 1950", they created the welfare state as we know it today.

The War Years 1939-1945. Before 1939 most of the wealthier people in Britain agreed that the poor needed help. Few of them, though, really knew much about life in the slums of the industrial cities. They had read their newspapers and some had studied books and official reports, but their knowledge was second-hand. Not surprisingly they had no wish to go to the slums, but what happened in the early years of the war was that the slums came to them. As the bombing began, thousands of children were taken from the cities and billeted on prosperous middle class families in safer areas. In many homes, the evacuees caused more upset than the Germans. No-one who took a child from a slum was left in any doubt about the need for social reform.

At the same time the Government started planning for the future and appointed a Committee under Sir William Beveridge to prepare a report. It appeared in 1942 under the title "Social Insurance and Allied Services", though it is usually known as the "Beveridge Report". It roused a good deal of interest, and well over half a million people bought copies. Millions more read about it in their newspapers, or heard about it on the radio.

Beveridge said there were five giants that stood in the way and would have to be destroyed. They were Want, Disease, Ignorance, Squalor and Idleness. His report was mainly about the first two.

To deal with want there was to be a scheme of national insurance against unemployment, with pensions for widows, orphans and the elderly. To cope with disease, there was to be free medical treatment. Such ideas were not new. Lloyd George had already put both into practice in 1911, but what was revolutionary in the Beveridge plan was that it said they should be for everyone. Originally, they were only for the less fortunate members of the working classes, and everyone else scorned to take a helping hand from the State. Now all were to be involved, and a man should have no feeling of inferiority if he drew insurance benefits, or if he had free medical treatment from the national health service. In the good times he paid into the fund, and in the bad times he took from it, as was his right.

The Labour Government 1945-1950. When the Labour Government came to power it was able to turn Beveridge's hopes into something like reality. Not only did it have a majority, but the Conservatives offered little opposition. Indeed, Sir Winston Churchill's coalition government had taken two important steps even before the general election. They had set up a Ministry of National Insurance and had started Family Allowances.

Collecting the Family Allowance—1946   299

Under the Labour Government one of the most important measures was the National Insurance Act of 1946. There has to be a National Insurance Contribution each week, for every person in work. An employee pays part of it himself, and his employer the rest; there are special arrangements for people who work for themselves, but all have to pay. The money goes into a central fund, to which the Treasury adds at least as much again from the taxes. The fund is used for unemployment benefits, pensions of all kinds, maternity grants, birth grants and death grants. It also goes to finance the National Health Service. The state will help us, even before we are born, and then through every sort of misfortune and difficulty until we die.

The National Health Service Act was also passed in 1946 and it, too, was far-reaching.

In the first place, Local Authorities have important duties. They organise services such as nurses and ambulances, and they are responsible for providing a healthy environment with good water supplies, sewage and scavenging.

Next, there is a Hospital Service. The state took over all hospitals, some of which had been run by local authorities, and some by charity. The country was divided into twenty areas each with a Regional Hospital Board; every hospital has a Management Committee responsible to its Regional Board.

There is also a General Practitioner Service, though it was set up with some difficulty. Doctors were suspicious of the National Health Service because they were afraid they would become little better than salaried civil servants—and with rather low salaries into the bargain. They finally agreed to join, on the understanding that they could keep their freedom and their private patients.

They are paid a fixed amount for each national health patient they have on their books, and they have the same amount whether they see the patient often or whether they do not see him at all. The payment was originally 75p a year but has increased from time to time and more than once the doctors have won money for themselves by threatening to leave the National Health Service altogether. Nurses and hospital workers have been less fortunate.

There are also dentists, opticians and pharmacists. Dentists and opticians are paid according to the work they do, pharmacists according to the number of prescriptions they handle.

To round off the social security system there was the National Assistance Act of 1948, which meant the end of the Poor Law. There will always be people who are in such misfortune that their National Insurance benefits are not enough, and they can have help from the taxpayer just as in the old days they had help from the Poor Rates. The differences are that National Assistance is government money and does not come from the rates, while the scheme is administered by the central authority, not a local one. None the less, taking National Assistance means drawing from a fund to which you have not contributed, so it looks like charity, and there are people who prefer to suffer and go without.

Perhaps even more important than their social security schemes, was the government's policy of full employment. For a long time after the war practically no-one was without a job. People who are in work do not draw national insurance benefits, and they can also feed, clothe and house themselves decently, so they are less likely to be ill. As Edwin Chadwick had never tired of saying a hundred years before, it is better to have a prosperous, healthy environment than to allow poverty and disease, and then provide expensive cures for them.

Full employment was partly due to the economic conditions in the world as a whole, but the government also did a great deal. So many industries have been nationalised and taxation is so high, that the government has a lot of power. When it sees that unemployment is rising it can create jobs directly, for example by providing new equipment for the railways, building power stations, or constructing new roads. It can also give people more money to spend by cutting taxation. They use the money to buy goods, so the factories increase production and there are more jobs available.

There is a disadvantage. The government deliberately sets too much money to chase too few goods, so prices are bound to rise. Inflation has been a serious problem ever since the war. We have seen, too, how employing people in the public sector has robbed industry of the workers it needs.

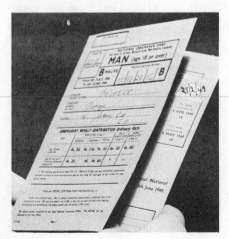

Questions
1. What document is shown here?
2. Who has cards like this?
3. When do they first acquire them?
4. What is the table, just over half way down on the front?
5. What has been stuck inside the card? What does it prove?
6. A man who has been dismissed from his job might say he had "been given his cards." Why does he need them?

EFFECTS OF THE WELFARE MEASURES IN YORK

	1936	1950
Percentage below the poverty line	31.1	2.77

If there had been no new welfare measures after 1936 the percentage for 1950 would have been 22.18.

EXAMPLES

(Deficit is the amount a family is below the poverty line, and surplus is the amount they are over it.)

A. *Widower 85 and invalid daughter 50.* Old Age Pension £1.30, allowance for daughter £1.30. Value of home grown vegetables 12½p. Total income £2.72½. Deficit 19p per head. Although they still suffer privation their main feeling is gratitude for the welfare legislation. Before, they lived on 87½p between them, half of which went in rent.

B. *Man, wife and four children.* Man is a labourer and earns £5.20. Family allowances 75p. School and cheap milk 20p. Home grown vegetables 12½p. Total £6.27½. Deficit per head 5p. Wife complains that they cannot buy enough food or adequate clothing. Husband complains of having to keep children at school until 15. He says not only ought they to be earning, but that in their last year they demand pocket money. Through unskilled management this family probably suffers more than it need.

C. *Man, wife and three children.* Man is shop assistant earning £5.33 per week. Family allowances 50p. School and cheap milk 16p. Total £5.99. Surplus 9p. per head. Main worry is clothing.

D. *Man, wife and three children.* Man is electrician earning £8.75. Family allowance 50p. School and cheap milk 16p. Total £9.41. Surplus 63p per head. Prosperous and contented. They have an 8 h.p. car.

(Rowntree—*Poverty and the Welfare State.*)

Questions

1. *How far were the new welfare measures responsible for the decline of poverty in York?*

2. *Draw bar diagrams to show where each of the four families came in relation to the poverty line (a) as they are and (b) where they would have been without their benefits.*

"JOB-DODGING" IN THE 1970's

Among the increasing ranks of the unemployed are professional job-dodgers who avoid offers of work so that they can draw dole money. The majority are men in the 18 to 36 age group who are idle to the backbone and twice as devious. They boast of the jobs for which they have been rejected and smirk at the stupidity of the social security authorities.

The formula for job failure is simple: Dress scruffily, be surly, rude, and make your general unsuitability for employment obvious. If that fails, claim that the conditions of work are not quite what you were used to. As a last resort, threaten your prospective employer with "sanctions." As one man said, "You had better mark me unsuitable, because if you do employ me I bloody well will be unsuitable within two weeks." Then there was a heavy goods vehicle driver who was consistently turned down for jobs. Benefits officers found that during interviews he "let slip" that he was a militant union man involved in a lot of past industrial action. In fact he was nothing of the kind. Some job-shirkers are nothing if not direct. One looked shocked when told his weekly wage would be £50. "Come off it governor," he said. "I'm getting £38 a week off the State for doing nothing." He did not get the job. Benefits can be cancelled, but this depends on local officers "getting to know" about abuses. They learn of them all too infrequently.

(*Daily Telegraph*—July 27 1976.)

Questions

1. *Why do some men not want work?*
2. *What do they do to avoid offers of work?*
3. *What can be done about people who behave in this way? Why does it not often happen?*
4. *Compare this situation with the problem of the able-bodied pauper of the 1830's.*

5. How would you prevent "job-shirking" without injuring families in real need?

Questions—Chapter Forty-Six
1. How did the war show the need for social reform?
2. What Report was produced during the war?
3. What two problems did it examine?
4. What did it say should be done about them?
5. What new idea was there in the Report?
6. What government was mainly responsible for the welfare state?
7. When was the National Insurance Act passed?
8. What are the three sources of money for National Insurance?
9. In what ways is it spent?
10. When was the National Health Service started?
11. What duties do Local Authorities have?
12. How was the Hospital Service re-organised?
13. Why were doctors reluctant to join the National Health Service?
14. On what conditions did they join?
15. How are they paid?

16. What other professional people work for the National Health Service? How are they paid?
17. Why is National Assistance necessary?
18. How is it different from the old system of Poor Relief?
19. How does full employment help the welfare state?
20. How can a government create full employment? What problems are caused as a result?

Further Work
1. Talk to someone who was evacuated, or received evacuees, during the war. Ask what they remember.
2. Ask your parents, or other adults, how the system of National Insurance affects them.
3. What are your experiences of dealing with the National Health Service? What changes would you suggest?
4. Collect items from newspapers on different aspects of the welfare state. What are the problems? How serious are they?
5. "The state in organising security should not stifle incentive, opportunity, responsibility—Beveridge Report. What do you feel has happened?

CHAPTER 47

Trade Unions

Before 1939 the trade unions found themselves in one kind of difficulty after another, suffering a particularly heavy defeat when the general strike of 1926 collapsed. Since the Second World War, though, they have grown in importance and now have considerable economic and even political power.

1900-1914. During the years 1900-1914 the trade unions had a variety of problems.

In the first place it was a time when prices were rising, and wages did not keep up with them. There were strikes, with a good deal of violence, as for example, the coal strike of 1911 and the transport strike of 1912. Both failed, adding to the bitterness of the working classes.

Under these conditions an extremist movement calling itself "syndicalism" was able to grow. It took its ideas from a French trade unionist called Georges Sorel, and he in turn had been inspired by Robert Owen. The plan was that the workers in each industry should carry out strike after strike until they had crippled it. When that happened, they would take it over, and run it for their own benefit. Most trade union members did not agree with such an idea, and in 1912 the T.U.C. rejected it with a large majority. However, though it was easy to condemn the extremists, it was not so easy to control them.

Finally, there were two complicated battles with the law. The first was the Taff Vale Judgement of 1901. There had been a strike on the Taff Vale Railway, and when it was over, the Company won damages from the Amalgamated Society of Railway Servants for the money it had cost them. Clearly no union would be able to call a strike if it was going 304 to have to pay for the employers' losses.

The law was changed by the Trade Disputes Act of 1906 which said that unions could not be made to pay compensation for money lost during a strike.

The other legal problem was caused by the Osborne Judgement of 1908. A member of the Amalgamated Society of Railway Servants, W. V. Osborne, said that his Union needed his permission before giving part of his subscription to the Labour Party. The courts held that he was right. Labour candidates and M.P.s badly needed money, but now the unions had great difficulty in finding it for them.

Again Parliament came to the rescue, and passed the Trade Union Act of 1913. It gave Unions more freedom to help their political friends with their funds.

During these difficult years the trade unions tried to strengthen themselves by taking part in politics. They began in 1900 when several of them joined with some socialist societies, like the Independent Labour Party and the Fabians, to form the Labour Representation Committee. Their aim was to bring about the election of Labour M.P.s. This would cost money, so at first most of the unions were not too keen. However, after the Taff Vale Judgement, they saw they would need friends in Parliament if they were to have the law changed. They backed the L.R.C. which fielded 50 candidates at the general election of 1906, 29 of whom were elected. The Labour M.P.s worked in alliance with the Liberals, who were anxious to please them so that they could keep the working class vote. This was why they passed the Trade Disputes Act of 1906 and the Trade Union Act of 1913.

1918-1939. After the First World War, the trade unions tried to improve their organisation. Small, local unions joined together to become much more powerful. A good example was the Transport and General Workers' Union, which was largely the creation of Ernest Bevin.

There was also the General Council of the T.U.C. Congress only met once a year, but now they also had a General Council permanently in session.

For all this, the trade union movement was not strong. Unemployment was never less than a million, which made it easy for employers to beat down wages. There was, for example, a trial of strength in 1921 when, after a bitter strike, the coal owners made the miners work longer hours for less pay.

More serious trouble came in 1926, and again it began with a miners' strike. They wanted the government to pay a subsidy to keep up their wages and they asked the T.U.C. for help. The T.U.C. supported them by calling a mass sympathetic strike that was known as the General Strike. Two and a half million men came out and work stopped on the railways, in road transport, the docks, power stations, printing works 305

A bus travels under police supervision during the General Strike.

and several other industries. The strike lasted nine days, and then collapsed.

Baldwin's Conservative government was prepared. It organised troops and volunteers to keep essential services going. It beat the printers' strike with its own news sheet, the "British Gazette", and by broadcasting. It won public opinion over to its side. On the other hand, the T.U.C. had drifted into a crisis for which it was not ready. Moreover, it found that the miners were uncooperative. The problem was to decide who should order a return to work. Naturally the T.U.C. felt that it was their right, but the miners said the strike must go on until they had the terms they wanted. The T.U.C. replied, in effect, that if the miners wanted to conduct the strike in their own way, they must conduct it on their own. They hung on for another six months and went back to work only when their families were starving.

After the General Strike, the government pressed home its victory by passing the Trade Disputes and Trade Union Act of 1927. This made it illegal to try and coerce a government by strike action and also repealed the Trade Union Act of 1913. It was now much more difficult for unions to raise money for the Labour Party whose income was cut by one third.

There was a change of heart in the Labour movement which was 306 shown in 1928, when Transport House opened. It was the work of one of the greatest trade union leaders of this century, Ernest Bevin. Transport House was to be the headquarters, not only of his own Transport and General Workers Union, but also of the T.U.C. and the Labour Party. It proved that the extremists were out of favour, and that for the time being the unions would work for their political aims, in the legal way, through their allies in Parliament.

The Trade Union Movement since 1945. Following the defeat of 1926, the trade unions had to tread carefully. However, they began to revive in the 1930's and then, after 1945, they became powerful. The reason was full employment. A man who is in work is willing and able to pay his union subscription, so membership increased.

The trade unions have used their power in many ways. The most important was to win regular wage increases for their members. Full employment means inflation, but this has not bothered the big unions unduly. They have seen that their members' wages have kept up with prices and in the meanwhile others have suffered.

In some industries unions have become so powerful that they can operate a "closed shop". This means that they will not allow an employer to take on a man, unless he is a union member.

The unions have gained political power as well. They have enough money to make large grants to the Labour Party who, as a result, have frequently been in power since the war. Naturally, any Labour Government is influenced by the trade unions. Sometimes the unions can even use their industrial power to bring political changes directly. For example, in 1974 a miners' strike toppled Edward Heath's government—a long delayed revenge for 1921 and 1926.

Another development is that the extremists in the movement have once again raised their heads. Because the unions are so powerful, and because they have such control in the unions, they can have an influence over the country quite out of proportion to their numbers. The Communist Party has used the trade union movement for its own ends. Since the 1950's they have been unable to muster enough support in any constituency to return a single member to Parliament but in certain Unions many of them are officials, and once elected it is often difficult to dislodge them. In 1961 it was shown that communist officials of the Electrical Trades Union had been rigging elections and it was only determined action by the T.U.C. that brought their removal. Shop stewards have become important men and some are decidedly militant. From time to time they will even defy their unions and call unofficial strikes.

There is no doubt that the abuse of power by some Trade Unions has added to Great Britain's economic problems. They have forced up inflation, and they have lost production through strikes. However, most 307 unions are responsible organisations so it is wrong to blame them for misfortunes that have been created, in the main, by governments.

Questions
1. What does this picture tell you about the attitude of the Government to the General Strike?
2. How did the public as a whole feel about the General Strike?
3. On whom else did the Government call apart from troops and police?
4. What was happening in the Trade Union movement that gave some cause for alarm?
5. What, in your view, would happen if the Government called out troops during a strike today?

THE GOVERNMENT VIEW OF THE GENERAL STRIKE
The Trade Union leaders have felt bound to support the miners and have, therefore, called a general strike. They believe that this threat will compel the Government to grant an indefinite prolongation of the subsidy to the coal trade at the expense of the tax payer. This has been shown to be a foolish policy, no better than drinking salt water to relieve thirst. If Parliament were to allow its considered judgement to be over-ruled by the cruel assault of a general strike, the economic disaster would only be a part of a much greater disaster. It would be established that the

weapon of a general strike is irresistible. The Trade Union leaders would in fact become the masters of the whole country and the power of Government would have passed from Parliament into their hands. Instead of the representatives of the nation duly elected on a franchise almost universal, our destinies would be in the hands of a body of men, who, however well meaning most of them may be, represent only a section of the public and have derived no authority from the people comparable to that of the House of Commons. While, therefore, there is plenty of room for negotiation about the coal trade, there can be none about a general strike. This is not a dispute between employers and workers, it is a conflict between Trade Union leaders and Parliament and that conflict must only end, and can only end, in the distinct and unmistakable victory for Parliament. This victory His Majesty's Government is determined to secure.
(The British Gazette—May 5th 1926.)

Questions. According to this newspaper:
1. Why were the miners on strike in 1926?
2. How reasonable were their demands?
3. What does the T.U.C. hope to achieve with the general strike?
4. What would happen to the Government if they won?
5. What sort of conflict is the general strike?
6. Who must win it and why?

A LEFT-WING VIEW OF THE GENERAL STRIKE
The idea of representing a strike which arose entirely out of industrial conditions and had entirely industrial aims as a revolutionary movement was mainly Mr. Churchill's. No-one believes in it—least of all Mr. Baldwin. Mr. Churchill jumped in with it as soon as the break came, made himself super-editor of the British Gazette,

and ran it there for all it was worth. It has turned out to be worth very little. All the efforts to make the nation's flesh creep have failed. The big employers are angry. They say, "We have to work with Trade Unions afterwards. A fight to the finish such as Churchill talks about is all nonsense." The leaders of all the Churches have told Mr. Baldwin as plainly as possible that the talk about revolution is rubbish, and that the dispute concerns miners' wages. It was significant that Mr. Baldwin dropped the revolution stunt in his broadcast on Saturday. Thus all the display of steel helmeted troops, all the tearing about of motor cars filled with special constables, all the hints of the Home Secretary that the regular police are wanted "for perhaps sterner work," all the clatter about the country being in danger of civil war, have failed of their object. The nation has kept its head in spite of the alarming tricks played upon it. Mr. Churchill has failed again and everyone knows it.

(*The British Worker*—May 10th 1926.)

Questions. According to this newspaper:
1. What was the cause of the general strike?
2. What are its aims?
3. What does Mr. Churchill say they are?
4. Who was Baldwin? What are his views?
5. What are the views of employers and churchmen?
6. What government measures have been taken?
7. What was their object?
8. What does the country as a whole believe?
9. How would the writer of this article disagree with The British Gazette?

Questions—Chapter Forty-Seven
1. Why was there much discontent just before 1900?
2. What plans did the syndicalists have?
3. What problem did the Taff Vale Judgement create?
4. What Act of Parliament solved it?

5. What problem did the Osborne Judgement create?
6. What Act of Parliament solved it?
7. What organisation was formed in 1900? What were its aims?
8. What persuaded the Unions to support it actively?
9. How did unions try to become stronger after 1918?
10. How did unemployment help employers after 1918?
11. How did the miners' strike of 1926 lead to the General Strike?
12. How many workers struck? How long did the strike last?
13. What actions did the Government take?
14. What problems did the T.U.C. have?
15. How was the law changed after the strike?
16. What is Transport House? What did its opening prove?
17. Why were the Unions more powerful after 1945?
18. How did the Unions use their power?
19. How have the Unions gained political power?
20. How have extremists used the Trade Unions?

Further Work
1. Find out what you can about Ernest Bevin.
2. Read more about the General Strike, and discuss it with people who were alive at the time.
3. Find out what you can about the careers and views of prominent Trade Union leaders today.
4. Talk to an adult who is a member of a Trade Union. Ask why he has joined, and what he hopes his Union will do for him.
5. Take notice of any Trade Union news that may appear in the press. Read what newspapers with different political views say about it.
6. List the ways in which Trade Unions can influence the affairs of the country. In your view, have they become too powerful, or are they not powerful enough? Have the British Gazette's fears come true?

309

CHAPTER 48

Secondary and Further Education

By the end of the nineteenth century the state was giving every child an elementary education; during the twentieth century it went on to provide secondary education as well.

State secondary schools grew out of the elementary schools in the 1890's. Their development was encouraged by the Education Act of 1902 but at first they were only for the brighter children. Then, in 1944, another Act provided secondary education for all. On top of that there are today Technical Colleges, Polytechnics and many more Universities as well.

For a long time the wealthy had had a private secondary system of their own, but the state system did not absorb it. Instead it grew alongside it so that children from different social classes still go to different schools. None the less, there are opportunities for everyone, but poorer children, in the main, do not take them. They go into jobs much the same as those of their parents, and there is little the schools can do about it.

Education and the Class System. The education a child receives depends on the social class to which he belongs.

The men of the Middle Ages who founded the public schools and the Universities of Oxford and Cambridge had meant them for the children of the poor, but by the nineteenth century, and indeed long before, the rich had purloined them. It was relatively easy for an upper class child to go from his preparatory school, or private tutor, to a public school, and then on to one of the ancient Universities. Up to a point this is still true, though the Universities are now setting much higher standards. Even so, half the students at Oxford and Cambridge still come from the public schools, which provide for only a tiny minority of the nation's

children.

Like the upper class children, those from middle class homes have always found it fairly easy to go through secondary education and then on to a University. Most of them, though, tended to follow a different road. Rather than be boarders at expensive preparatory and public schools, they have been day pupils at private schools and the old endowed grammar schools. From there they have gone, mainly, to the newer "redbrick" Universities, though some do go to Oxford and Cambridge.

There have been changes. The endowed grammar schools became direct grant schools, but more important, as the state schools have improved, the middle classes have taken over the best of them—quite often pushing out working class children as they do so. They will send their children to a state primary school if it serves a "nice" area, and they are usually happy with state grammar schools. They want their children to mix with their own kind, and they want the school to coach its pupils to win good examination results and prepare them for professional careers. If they cannot have these things, then they prefer to send their children elsewhere, even though it means paying school fees.

Providing secondary and further education for working class children has been a much more difficult problem. In the first place, since the parents neither can nor will pay anything for the education of their children, every penny has to come from public funds. Secondly, for many working class children, education is something they resist, and they escape from it so that they can earn money as soon as they possibly can.

Origins of State Secondary Schools. By the 1890's the elementary schools were so well established that some of their pupils were ready and willing to have secondary education. Two types of school appeared.

One of these was the Higher Grade School. In any elementary school a few pupils only would be likely to stay on into the higher standards. Usually there were not enough of them to make a class, so it was more economical for a School Board to open a separate school for all the children in the town wanting to go through the higher standards.

The other kind was the Technical School. Britain was losing her place as the world's greatest economic power and many people blamed our lack of technical education. As a result, in 1889, Parliament passed the Technical Instruction Act, allowing County and County Borough Councils to open Technical Schools. Most of the pupils in them came from elementary schools.

Both types of school had money from the rates, but they also had grants from the Science and Art Department at South Kensington, so they had a strong technical and scientific bias.

The Balfour-Morant Act of 1902. One problem with the system that had grown up in the 1890's was that secondary education was in the hands of two authorities—the School Boards and the County and County Borough Councils. Another problem was the fact that many School Boards were too small and too poor to build higher grade schools. The answer to both problems was to abolish School Boards. This was done by the Education Act of 1902. Balfour was the politician who introduced it to Parliament, and Morant was the civil servant who did most of the work preparing it. Having abolished School Boards, the Act allowed County and County Borough Councils to "supply or aid the supply of education other than elementary".

Councils all over the country now built new secondary schools, or converted higher grade and technical schools into secondary schools. Guided by Morant at the Board of Education, these schools lost their strong scientific and technical bias, and gave a more general education, even teaching Latin like the grammar and public schools. This made them more attractive to the middle classes than to the working classes.

Moreover they charged fees, so that working class children could not afford to attend them. The government tried to put this right in 1907 by allowing each school to give a number of free places. Children from the elementary schools competed for these places by taking examinations.

312   *A State Secondary School in the 1920's*

Here was the beginning of 11 + selection. It was better than no working class children having a secondary education, but it still seemed most unfair that only the cleverest children from poor homes could go to a secondary school, while there were places for almost all those who could afford to pay.

The Butler Act of 1944. In 1926 the Hadow Report was published, and it recommended secondary education for all. It said there should be two kinds of secondary school—grammar schools and modern schools. They were supposed to be equal, but the grammar schools were to take the brighter children.

Due to economic problems little was done about the Hadow Report until nearly the end of the war. Then, in 1944, R. A. Butler introduced an important Act to Parliament. This organised education in three stages—primary, secondary and further. All children now had to go to a secondary school, and they also had to stay an extra year, since the school leaving age was raised to 15. Fees were abolished in all state schools, so a middle class parent could no longer buy his child a better education, unless he went outside the state system.

The Act did not say how local authorities were to organise their schools, but most of them adopted the Hadow plan. People at the time thought it was possible to select fairly by using intelligence tests. It was also hoped that modern schools would have as high a reputation as grammar schools. However, grammar schools, which took the brighter children, were bound to have more status. Also, accurate selection is almost impossible. It is easy enough to pick out the very bright and the very dull; the problems come when trying to sort out the borderline cases. Finally, in spite of the abolition of fees, middle class children took most of the places in the grammar schools.

It seemed, then, that a child from a wealthy home still had a better chance of a good education than one from a poor home. In view of this, many local authorities went over to comprehensive schools, and this became the official policy of the Labour Party. However, even within the comprehensive system, middle class children have the advantage. They do better at examinations and are more likely to stay on into the sixth form and go from there to the University.

Further Education. One important development is the increase in the number of Universities. Many have been founded since the Second World War, as, for example, Kent, Sussex and East Anglia.

Technical education has grown considerably. It is so unlike the traditional education of the upper and middle classes that it has only just become respectable. In the first place Technical Colleges have 313 grown. They provide a variety of courses from day release in industrial work to "A" levels in academic subjects. Some have been made into Colleges of Advanced Technology where students can work for degrees or similar qualifications. Finally there are the Polytechnics which rank almost with the Universities.

Questions

This picture is of a London Comprehensive School in 1956.

1. *What do you understand by comprehensive education?*
2. *What system was more usual just after 1944?*
3. *Which political party is in favour of comprehensive education?*
4. *How are comprehensive schools supposed to help working class children?*
5. *In your opinion, do they succeed?*
6. *What would you suggest as the likely number of children attending this school?*
7. *Why has it been thought necessary to make comprehensive schools so large?*
8. *Are you in favour of large schools or small ones? Why?*

GRAMMAR SCHOOL CHILDREN

An investigation in 1951 showed that the middle class was still heavily over-represented in the grammar schools. Children from professional and managerial families account for 15% of the total population, 25% of the grammar school population and 44% of the sixth-form population. The reason must be looked for partly in social influences—the less educated parents, the more crowded and noisy homes, the smaller opportunities for homework; and partly in financial factors—a child continuing at school is a heavy financial strain on working-class parents.

(C. A. R. Crosland—*The Future of Socialism*. 1956.)

Questions

1. What proportion of children are middle class?
2. In 1951 what proportion of children in Grammar Schools and in Sixth Forms were middle class?
3. What explanations does Crosland give?

TWO MODERN SCHOOL CHILDREN—TOM AND SHEILA

Tom's father, a works manager, thought of sending him to private school, but found that boys were entering his firm having passed G.C.E. examinations in secondary modern schools. As a result he rented accommodation so that his boy could come to us. We found that the boy had an immense fund of general knowledge, but at the end of his second year he still had difficulty with arithmetic and basic English skills. Individual coaching in these subjects was arranged. In the meantime Tom was featuring in school plays and played in the rugger team. In the fourth year, following great efforts, he made a marked advance. He obtained Group One passes in G.C.E. in chemistry and history and also passed in language and literature. At the moment he is taking five more subjects. He has been recommended for a Sixth Form Scholarship at an independent school open to outstanding boys from secondary modern schools. He is Deputy Head Boy.

Sheila is the eldest of five children. Her father, a capstan lathe operator, lives on a housing estate where many of the families come from slum clearance areas. All his children attend school badly, and Sheila missed twenty weeks' work in her third year. Her father did not always know of these absences, but even after warnings from the attendance officer did not enforce his authority. In her fourth year Sheila worked in a café on Saturdays and was seen working there when she was supposed to be absent because of illness. She did not do well in any school work. She did not work to capacity, and her absences made it difficult to interest her and gain her co-operation. She never joined any school societies and did not do well in games or P.E.

During her last two years at school she was very interested in boy friends.

(*Half Our Future*—Newsom Report. 1963.)

Questions

1. To what social class does Tom belong?
2. How did his father choose a school for him?
3. What decided the father's choice of house?
4. What problems did Tom have at school?
5. How were they overcome?
6. What school activities did Tom join?
7. What G.C.E. passes did he obtain?
8. Where is he to go when he has finished at his present school?
9. What do Tom and his parents feel about education?
10. How has their attitude affected his progress?
11. To what social class does Shelia belong?
12. How big is her family?
13. Where does she live?
14. What is her father's attitude to bad attendance?
15. Why is she backward in her school work?
16. What out of school activities did she join?

17. *What is her main interest?*
18. *How has her progress been affected by her own attitude and that of her parents?*

Questions—Chapter Forty-Eight

1. To what schools and universities have (a) upper class and (b) middle class parents sent their children?
2. To what state schools will middle class parents send their children willingly?
3. What do middle class parents expect from schools?
4. State two reasons why it has been difficult to give working class children secondary education.
5. Why were Higher Grade Schools started?
6. Why were Technical Schools started?
7. Where did both find their money?
8. What two problems were there with the secondary education system of the 1890's?
9. Who was responsible for the 1902 Education Act?
10. What did the Act say?
11. What education was given in the new secondary schools?
12. How was it possible for working class children to attend them?
13. What did the Hadow Report recommend?
14. Who was responsible for the 1944 Education Act?
15. What stages of education did the Act require?
16. How did most local authorities organise secondary education?
17. Name three problems created by the system.
18. Why did many local authorities adopt comprehensive education?
19. Name some of the universities founded recently.
20. Name three kinds of technical institutions.

Further Work

1. What is being done today to ensure that working class children have good educational opportunities?
2. Ask your parents and grandparents about their secondary education. Compare it with your own.
3. Find out when each of the secondary schools in your area opened and, if it was not a new one, what it was at the time.
4. Write the history of secondary education in your area.
5. What opportunities have you for further education?